To Follow the Lamb

To Follow the Lamb

A Peaceable Reading of the Book of Revelation

TED GRIMSRUD

CASCADE *Books* • Eugene, Oregon

TO FOLLOW THE LAMB
A Peaceable Reading of the Book of Revelation

Cascade Books
An Imprint of Wipf and Stock Publishers
199 W. 8th Ave., Suite 3
Eugene, OR 97401

www.wipfandstock.com

PAPERBACK ISBN: 978-1-6667-3224-5
HARDCOVER ISBN: 978-1-6667-2569-8
EBOOK ISBN: 978-1-6667-2570-4

Cataloguing-in-Publication data:

Names: Grimsrud, Ted, author.

Title: To follow the lamb : a peaceable reading of the book of Revelation / Ted Grimsrud.

Description: Eugene, OR: Cascade Books, 2022 | Includes bibliographical references.

Identifiers: ISBN 978-1-6667-3224-5 (paperback) | ISBN 978-1-6667-2569-8 (hardcover) | ISBN 978-1-6667-2570-4 (ebook)

Subjects: LCSH: Bible N.T. Revelation—Criticism, interpretation, etc.

Classification: BS2825.52 G75 2022 (paperback) | BS2825.52 (ebook)

03/29/22

For Kathleen Temple,
my best friend and most important intellectual inspiration

Contents

Acknowledgments

It took me a long time to finish this book. I never would have made it if not for the help of many people along the way. With these few words here, I want to note with gratitude the most important helpers.

Shalom Mennonite Congregation gave me the opportunity to preach through the entirety of Revelation. Even better, we had feedback sessions after each sermon that helped me immeasurably to see what needed more (and less) elaboration.

Eastern Mennonite University since 1996 has provided a hospitable environment for my work in peace theology. Especially my class "Biblical Theology of Peace and Justice" gave me a chance to discuss Revelation in the context of the Bible's witness to shalom. I am grateful to the students in that class who questioned, challenged, and (at times) affirmed what I had to say.

Eastern Mennonite Seminary gave me a last-minute opportunity to teach a class on Revelation in the spring of 2020. It was quite stimulating to examine the book's content amidst the disruptions and fears caused by the great pandemic that midway through the semester forced us to finish the class online. I appreciate how those in the class rolled with the stresses of that time and contributed to a genuine community of learning that helped me so much to put the finishing touches on this book.

Most of all, as always, I am grateful to my life partner, Kathleen Temple. Kathleen was present with me back in the 1970s when I started paying attention to Revelation and has been my co-seeker ever since. I would never have been able to write these pages without her constant insights and affirmations. Though our son Johan, daughter-in-law Jill, and grandchildren Elias and Marja had little to do with this particular project, their presence in my life spurs me on to seek wholeness however I can.

1

Introduction

Why This Book Matters

When it comes to the Bible, the book of Revelation is like the unruly youngest child in a large family. Many of the more stable and conventional family members frown at this child and may even wish that it wasn't part of the family. Revelation was somewhat marginal in early Christianity and was included with the rest of what became the New Testament in only some collections. In time, though, Revelation came to be accepted (albeit reluctantly) by various Christian groups as part of their Scripture.

Revelation's ultimately accepted place in the New Testament did not mean the book would get equal attention with the other parts. Famously, the sixteenth-century Reformers Martin Luther and John Calvin both ignored Revelation as they wrote voluminously about most of the rest of the Bible. Various lectionaries that provide schedules for the reading of the Bible in Christian worship services usually leave Revelation aside and only occasionally list small snippets of the Bible's last book.

THE ATTRACTIONS OF THE BOOK OF REVELATION

On the other hand, and perhaps not coincidentally, Revelation did draw a great deal of attention from various marginalized, heterodox, and visionary groups on the edges of mainstream Christianity. If the established church was not going to provide authoritative teaching about the contents of this wondrous book, nonestablished prophets and seers would fill the vacuum.

I didn't know anything about the reputation of Revelation when I first encountered it after my conversion to Christianity just before my senior year in high school. It turned out that my initial immersion in roiled waters of Revelation study came in a faith community that was on the edge of mainstream Christianity—though I wasn't aware of this marginality at the time.

I joined a rural Baptist congregation where the pastor preached continuously about how we lived in the last days and that we could be raptured out of life on earth at any moment to be with God. The signs of the times all pointed toward Jesus's soon return. These were the early 1970s. The war on Vietnam raged nightly on television. The Communist threat loomed large. Race riots spread widely, and the sexual revolution was making clear just how decadent American society had become. And all the long-haired hippies!

I didn't know much about the Bible or about Christianity in general, just that I did want Jesus to be my Savior. The people in my church were warm and welcoming to me. I was bright and curious and ready to learn what I could about this new faith I was becoming part of. I read avidly and listened to taped sermons. Names I remember are Jack Van Impe, Salem Kirban, Dwight Pentecost, and John Walvoord. And, most importantly, Hal Lindsey.

Lindsey's book *The Late Great Planet Earth* had been published the year before my conversion. It quickly became the go-to book for those interested in future-oriented biblical prophecy. It sold millions of copies and became the best-selling book, secular or religious, in the United States during the decade of the 1970s. I read it several times along with others of his books. I also listened to dozens of Hal Lindsey tapes.

I now have negative feelings about the few years that followed my conversion. I remain grateful that I was treated well in that church community. People were kind and generous throughout my time there. However, I believe now that the theology I learned (especially what I was taught about Revelation and the end times) had a doubly hurtful impact on me.

First, it was bad theology that gave me wrong ideas about every other element of my faith—salvation, who Jesus is and what he cares about, heaven and hell, how to read the Bible, the meaning of the church, and on down the line. I had a lot to unlearn later. As it turns out, thankfully, that unlearning was not particularly difficult or traumatic once my sensibility changed. But I wish I would have had a more intellectually healthy introduction to the faith.

Second, and more subtly, I believe that my immersion in the version of Baptist fundamentalism I encountered cost me a college education. I was inoculated against the kind of natural curiosity and excitement that I think would have characterized my college experience had I been educated differently as a new Christian. I was taught to be suspicious of ideas, questions, and intellectual diversity. Instead of getting a background that would serve me later in graduate studies, I was encouraged to simply accept the simple doctrines I was presented with. I spent the first three years of college in an intellectual fog, learning very little and living with a sense of suspicion toward the entire enterprise of higher education.

Things changed dramatically for me at the end of my junior year. Interestingly, a crucial catalyst came in a conversation with a mentor in the small, nondenominational, conservative church I had joined when I moved for college. We were discussing end times theology. As he explained the different points of view among Christians, I was shocked to learn that the future-prophetic view I had been taught was not the only view that Christians had. In fact, my mentor said, most Christians don't hold that view. This revelation rattled me, but I happily took it as an invitation to explore some of the other views. If what I had been taught was not the only option, perhaps I could find something better.

As it turned out, I happened upon some writings a few months later that very ably explained why the future-prophetic view of the end times was, in fact, deeply flawed. As an indication that my convictions about that viewpoint were not nearly as deep-seated as I might have imagined, I quickly rejected that entire theological orientation.

My final year of college became a time of intense reading and talking as I entered with enthusiasm the world of academic theology at an introductory level. A key resource for me was Francis Schaeffer, who confirmed my rejection of the future-prophetic schema and who encouraged me to ask questions and to pursue truth wherever it led me. As it turned out, such a pursuit actually led me away from Schaeffer's own narrow theology.

With the end of my fixation on the end times, I lost interest in Revelation for several years and pursued other interests. After Schaeffer, I turned to Dietrich Bonhoeffer and Jacques Ellul as important thinkers. And, partly under their influence, I embraced pacifism as a core conviction (this was the end of the Vietnam War years and I had faced the possibility of being drafted and going to war). The excitement about pacifism led to discovering the writings of John Howard Yoder and other Mennonites and to some intense discussion in our little church.

At some point, perhaps 1978, our church had a formal debate about pacifism. The person arguing against pacifism asserted that while Jesus certainly was nonviolent during his life on earth, we know from both the Old Testament and the book of Revelation that God at times approves of war.

Now, I had read a bit on the issue of the Old Testament and war and felt like I had a good sense of how to counter that argument. But his point about Revelation had me stumped. From what I remembered of Revelation, I had to agree that it seemed to be pretty okay with violence, some of which would be initiated by God. Since becoming a pacifist, I hadn't really thought about Revelation.

The tension I felt at that time stemmed from two powerful convictions. The first was that Jesus would have us be pacifists (that is, never support or participate in war or in other death-dealing violence against human beings). The second was that the Bible was true, from Genesis to Revelation, and it came from God. Thus, since God wants us to be pacifists, and the Bible is God's word, the Bible must support pacifism. But were both of these convictions actually correct—at the same time?

As I mentioned, I had come to some peace of mind about the Old Testament. It would be a challenge to work through all the issues related to divinely initiated and divinely supported violence in the Old Testament, but I was confident it could be done. But what about Revelation? I realized that I had to figure this one out. So, I started to read Revelation and read about it. It was an exciting project because I discovered that the anti-pacifist assumptions expressed in our church debate did not reflect the scholarly consensus on Revelation.

As with the Old Testament, the scholarship on Revelation concerning divinely initiated violence was diverse. Not only fundamentalist Baptists argued that the Bible affirms violence. However, many argued a contrary view. I fairly soon learned of what I now call the peaceable Revelation stream of interpretation. A key figure was British scholar G. B. Caird[1] who wrote an influential commentary in the mid-1960s. Writers such as J. P. M. Sweet[2] and Richard Bauckham[3] furthered Caird's pacifist-friendly reading of Revelation. Also, an Anabaptist scholar, Vernard Eller,[4] wrote a quirky but convincing (to me!) commentary that explicitly argued for pacifism.

My wife (Kathleen Temple) and I decided to attend the Anabaptist Mennonite Biblical Seminary in the 1980–1981 school year. During that year our education in peace theology deepened and we decided we wanted to become Mennonites. I took an excellent class on Revelation from Gertrude Roten at AMBS, and also took several classes from pacifist biblical scholars such as Millard Lind and Willard Swartley.

1. Caird, *Commentary*.
2. Sweet, *Revelation*.
3. Bauckham, *Theology*.
4. Eller, *Most*.

After AMBS, I continued to learn more and more about Revelation. As an interim pastor, I began to preach by working through Revelation in a series of seven sermons. These were well-received in our congregation and ultimately published in the weekly magazine of the Mennonite Church, ~~The~~ *Gospel Herald,* over seven consecutive weeks in 1983. I felt the courage to expand the articles into a popular-level commentary that was published in 1987.[5]

Since then, I have gone on to present academic papers, preach sermons, lecture in college classes, edit books, and read much about Revelation. My views have evolved, but more than ever I still believe that Revelation is a book of peace. Even though a strong interpretive stream treats Revelation as peaceable, I do think we could use a book on Revelation that makes the peace theme more central and obvious than has generally been done. Hence, the present book.

I began to direct my interests in Revelation toward writing a new book several years ago and preached another long series of sermons on it. The context for this more recent set of sermons was a congregation filled with what I call, only partly facetiously, "cultured despisers of the book of Revelation"—people who are skeptical that Revelation has much that is redemptive to offer for peaceable Christians. I hoped with those sermons, and hope now with this book, to persuade such skeptics of the value of Revelation for transformative living in our current world.

I approach Revelation as a theological ethicist who draws on biblical and theological resources for guidance and courage for living peaceable lives. I write with strong convictions about the need for radical social change in our broken world and with strong convictions that that change needs to be anchored in nonviolent convictions and practices. I am inspired by the teaching and practice of Martin Luther King Jr., and I believe that Revelation actually supports such an approach.

I am not very interested in the technical aspects of critical study of the Bible (see David Aune's[6] three-volume commentary for an exemplar of that type of work). I believe such work is important and I benefit from it. However, I take a more engaged approach asking at every level what Revelation has to offer for our peacemaking work. In the several decades since publishing my earlier commentary, I have only had my views about Revelation as a peace book deepened and strengthened. I hope what follows will show why.

---

5. Grimsrud, *Triumph.*
6. Aune, *Revelation.*

WAYS OF INTERPRETING REVELATION

During the conversation I had with the friend who informed me (and thereby changed the trajectory of my life) that the end times theology I had been taught was not Christianity's only position, I learned for the first time of the term "dispensationalism." This is the label for the school of thought that expects an imminent rapture that will take Christians out of the world and prepare the way for the great tribulation and Jesus's soon return. It turns out that rather than being the standard Christian view, dispensationalism dates back only to the 1830s and the teaching of an Irish Anglican priest named John Nelson Darby. And it never was accepted in mainstream Protestant, Catholic, or Eastern Orthodox churches.

Going back to earliest Christianity, Revelation has a colorful history and has attracted an extraordinarily wide range of interpretations. The suspicion with which establishment Christianity has always treated Revelation surely has contributed to the wide variety of interpretations, since authorized theologians and church leaders have never been particularly interested in it and hence have not established official interpretations.

From the time Revelation began to be circulated with the other writings that make up the New Testament, some have been attracted to a futuristic interpretation that reads Revelation as containing predictive prophecies that inform those with the insight to see about what will be happening in the future. This approach has always been controversial. Dispensationalism is only one of the many future-prophetic schemas that have emerged, though it is the main one in recent history that has gained a following.

We may identify three general approaches to reading Revelation in Christian history: the future-prophetic view, the historical-symbolic view, and the "problematic view."

(1) The future-prophetic view's emphasis on predictive aspects has made the book attractive for many who were on the margins of society and church. Dissatisfaction with the established order may fuel a desire for readings that promise something different in the future. So, Revelation has been a playground for theologies that promise some kind of major change in the future—be it in history for various groups of revolutionaries such as the Taborites in fifteenth-century Europe or the Peasants' Revolt rebels a century later, or be it those who hope for a paradise after the end of history that will reward the dispossessed and punish their oppressors.

(2) The historical-symbolic approach has been typical for those interpreters who have been part of mainstream theological communities. However, these interpretations were not widespread or influential on a popular level, perhaps mainly because of the general lack of interest in Revelation.

Revelation has been virtually absent from the lectionaries that determine what passages from the Bible will be read in the mainstream church's worship service. This absence has surely led to little attention being paid to Revelation in the training of pastors in colleges, seminaries, and congregational Christian education classes.

The historical-symbolic approach recognizes the importance of viewing the historical setting of the book in similar ways that the historical setting of, say, Jeremiah or Romans have been important for interpretation. Revelation, though, contains a much greater number of difficult to interpret images and numbers than other biblical books. So, effort must also be spent on discerning the meaning of all that symbolism. This approach tends to read Revelation as simply another document from early Christianity with exhortations and instructions that are best interpreted in light of their meaning to their original audience—and relevance to the present being discerned in relation to parallels between the present and the original setting.

(3) From the start, many in the mainstream or established church have seen Revelation as problematic. The attraction it has had for marginal Christians has been cause for much of this suspicion by those in the center of power. A significant influence on later theology may be found in the theology of Augustine, who is considered the father of the "amillennial" view that removes the message of Revelation from historical embodiment. Rather than looking for a "millennium" in history that would involve a transformation of the present status quo, Augustine advocated a stance where Christians could be much more comfortable with the social and political and ecclesial status quo. Augustinian theology influenced the Protestantism of Martin Luther and John Calvin to disregard or dismiss Revelation as an important source for Christian theology.

In later generations in Western Christianity, under the influence of the age of reason, the bizarre and cataclysmic visions of Revelation were seen as absurd and unbelievable—and problematic in their influence on many non-enlightened Christians. The resultant hostility toward Revelation may be seen in writers such as the British novelist D. H. Lawrence (who famously characterized Revelation as full of "flamboyant hate and simple lust for the end of the world").[7] The contemporary popular scholar of the historical Jesus, John Dominic Crossan[8], is another cultured despiser of Revelation. Perhaps the harshest takedown is Los Angeles Times journalist Jonathan Kirsch in his book, A History of the End of the World: How the Most

7. Quoted in Kirsch, History, 15. See Lawrence, Apocalypse, 9.

8. See Crossan, God, chapter 5, "Apocalypse and the Pornography of Violence," 191–235.

Controversial Book in the Bible Changed the Course of Western Civilization. Feminist theologians such as Catherine Keller[9] and Tina Pippin[10] have also written sharp critiques of Revelation.

A much more positive disposition toward Revelation may be found among progressive Christian social activists beginning in the last part of the twentieth century. Global crises such as the spread of nuclear weapons and environmental devastation have demanded a deep, cosmic response. Writers such as William Stringfellow,[11] Daniel Berrigan,[12] Elisabeth Schüssler Fiorenza,[13] Dale Aukerman,[14] and Barbara Rossing[15] have used Revelation as a resource for their advocacy. The influential theologian activist Walter Wink[16] utilized Revelation's portrayal of the powers such as the dragon and the beast for his insights into the dynamics of human social life and the ways structures, institutions, and ideologies shape us for evil.

HERMENEUTICS

The debates about how to interpret Revelation seem impossible to fully resolve. What one finds in Revelation will be decisively shaped by one's assumptions when one picks the book up. Some questions that shape what will be perceived about Revelation include whether the book is making predictive prophesies or not, whether the reference to Jesus Christ in Revelation 1:1 should be seen as a direct link to the Jesus of the Gospels or an allusion to a Jesus of the end times who has a different agenda, and whether when we read Revelation we should expect ethical directives that take a peacemaking approach or actually point in a pro-violence direction.

Let me briefly sketch my agenda as I approach Revelation. I begin by accepting that it is a valid part of the Christian Bible. I expect it to be a source of guidance and inspiration. So, I read Revelation in an engaged, optimistic way. When I encounter parts of the book that seem not to be encouraging, I scrutinize them closely, looking for ways to read that do respect the integrity of the text and test whether an encouraging view might be possible. Because it's part of the Christian Bible, I read Revelation in relation to what comes

9. Keller, *Apocalypse.*

10. Pippin, *Death.*

11. Stringfellow, *Ethic.*

12. Berrigan, *Nightmare.*

13. Schüssler Fiorenza, *Revelation.*

14. Aukerman, *Reckoning.*

15. Rossing, *Rapture.*

16. Wink, *Engaging.*

before in Scripture and expect that it will echo more than contradict the core teaching of the big story the Bible tells.

I seek to interpret the text as accurately as possible. The best way to do that is to read the book of Revelation as a whole, allowing the whole to shape how we read the parts, looking for interpretive guidance from the entire book when engaging particular verses. Beyond reading the book as a whole, I also read it as part of the New Testament and as part of the Christian Bible.

In reading Revelation as a positive resource that guides and encourages those who seek to follow Jesus, I look for ways that the book might speak to our present context. However, I do not do this by looking for predictions of events soon to happen. Rather, I look for analogies between John's context and ours. I expect that John's wisdom for his time will be relevant for ours.

I approach Revelation as a piece of first-century literature without any special magical properties. The relevance that Revelation might have for us must follow from the relevance it had for its original audience. It has the form of a "classic text" that over time has provided meaning and insight to its readers, the product of the insights of its original human author. We understand Revelation best through the faculties of our human discernment efforts. We draw on our knowledge of the book's context, our analysis of its content, our conversations with other readers, and our commitment to find meaning and guidance for faithful living from its words.

We try to recognize the role our own social context and convictions play as we read the Bible—and as we apply what we learn from the Bible to our lives. We have an ongoing conversation as we continually move back and forth between the text and our present world. We ask questions of the text based on our current context and allow the message we find in the text to shape how we respond to our world. The element of my current context that I bring to bear most directly to our engagement with Revelation is the violent ideology of the American empire. I ask questions of the text that relate to the possible relevance of John's engagement with the violent ideology of the Roman Empire for our engagement in our day.

THE FUTURE-PROPHETIC SCHEMA

I do not expect accurate predictive prophecy from Revelation, so I approach it in ways that are profoundly different than those who follow a future-prophetic reading strategy. However, given the popularity of that approach, it seems likely that most readers of this book would benefit from a short critique even if they are interested in a more peaceable reading.

John Nelson Darby (1800–1882), an Irish Anglican priest who left the priesthood and founded the Plymouth Brethren movement in the mid-1830s, was one of the great theological innovators of the past two hundred years in English-speaking theology. His approach, often labeled "dispensationalism" due to its reading of Christian history in terms of seven "ages" or "dispensations," remains the standard template for future-prophetic interpretation of Revelation (recognizing, of course, much diversity among Darby's various theological descendants). Certainly, both Hal Lindsey and Tim LaHaye (the co-author and theological source for the Left Behind books and movies) remain pretty close to Darby in their viewpoints.

One key idea in this future-prophetic schema has been that the course of history, especially the events that will usher in the end of the world, are foretold in the Bible and may be discerned if we read the Bible correctly. The phrase "rightly dividing the word of truth" from 2 Tim 2:15 became a catch-phrase for dispensationalist teacher C. I. Scofield, of this type of reading. Scofield authored an enormously popular series of notes for interpreting the Bible that were published with English Bibles in the "Scofield Bible" early in the twentieth century.

According to the dispensationalist scheme, at the beginning of time God determined a specific, detailed plan for history's last days. This plan involved seven dispensations, each with a distinctive plan for salvation. We currently live near the end of the fifth dispensation and at any moment it will end when God takes God's people out of the world (the "rapture") and initiates a horrendous period of chaos and violence (the "great tribulation") that will end with a massive war ("the battle of Armageddon"). Then will come the sixth dispensation (the "millennium") that will end with the final judgment that will usher in the final, eternal paradise.

Two events have played key roles in recent expressions of this schema: the creation of nuclear weapons and the establishment of Israel as a nation-state. Nuclear weapons have made it much more believable that a sudden catastrophe that ended life on earth is a realistic possibility. And Israel's formation in 1948 was seen as the fulfillment of predictive prophecies and as the key moment signaling that human history has entered its final stage.[17]

This perspective takes several important theological steps. God is all-knowing, in control of the events of history, and the bearer of irresistible power. Human history is on a downward trajectory as things continually get worse and will require God's direct intervention to avert total self-destruction. Jesus is a radically different character between his first coming

---

17. For an excellent historical treatment of the career of the future-prophetic schema, see Boyer, *When*.

as a nonviolent willing sacrificial victim and his second coming as a violent judge. Human beings are profoundly fallen, sinful creatures decisively inclined toward destructive self-deception. Our problems as humans are greatly exacerbated by a powerful and ever-deceiving personal Devil. In the end, God will conquer Satan, throwing him into the lake of fire, a place of eternal punishment. Joining Satan in the lake of fire will be all human beings who have not accepted Jesus as their savior.

I believe the future-prophetic schema is enormously problematic: (1) It proposes a deterministic notion of God where the predicted events from centuries ago are set in concrete. This is a puppet master kind of God who does not allow for human free will or, actually, the dynamics of love where God respects God's creatures and allows us to grow and learn and contribute to the working out of God's will for humanity.

(2) It suggests that the true meaning of Revelation was not apparent to its writer and first audience. In fact, the meaning of Revelation has been hidden for most of the history since it was written, only now being made apparent to true believers who understand the predictive prophecies. This is a strange view of the writing of the Bible where the authors themselves are ignorant of the meaning of what they write.

(3) Thus, the future-prophetic view presupposes an extraordinarily "high" view of the inspiration of Scripture, as if it is simply made up of direct revelations from God that bypass the human concreteness of the Bible's writers. This view not only presents a troubling view of God as controlling, it also denies the humanity of the Bible.

(4) The future-prophetic approach has centered on the United States. Not coincidentally, throughout the history of this school of interpretation, the enemies of God in Revelation (and elsewhere in the Bible) have been enemies of the United States. Whereas in Revelation, the Roman Empire as the world's dominant superpower is seen as a manifestation of rebellion against God, for present-day future-prophetic believers, the world's dominant superpower (the United States) is presented as being on God's side. The tendency to weaponize the Bible for the sake of one's own nation's ends has a long and devastating history in the past 1,600 years.

(5) Finally, in general the future-prophetic approach to Revelation reflects a fearfulness that actually contradicts the book's own message of courage and resistance in the face of suffering. This approach often reflects fears of other cultures, of an uncertain future, of an open universe, and of the responsibility to work to manifest new Jerusalem. Such fearfulness seems to reflect a lack of trust in the mercy and loving patience of the One on the throne and of the Lamb.

In contrast to the future-prophetic schema, my approach takes seriously Revelation's historical context as we seek to learn from it so that we might better be peacemakers in our own historical context. What may we say about Revelation's historical setting?

PLACING REVELATION IN ITS HISTORICAL CONTEXT

The book of Revelation presents itself as a letter written by a church leader to seven congregations in "Asia," the name for a province of the Roman Empire located in the western part of present-day Turkey. We may call Revelation a "pastoral letter." To call it "pastoral" is to note that John has in mind the people in the churches to which he writes—in their time and place. The practical spiritual needs and concrete social issues John's audience faced had nothing to do with the kinds of speculation about the far distant future that many interpreters see in Revelation. John hoped to encourage faithfulness and hope for his readers in their world.

To call Revelation a "letter" is to note that it was written for particular people known to its author and addresses their issues. It is "public" in the sense that it was written for the "people in the pew." On the other hand, it was not "public" in the sense that it was not written for the general public in the wider world who would be mostly unknown to John. Like Paul and Paul's letters, John seems to have written Revelation as a way to make his voice present to his churches even when he was physically absent. Our challenge, as with Paul's letters, is to discern what John meant in addressing his direct historical audience. Only then might we be enabled to sense what his words might mean to us.

This "John" seems to have been a character most likely unknown to us except through this book. A scholarly consensus (though far from unanimous) holds that this is likely not the "John" of Jesus's twelve disciples nor the author of the Gospel of John and the letters of John in the New Testament. This is simply "John," a self-styled prophet who appears to be suffering persecution due to his witness to the way of Jesus.

John writes during what appears to have been an unsettled time, probably during the last decade of the first century of the Common Era. The area where he ministered was evangelized by Paul maybe a generation earlier. One of the congregations mentioned in Revelation is known to be a place where Paul worked (Ephesus) and another not named in Revelation was nearby (Colossae). We know a bit about some general upheaval in this part of the world in the years not long before Revelation was written—wars, famine, earthquakes, the eruption of the volcano Vesuvius (79 CE). So there likely was a widespread sense of uncertainty in that region.

Persecution was in the air. Christians often (though not always, as we will see) refused fully to participate in public religious and civic festivals and other meetings. Generally, Christians came from the non-elite segments of society and so may have had a sense of alienation from the economic and political establishment. Probably difficult dynamics existed between Christian and non-Christian Jewish communities. Christianity increasingly attracted believers who did not come from a Jewish background. At this time, Jews were granted a significant level of tolerance and released from some of the religious expectations. This tolerance likely was increasingly withheld from Christians, who were less and less assumed to be Jews.

Probably the most immediate fraught issue for Christians followed from the intensifying dynamics of emperor worship. The demands for religious obedience to the emperor were growing. The emperor Domitian (who ruled from 81 to 96) increased these demands. Christians debated among themselves how to respond to emperor worship and the broader sense of empire-inspired public religiosity (something we could liken to a kind of civil religion[18]). For stricter Christians, such as John, the demands of the empire and emperor directly contradicted the expectation that they give their highest loyalty to the God of the Bible, the God of Jesus.

Christians responded in several different ways. Some renounced their faith and joined fully with the empire, a move that greatly enhanced their potential for higher social status. Many who remained in the churches believed that compromise was possible, Christians could participate publicly in the empire religiosity and remain active Christians in private (the empire did not restrict private religious practices, only expected concurrent participation in their festivals, et al). Or Christians could take a more rigorous and exclusivist stance and refuse to take part in the empire religiosity due to the conflict of loyalties.

John strongly advocated for the rigorous option and warned of negative consequences for those who went along with the empire. He expected readers who accept his exhortation would face trouble. Widespread persecution against Christians just because they were Christians does not seem to have been happening. However, should Christians defy the empire's call to give it religious devotion the consequences could be enormous. On the other hand, John insists that the consequences of accommodation would be even greater: separation from God.

18. Gorman, *Reading*, 40–56.

REVELATION AS AN "APOCALYPSE"

Our book gets its English title from the first word of the book in Greek: *apokalypsis,* translated into English as "revelation." This Greek word also gives us our English word "apocalypse." This is a common word in the New Testament, though the only place it is used in Revelation is at 1:1. Elsewhere, it has the general sense of the revealing or unveiling of truths from God. This is how Paul talks about how he received the gospel (Gal 1:12; Rom 1:17). By calling what follows an *apokalypsis,* John makes high claims for what he discloses.

Later readers noticed similarities between Revelation and various other writings from that era—most notably the book of Daniel in the Bible (though neither Daniel nor the other writings used the term *apokalypsis* to describe their contents). Among modern scholars, the term "apocalyptic" has been used of these various writings that were produced from the second century BCE through the second century CE. Except for Revelation, Daniel, and a section from the Gospel of Mark (with parallels in Matthew and Luke), none of the other "apocalyptic" writings were included in the biblical canon. Writings such as the Book of Enoch, and the Apocalypses of Baruch, Paul, and Peter (some Jewish, some Christian) did get wide circulation.

The books usually included in what is called the genre of apocalyptic writings typically shared many common characteristics. A few of the key ones include addressing a context where the audience (presumed to be God's people) feels besieged by political and cosmic forces. Life is a struggle between the forces of good and evil and the writings proclaim the ultimate victory of God, often occurring in the age to come. They tend to contain visions of catastrophe, often with extreme symbolic imagery and massive violence. Human beings must take sides in this battle.[19]

Helpful as it might be to compare Revelation to these other writings, I also believe it is important to recognize important differences, characteristics that mark Revelation as something more than simply another example of the apocalyptic genre. We should note ways that Revelation employs "apocalyptic" literary devices that make Revelation distinctive in the New Testament. However, we should also recognize that to label it too narrowly as "apocalyptic" might lead us to misunderstand the book.

The date and origin of Revelation is relatively clear. The book makes no attempt to shroud its actual provenance, as is usually the case for apocalypses. This means that John intended to speak directly to an audience of his

19. Gorman, *Reading,* 15.

own time and place. None of the other "apocalyptic" writings have a section like Rev 2–3 where John makes transparent his setting and his agenda.

Generally, apocalyptic literature presents a clear distinction between the present age of brokenness and a future age of healing. In Revelation, the key event has happened in the past with the life, death, and resurrection. Often, interpreters of Revelation who read it as a member of the apocalyptic genre project a futurist orientation and miss the significance of what we could call Revelation's "realized eschatology." One of the important elements of seeing Revelation as having a sense of present fulfillment is that such a sense underscores the significance of John's call for *present* faithfulness. As well, seeing Jesus's nonviolent life, death, and resurrection as the only victory that matters refutes the notion that Revelation teaches some future literal war between God and God's people versus the spiritual and human enemies of God.

Revelation certainly portrays a struggle of good versus evil. However, unlike many apocalypses, this conflict is surprisingly one-sided. We find no strong dualism that pictures the forces of God entering into an open-ended battle with the forces of the evil powers where the outcome is up for grabs. Revelation from the very beginning affirms the victory of God and the Lamb as already in place. The powers of evil may deceive human beings, but when confronted with God, they simply surrender, are captured, and sent into the lake of fire.

Revelation itself identifies with the writings of the Old Testament prophets. As a prophecy in the biblical sense, Revelation intends to "forthtell" God's agenda for humanity in the present world, making allusions to the future not to "foretell" events yet to happen but rather to stimulate its audience to live faithfully in their own time and place.

Revelation's message complements the fully public and easy to understand story of Jesus told in the Gospels. Jesus, the Lamb, already won the victory over the powers through his faithful life, his authoritative teaching, his courage in the faith of a violent death, and his vindication by God in resurrection. This message is quite different from the much more confusing, convoluted, and deliberately mysterious messages of various other apocalypses.

REVELATION'S PEACE THEOLOGY

In the commentary that follows, I make the case verse by verse for reading Revelation as a peace book. Here is an overview of that argument against the standard understanding among interpreters that Revelation is a pro-violence book.

First, while many commentators *assume* that John has a vengeful orientation and thus read the evidence of the book in a pro-violence sort of way, I take up Revelation with a skepticism toward the idea that John's orientation is fundamentally vengeful. That John is vengeful has to be shown when I approach Revelation. My main reason for not assuming that Revelation has a vengeful orientation is that this book is part of the New Testament (which, overall, does not have a vengeful outlook). The very first sentence of Revelation tells the reader that it is a "revelation of Jesus Christ." Now it could be that John's Jesus will be different from the Jesus of the Gospels, but that is something I think needs to be established, not assumed.

As I read Revelation, I recognize it as part of the New Testament. Thus, I expect it to elaborate on central New Testament themes such as God's healing love and the call to follow the way of Jesus. Of course, the book must be studied for what it actually says, but what we see will be shaped by what we expect to see. What reason would we have to *assume* that John has a vengeful orientation—and then inevitably to allow that assumption to take away the need to *establish* that this is John's orientation? I am skeptical that we have a good reason.

Because they tend to assume Revelation has a vengeful orientation, many scholars are not actually "neutral" in how they read the book. Yet they write with a detached, "scholarly," tone more than a stance sympathetic with Revelation's mode of resistance versus the Roman Empire and the domination system in general. I choose not to take a detached, scholarly approach but rather read Revelation "from the inside" (that is, read Revelation as part of my story [as the reader] of seeking peace—or, stated alternatively, I read Revelation as a part of the Christian canon from the point of view of one who accepts that canon as providing a normative source for *my* theology/ethics).

To read Revelation as a peace book, we start with this question: What does this book have to teach us about peace? If we take a detached view without presuppositions about the book's meaningfulness and simply treat it as an artifact to analyze, we won't be likely to see it as very peaceable. I'd say that this latter approach, though, makes it less likely that the interpreter would be able to understand the *message* of Revelation accurately. We face a dilemma—may we truly understand Revelation if we don't try to read it the way it was meant to be read? What follows are a few suggestions of what Revelation might have to teach us about peace.

(1) The centrality of the slain Lamb who stands and is worshiped

The vision contained in chapters 4 and 5 may be seen as a key to the message of the entire book (and to the message of the New Testament as a whole and of the Bible as a whole). These two chapters portray a worship service that begins and ends with worship by all of creation. The beginning focuses on worship of the one on the throne, the ending focuses on worship of the Lamb. In between, we learn why the Lamb is worshiped. Due to his persevering love that led to his death and his vindication by the one on the throne through resurrection, he demonstrates what allows "the scroll" to be opened (5:6)—that is, what allows history to reach its healing culmination.

Everything that follows in Revelation should be read in light of this vision. There are, of course, images that seem to be in tension with the peaceable message of Rev 5. However, just about all of those images are ambiguous and open to different interpretations. None of them flat out contradict Rev 5. If those discordant but ambiguous images are seen as intended by John to support the vision of the slain Lamb standing and being worshiped, they will be seen quite differently than if they are seen as intended to convey a message of punishing vengeance.

That the resurrected Lamb stands "as if slaughtered" (5:5) underscores the centrality of the "blood" metaphor to the book as a whole. It is fascinating and enormously instructive to trace the use of blood in the book. Remarkably, in tension with those views that portray Revelation as vengeful and violent, never once in the entire book are we told that any of God's human enemies have their blood shed. One possible exception is the picture in Revelation fourteen of blood rising to the bridle of a horse (14:20)—this is a key ambiguous image that reads quite differently in light of Rev 4 and 5 and the way "blood" is used everywhere else in the book. As I discuss in the commentary, we have good reasons to read the "blood" in 14:20 as another allusion to the blood of Jesus and his martyred followers.

The "blood" in Revelation is shed by Jesus or by his followers. Jesus's blood signifies his faithful witness in his life, and it heals those who follow his path. The "blood" of Jesus is in fact the "weapon" that defeats the powers of evil (12:11). The conquering that God, the Lamb, and their people do in Revelation is the conquering of persevering love. The "Lamb's war" is fought with the weapons of the word of truth and the faithful witness of Jesus's message.

(2) Overcoming the powers

The story Revelation tells makes a crucial distinction between human beings who stand against God and the spiritual forces of evil personified by the dragon, beast, and false prophet. Revelation holds out the possibility that human enemies of God ("the inhabitants of the earth" and "the kings of the earth") may remain committed to the dragon and join it in the lake of fire. However, only the evil powers are *explicitly* throne into that lake. The "destroyers of the earth" who are "destroyed" are the powers, not the people. The presence of the kings of the earth in the new Jerusalem and the healing of the nations who opposed God indicates that the focus of judgment is on these powers, not on human beings. And when the powers are gone, the humans who had allied with them have hope for healing.

One of the difficult to interpret elements of the story is the jarring juxtaposition of the Lamb who conquers through persevering love in chapter 5 and the Lamb who breaks the seals of the scroll beginning in chapter 6, leading to a series of terrible plagues of violence and death. What we actually have with these seemingly contradictory pictures may be a sophisticated attempt by John to navigate the perennial tension that comes with belief in a good God and awareness of terrible suffering and injustice in the world. John actually gives us a picture of God being somewhat removed from the plagues—with a sense that the main forces that directly cause destruction are actually the evil powers. These powers serve God's "wrath" in the sense that they contribute to the consequences in the world of human beings turning from God.

Here the vision in chapter 5 (and how the book's emphasis on the faithful witness of the Lamb and his followers reinforces that vision) becomes crucial. If we see this vision as central, we will likely understand the plague visions to convey that the world is home to violence and injustice driven by the oppression of the dragon and its servants (including the great empires such as Rome). How does God "conquer" those powers and bring healing in face of the violence? If God tried to conquer using vengeance and divine violence, the spiral of death would only be accelerated. Instead, God breaks the spiral through persevering love. Crucially, Babylon goes down due to drinking the blood of the saints (chapters 17–18) and the rider on the white horse rides forth to battle with his blood already having been shed and armed only with his word of testimony (the sword coming out of his mouth, chapter 19).

(3) Salvation for the many

Does John's vision hold out hope for only a tiny remnant while the vast majority of humankind faces the vicious sword of God's condemning judgment? I think not. Only a selective reading of the book, following the *assumption* that the book is mainly about vengeance, could fail to see the strong universalistic tendencies that are present throughout.

Throughout the book we have worship scenes. These scenes are not peripheral tangents, but actually help make up the core message of the book and help us understand the plague visions. The worship scenes are notable in how all-encompassing the worshiping community is understood to be. Over and over again we read of the worshipers coming from *every* tribe and nation and language. The victory is for everyone!

A key vision comes in chapter 7. An accurate understanding of this vision would turn the standard view of the famous number 144,000 on its head. This is not a number that denotes a limited sense of salvation but actually symbolizes an expansive sense of salvation. In chapter 5, John *heard* a narrow view of messiahship, but *saw* the Lamb worshiped by all creation. Then, in chapter 7, John *hears* the 144,000 but then *sees* an uncountable multitude. These two groups are the same—the 144,000 defines the group as the people of God; the uncountable multitude tells us who makes up this people.

This universalistic inclination is supported elsewhere in the book, culminating with the key mention of the kings of the earth (who symbolize God's human enemies) healed and present in the new Jerusalem where, crucially, the door is never shut.

FOR FURTHER ENGAGEMENT

1. What is one point in this introductory chapter that you found particularly helpful and one point that left you with a question or concern?

2. How do you respond to the discussion of the "future-prophetic schema." In particular, how persuasive do you find the author's five points of critique? Can you think of other points (positive or negative) about that approach that could be made?

3. While Revelation seems to be deeply concerned with how followers of the Lamb live their lives in engagement with their wider culture, its author does not appear to be outlining a detailed political program for readers to adapt. What do you think his political agenda was?

4. In your initial impression of Revelation, how would you describe its emotional impact? What kind of feelings does it evoke for you? Do those feelings make you want to engage Revelation more closely or to set it aside?

In this chapter I have hopefully established that it is not out of line to expect that Revelation will line up on the side of peace. As a Revelation of Jesus Christ, the book may reasonably be read as a book of peace. That will be my argument. In what follows, we will look more closely at John's presentation to see if my assertions are worthy to be affirmed.

2

A Revelation about Jesus

[Revelation 1]

The first chapter of Revelation makes it clear that we must take with all seriousness the book's focus on Jesus Christ. We begin with the self-identification: This is a "revelation of Jesus Christ." Whatever we may think "revelation" (the Greek word would be literally translated as "apocalypse") may mean, what is being revealed has to do with Jesus.

We then get a quick christological primer. This Jesus has a three-part identity: "faithful witness," "first born of the dead," and "ruler of the kings of the earth." We can expect the meaning of these titles to become clearer as the revelation unfolds. He is a savior whose "blood" brings liberation, another concept to be illuminated as we proceed. This Jesus is "coming," as is "his God and Father." We will learn more about what "coming" means as the story unfolds. Already, we get the clear sense that Jesus and "his God" will be portrayed as quite closely linked.

In the second half of the chapter, we are given a striking description of Jesus, drawn from various Old Testament images and full of symbolism. The key point comes at the end of the chapter. This Jesus, first born of the dead, is "alive forever and ever" and ever present among his people. This presence, we will learn, is to be understood as both a blessing and a challenge. He will, as has been said, comfort the afflicted and afflict the comfortable.

REVELATION 1:1–8

> The revelation of Jesus Christ, which God gave him to show his servants what must soon take place; he made it known by sending his angel to his servant John, who testified to the word of God and to the testimony of Jesus Christ, even to all that he saw. Blessed is the one who reads aloud the words of the prophecy and blessed are those who hear and who keep what is written in it; for the time is near. John to the seven churches that are in Asia: Grace to you and peace from him who is and who was and who is to come, and from the seven spirits who are before his throne, and from Jesus Christ, the faithful witness, the firstborn of the dead, and the ruler of the kings of the earth. To him who loves us and freed us from our sins by his blood, and made us to be a kingdom, priests serving his God and Father, to him be glory and dominion forever and ever. Amen. Look! He is coming with the clouds; every eye will see him, even those who pierced him; and on his account all the tribes of the earth will wail. So, it is to be. Amen. "I am the Alpha and the Omega," says the Lord God, who is and who was and who is to come, the Almighty.

From the very beginning of the book, we are required to settle on a reading strategy for Revelation. I can think of three distinct broad options that highlight different terms and motifs at the beginning. These distinctive emphases lead to divergent ways of reading the book as a whole.

One option picks up on the book's first word, "Revelation." The Greek word is *apokalypsie*, the source for our words "apocalypse" and "apocalyptic." This emphasis places the priority on Revelation as apocalyptic writing, part of a distinctive genre of literature that flourished in the ancient Near East in the generations prior to and following after Jesus's time. With this emphasis, Revelation is read first of all in relation to other apocalyptic literature, with the focus on its distinctiveness among the biblical writings.

A second option emphasizes the phrase, "to show his servants what must soon take place." For those with this emphasis, Revelation is read first of all as predictive literature, providing information about future events. Best-selling books such as Hal Lindsey's *The Late Great Planet Earth*[1] and Tim LaHaye and Jerry Jenkins's Left Behind series[2] have popularized this emphasis.

---

1. Lindsey, *Late*.
2. LaHaye and Jenkins, *Left Behind*, is the first in a long series of books.

I will read Revelation in line with a third option. This approach places the emphasis on the second and third words of the book, "Jesus Christ." Revelation may (I would say *should*) be read in the context of the New Testament and broader biblical story of salvation that culminates in the life and teaching of Jesus Christ. When we place the priority on the "Jesus Christ" emphasis, we will read this reference to Jesus Christ as a signal that the book of Revelation self-consciously places itself within the gospel story. Then we will assume that Revelation is best read in continuity with Jesus's message.

To link "revelation" (apocalypse) closely with Jesus Christ leads us to a more mundane understanding of this term. As an "apocalypse" *of Jesus*, what follows intends to provide insight into the meaning of Jesus's life, teaching, death, and resurrection. We refer here to "revelation" as illumination and insight. We do not think of it as future predictions or esoteric visions meant to provide otherwise unavailable information concerning catastrophic judgment and the ending of history.

"What must soon take place," then, alerts John's readers that the visions to follow speak directly to their reality—with prophetic insight. "What must soon take place" does not signal literal predictions of the future. As with ancient Israel's prophets, this phrase means a call to attentiveness. Be aware and listen to John's message about the meaning of life, especially the meaning of what God has shown the world in the life, teaching, death, and resurrection of Jesus.

This "revelation" is said to originate with God. God gave the revelation to Jesus to show Jesus's followers ("servants"), which could be read as an inclusive population—all who seek to follow Jesus throughout time and geography. We will see that the book of Revelation has a particular geographical and historical context. However, in speaking directly to that context, the God of this book reveals the reality of Jesus's message in a way that speaks to all who would follow Jesus in all times and places.

God makes this revelation known to Jesus's followers through two mediators. God uses God's "angel" (which we should understand as a "messenger" about whom we know nothing else), the point being simply that God uses this messenger to convey the revelation to John. We are given no sense that this "messenger" has agency. All we know about the human recipient and second mediator of this revelation is that his name is "John." He is God's "servant," too, and he shares with Jesus and Jesus's servants the experience of persecution (1:9).

John testifies "to all that he saw." This includes both the "word of God" and the "testimony of Jesus." These two phrases presumably both allude to one basic message. The picture is of one of a number of places where Revelation links Jesus and God closely together. Here, the close connection specifically has to do with the unity in the message of Jesus with the will of God more than the metaphysical unity of later christological dogma. However, we will find as the visions unfold that they do not actually give literal pictures. More so, they are "literary" visions that often are impossible to imagine visually. So, what John "saw" actually refers more to what he read, heard, and imagined than to literal sight—but it is important to recognize that they are insights that he envisions.

The blessing with which the book begins goes to those who "read aloud" and "hear" the words of the "prophecy." This book is meant to be heard, as we will learn, by all the followers of Jesus. The audience will hear words of "prophecy." If we read Revelation in the context of the rest of the Bible, we will be inclined to understand "prophecy" in line with earlier prophets such as Amos, Jeremiah, and John the Baptist. Biblical prophecy speaks to present faithfulness. It is very different than the predictive soothsaying that is condemned many times in the Bible.

"For the time is near" (1:3) echoes "what must soon take place" in calling for attention from the readers and listeners. It should not be understood as a futuristic prediction about the soon end of history, but rather as a call to be aware of the presence of the kingdom of God and its demands in the world right now. This ethical sense is reinforced with the promise of blessing to those who "keep what is written" in the prophecy. Keeping what is written matters because, as Jesus taught, the kingdom of God is at hand, present among us, demanding our allegiance over against human kingdoms.

After this preface that identifies the book as a "revelation" and a "prophecy" given by God through an angel to "John," John himself enters the picture as the author of what is to follow. John addresses the prophecy to "the seven churches that are in Asia" (1:4). He packages what follows as a letter to those seven churches. I believe we should recognize that ultimately the human being John is the author of this book and that it captures his imaginative genius. We best see his casting the book as a revelation from God as a rhetorical strategy meant to convey his seriousness.

We are likely meant to understand the "seven churches" in two senses. They are seven actual congregations in the Roman province of "Asia Minor" in the northeast section of the Mediterranean region (the western edge of present-day Turkey). We will learn in chapters 2 and 3 more about these congregations, enough to realize that John means to speak to real people in actual churches facing concrete issues. John means this book to be practical for people in his present world.

At the same time that we recognize the need to keep the actual historical context for this prophecy always in mind, we also are encouraged to think in broader terms. That there are precisely *seven* churches spoken of (and portrayed in chapters 2 and 3) has significance. Numerous other congregations existed in that area in addition to the seven that are mentioned. So, John has something in mind when he addresses only seven. From the use of this number elsewhere in Revelation, we can be confident that at least part of what John had in mind was that when he addresses these seven churches, he also addresses the community of Jesus's followers more broadly. The number seven connotes completeness and thus encourages us to read Revelation as speaking to all Christian congregations in all times and places.

Like with much of the rest of the Bible, we do well to pay close attention to contextual clues we find in the book that will help us interpret and apply its message. We should assume that John has particular issues in mind that connect with the needs of the seven congregations he consciously addressed. However, addressing specifically seven churches (with seven's sense of completeness), John also aims his message at the broader set of congregations—both of his day and for the generations that follow (including ours).

John once more links God and Jesus closely together. This time, he also adds an allusion to the Holy Spirit in what is, at least in a loose sense, a Trinitarian allusion (1:4–5). John offers a salutation to these churches from God ("who is and who was and who is to come"), the Holy Spirit ("the seven spirits who are before his throne"), and Jesus Christ ("the faithful witness, the firstborn of the dead, and the ruler of the kings of the earth"). The key point here also seems to be the oneness of the message, the unity of these three sources of grace and peace.

For the chapters that follow, since this book is a "revelation of Jesus Christ," the description of Jesus here merits close attention. "The faithful witness" refers to Jesus's life of persevering love culminating in his execution at the hands of the Roman Empire. "Witness" translates the Greek word *martys* (also translated "martyr") making a clear connection between Jesus's life and his death. While Revelation emphasizes throughout both Jesus's close link with God and his exalted status, these elements of Jesus's identity remain inextricably linked with his life of vulnerable, persevering love. His faithfulness to the point of martyrdom provided the bases for his exaltation.

"The firstborn of the dead" refers to how God vindicated Jesus's faithfulness by raising him from the dead following his execution. The term "firstborn" implies that others are to follow. Later, Revelation makes clear that the promise of vindication through resurrection is also made to all those who "follow the Lamb wherever he goes." Just as Jesus as faithful martyr merits vindication, so too do his followers. The link is clear: the resurrection and the faithfulness go together. The reality of vindication underscores the book's optimism that those who follow the Lamb are on the winning side of history, even if for the present they suffer at the hands of the powers that be.

The phrase "the ruler of the kings of the earth" here emphasizes a paradox. The martyr is ruler! How can that be? We will have to figure this paradox out as we work through the rest of the book. At this point, we may note that John makes extraordinary claims about Jesus's ultimate power, about his role in the social and political events of the world, and about the nature of the world's rulers.

When held together, the threefold pattern of Jesus sets the stage for the revelation of Jesus Christ that is to come in this book. We will see more of how Jesus's life led to his martyrdom, of how God vindicated this life, and the relevance of these acts by Jesus and God for the politics of the world.

John continues in his opening message to the congregations by elaborating on the meaning of Jesus Christ he has brought before us. Jesus loves us and has freed us from our sins by his blood (1:5b). All three components must be held together: Jesus's love, Jesus's acts that provide for freedom, and the role of Jesus's "blood" in how he frees us.

The love stems from the love of the Creator for the creation, even in its brokenness and alienation. The underlying motivation for God that fuels "what must soon take place" is God's love. We have only a few explicit markers in the course of Revelation to remind us of the fundamental reality of God's love, so it is important to note John's beginning emphasis here.

Jesus's embodied work of love seeks to setting free the enslaved creation, especially enslaved humanity. The visions that follow reveal in powerful ways the identity of the agents who enslave and the consequences of the enslavement. John emphasizes from the start that everything Jesus does as God's agent in our world stems from love and purposes to free humanity from all that enslaves us. The "sins" referred to here are likely a general reality more than any particular acts—that is, Jesus frees us from our "sinfulness" or our "bondage to sin." The fundamental sin in the Bible is idolatry, trusting in things rather than in God. The consequence of idolatry is enslavement, wherein the idol seduces and controls the idolater.

Freedom from the control of sin and from enslavement to the principalities and powers that seduce humanity into idolatry comes through Jesus's "blood." As with elsewhere in the Bible, the term "blood" is used without a clear explanation of what precisely is meant. In the context of the rest of the Bible and of what is to come in Revelation, we may hypothesize for now that by "blood" John has in mind the overall life, death, and resurrection of Jesus. That is, it is not Jesus's literal blood that frees but what the blood symbolizes—Jesus's life of freedom from the powers and idolatry and sin, lived to the end in faithfulness even in face of violence and the most devastating kind of execution. God's vindication in making Jesus "firstborn of the dead" reveals to the cosmos that God's love survives the worst blood-letting of which the powers are capable.

The freedom Jesus provides is certainly a "freedom from": freedom from the powers and from idolatry and from sin, all the aspects of life that lead to enslavement. However, Jesus's freedom is even more a "freedom for." Jesus frees those who follow him so that they might be "a kingdom, priests serving his God and Father" (1:6). We must remember that "kingdom" is a political term, spoken of here in the present tense. The freedom-for is a freedom here and now to live as communities that embody the way of the Lamb and display to the cosmos that Jesus indeed is the ruler of the kings of the earth.

What follow in Revelation will be visions directly concerned with a struggle between two present and demanding kingdoms. The Roman Empire is a "kingdom," too. When John speaks of Jesus "making us a kingdom," he means to say that followers of Jesus have chosen to enter his kingdom and, in a genuine sense, to exit Rome's kingdom. The book will conclude with a clear juxtaposition of this choice, one of the fundamental choices energizing John's visions. Either Babylon (i.e., Rome) or new Jerusalem? These are the two rival kingdoms. John's burden is to present those in the churches with a vision of the realities and demands of God's kingdom. Those who are "priests" who serve Jesus's God do so through their embodied love and their resistance to the loyalty demanded by the kingdom that directly competes with God's.

The "priest" allusion links with the earlier reference to Jesus as ruler of the "kings of the earth." In Revelation, the Lamb demands a high level of commitment from his followers. This demand reflects the loyalty demanded of citizens of the Lamb's kingdom. The purposes of this commitment include the responsibility to witness to the kings of the earth and in doing so to contribute to their transformation. As we follow the references to the kings of the earth throughout the book of Revelation, we will see that for all its polarities and extreme drama, Revelation portrays genuine social transformation. With this transformation, the "glory of the nations" enters the new Jerusalem and contributes to the worship of God and the Lamb. The faithful witness of John's readers is a priestly mediation that will play a major role in this social transformation.

John follows his words of praise in 1:6 with a proclamation. Jesus is "coming with the clouds" (1:7). This statement alludes to Dan 7:13–14:

> I saw one like a son of man coming with the clouds of heaven
> . . . . To him was given dominion and glory and kingship, that all

peoples, nations, and languages should serve him. His dominion is an everlasting dominion that shall not pass away, and his
kingship is one that shall never be destroyed.

From Daniel, we have a reference to the "son of man" becoming king
of all nations. This vision fits well with John's comments here, more to reiterate John's points than add any new content. We will learn from the rest of the
book of Revelation the nature of the "kingship" of John's "Son of Man" (the
term Jesus used of himself in the Gospels).

The actual "coming in the clouds" with Jesus does not refer to a literal
return so much as emphasize Jesus's way of rule as the engine that ultimately
drives history to its healing conclusion. The statement "every eye will see
him," as well, emphasizes the universality of Jesus's message. We will have
to complete the book of Revelation to get a clear idea in what sense "those
who pierced him" will see him—and in what sense "all the tribes of the earth
will wail" (1:7). For now, we may remind ourselves to hold on tight to the
opening words: this is a "revelation" of *Jesus Christ*.

The affirmation of God as "Alpha and Omega" joins with several other
images scattered throughout the book that highlight God's universality and
ultimate supremacy. If we hold on tight to the close connection between
God and Lamb that John confesses, and the confession of God's love, we will
see these images of God's supremacy as reminders of the power of persevering love as the ultimate and victorious power of the universe. The use of
"Almighty" as the main title for God throughout the book (1:8; 4:8; 11:17;
16:7–14; 19:6, 15; 21:22) shows just how important the issue of God's power
is in Revelation.

REVELATION 1:9-20

I, John, your brother who share with you in Jesus the persecution and the kingdom and the patient endurance, was on the
island called Patmos because of the word of God and the testimony of Jesus. I was in the spirit on the Lord's day, and I heard
behind me a loud voice like a trumpet saying, "Write in a book
what you see and send it to the seven churches, to Ephesus, to
Smyrna, to Pergamum, to Thyatira, to Sardis, to Philadelphia,
and to Laodicea." Then I turned to see whose voice it was that
spoke to me, and on turning I saw seven golden lampstands, and
in the midst of the lampstands I saw one like the Son of Man,
clothed with a long robe and with a golden sash across his chest.
His head and his hair were white as white wool, white as snow;

his eyes were like a flame of fire, his feet were like burnished bronze, refined as in a furnace, and his voice was like the sound of many waters. In his right hand he held seven stars, and from his mouth came a sharp, two-edged sword, and his face was like the sun shining with full force. When I saw him, I fell at his feet as though dead. But he placed his right hand on me, saying, "Do not be afraid; I am the first and the last, and the living one. I was dead, and see, I am alive forever and ever; and I have the keys of Death and of Hades. Now write what you have seen, what is, and what is to take place after this. As for the mystery of the seven stars that you saw in my right hand, and the seven golden lampstands: the seven stars are the angels of the seven churches, and the seven lampstands are the seven churches.

John gives us as much information about himself in 1:9 as he will in the book. He calls himself the "brother" of the people in the "seven churches that are in Asia" (1:4). By calling himself their "brother," John implies that he does not have a formal role in relation to these congregations but is more their peer. He does make it clear in the book that he sees himself as a "prophet" (see especially Revelation 10 when he imitates Ezekiel by eating the "little scroll"). However, his authority in writing the book of Revelation is based on the vision he conveys, not on his positional status.

He shares with his readers "in Jesus the persecution and the kingdom and the patient endurance" (1:9). These terms evoke the earlier pattern of Jesus (faithful witness, firstborn of the dead, ruler of the kings of the earth). As evidence, John mentions that he is "on the island called Patmos because of the word of God and the testimony of Jesus" (1:9). About the significance of Patmos, no more is known about it than about John's identity itself. Traditionally, Patmos has been seen as a prison island, but we have no direct evidence that this was the case. It makes sense that John did suffer the fate of being imprisoned due to his witness to Jesus, but that must remain an inference.

The first vision of the book begins with "a loud voice like a trumpet" that commissions John to write what he sees. In this way, John makes it clear that he presents these visions as God's initiative, not simply his own imaginative creation. The voice tells John to describe these visions "in a book" and to send the book "to the seven churches . . . " (1:11). We again may see in this list of churches both a particular context (more on that in chapters 2–3) and a sense that John's visions speak to all churches (the number "seven" signifies wholeness).

In 1:11–12 we have the first of several cases where John initially hears a message then looks to see what the message involves. The contrast between the hearing and the seeing will be much more important in chapters 5 and 7.

Here, the main contrast seems to be between hearing "churches" and seeing "lampstands." That John is commanded to write what he "sees" emphasizes that seeing takes priority over hearing.

Amid the lampstands John sees a vision of a person. He clearly understands this to be the Jesus he has already mentioned as the content of the "revelation" to which this book witnesses. This is the first of a number of visions, all part of the one "revelation of Jesus Christ." The description of Jesus draws on a wealth of biblical images. In interpreting this vision and all the visions to follow, we best seek to hold the original content of the biblical images together with the distinctive picture being created by the allusions to those images in Revelation.

John is not a slave to his sources. In fact, even with his various allusions to Scripture (surely reflecting profound knowledge), John rarely if ever directly quotes from the Bible. What we have are new images that draw creatively on old images but with new purpose in some sense free from the original references (what British theologian Austin Farrar famously called "a rebirth of images"[3]). John does not write a research paper with an open Bible before him to quote from; rather he "sees" and "hears" his revelation of Jesus Christ and finds himself drawing on the store of images he had internalized over his years of immersion in the Bible.

John sees "one like the Son of Man" (1:13). He evokes both Daniel's vision (Dan 7:13) and the self-identification Jesus used in the Gospels. That Daniel's vision might especially have been in mind is supported by a second use of the term "Son of Man" in Rev 14:14 in a judgment scene. However, because John clearly does allude to Jesus, the gospel use must also be kept in mind.

The key point John makes in 1:13 is Jesus's presence with the churches—a presence we will learn that has both comforting and confrontive connotations for the seven congregations. The imagery of the golden lampstands evokes the golden menorahs that burn continually before God in ancient Israel's sanctuary (Exod 27:20–1; Lev 24:2–4). This image underscores how seriously God takes the vocation of these (and all other) communities of Jesus's followers.

The general description of Jesus here emphasizes his majesty, power, and might. In fact, the image of him with "head and hair . . . white as white wool, white as snow" evokes the Ancient of Days in Dan 7:9. This description is one of many places where Revelation emphasizes Jesus's close identification with God ("the one on the throne").

---

3. Farrer, *Rebirth*.

However, we should take care not to overemphasize the one side of the human/divine dynamic. John certainly sees Jesus as identified with the One on the Throne. However, in the end, we will see that this identification should inform our sense of the One on the Throne as least as much as it does our sense of Jesus (the human side of God alongside the divinity of Jesus). This is why we need to take seriously that the "Son of Man" metaphor alludes to Jesus's own earthly life and how he emphasized his own humanity. The statement by this "Son of Man" character, "I was dead" (1:18), points us to the life that Jesus lived that led directly to his persecution and execution by the very same forces who bedevil the followers of the Lamb throughout Revelation.

The "one like the Son of Man" has a "sharp, two-edged sword" that comes from his mouth (1:16). This image draws on biblical references to the word of God and to God's judgment (Isa 49:2; Wis 18:15–6; 2 Thess 2:8; Heb 4:12). As with the message of Jesus throughout Revelation, here we should think of prophetic words that convey the truth of God, truth either comforting or confrontive depending upon their content. We should recognize that his "sword" is the only weapon Jesus wields in this book (see also 2:12, 16; 19:15). It is clearly a "weapon" of proclamation, not a literal sword. We will see that Jesus himself wielded his weapon most decisively when he faced death due to his witness to God's love. Because he so wielded his sword, he "conquered" the powers of evil. Jesus conquers in a counterintuitive way— with his weapon held by his mouth and not by his hand.

John responds to the "Son of Man" by falling prostrate at his feet. Jesus responds with a call to a kind of resurrection: "Do not be afraid" (1:17); get up and "write what you have seen" (1:19). Jesus commissions John to service based on the reality that "I was dead, and see, I am alive forever and ever; and I have the keys of Death and Hades" (1:18). God's vindication of Jesus's faithfulness provides the basis for faithful discipleship with its implicit promise that God will likewise vindicate John and his readers. And, crucially for what comes, Jesus holds power over Death and Hades (and all those powers serving Death and Hades) from the beginning, before the rest of the book's visions are seen.

John sees "seven stars" that are held by Jesus, who tells him that the "seven stars" symbolize "the angels of the seven churches" (1:20). More than being specific beings with their own separate existence, we probably should understand the reference to the "angels" as a way of talking about each congregation's collective inner, spiritual reality. Jesus will address the "angels" of each of the seven churches in chapters 2 and 3 in a way that makes it clear that he speaks to each congregation's essence.

Each congregation has an existence of its own as a community made up of its members. This existence reflects not only the group's personality but also the social context of each. The cities and broader environment of which it is part deeply shapes each congregation. So, when Jesus speaks to the "angels," the point is not that we have discrete personal beings who mediate Jesus's message. Rather, it is that Jesus is speaking directly to the heart and soul of each congregation.

A REVELATION ABOUT JESUS

We face many interpretative choices when we read Revelation. Is it mainly predictions about the future or instead exhortation for first-century believers? Is it better read in relation to other, non-biblical writings in the so-called apocalyptic genre or instead read in relation to the New Testament? Are the plagues in Revelation from God or instead from the dragon and the beast?

Maybe the most important choice comes right away. When the first words of the book tell us this is a "revelation of Jesus Christ" do they mean a revelation *from* Jesus or instead a revelation *about* Jesus? Either reading is equally possible. Probably we should see both as being intended, at least to some degree. But I think we still have to choose which meaning to emphasize more. Though the Greek words themselves don't resolve the question, our choice will be important.

To emphasize more "a revelation from Jesus" may set a tone of distance between Jesus and the visions that follow. This distance makes it easier to see Jesus as describing terrible judgment that God visits upon the earth—and Revelation as a fear-inducing book. To emphasize more "a revelation about Jesus" may lead us to see Jesus as more directly involved in the visions; they reveal Jesus, not what Jesus describes. Which then leads to another choice: If this is a revelation about Jesus, does Revelation show us Jesus-as-judge, one who comes as a violent conqueror? Or does Revelation show us Jesus-as-servant, one who brings healing through compassion?

This is my choice: This book is most of all a revelation *about* Jesus that gives a vision of how compassion might work in our deeply flawed world. Such a choice of how to read Revelation will, I believe, open our imaginations to find in the intimidating visions of Revelation help for our healing work.

To put it in a nutshell, chapter 1 tells us that Jesus is very, very powerful. He is powerful in relation to the nations ("the ruler of the kings of the earth," "on his account all the tribes of the earth will wail"). He is powerful in relation to the churches with a loud, loud voice, addressing the angels of the churches and walking among the congregations themselves. He holds the keys to Death and Hades.

However, the issue of the *nature* of Jesus's power—and the nature of *God's* power, for that matter—plays a large role in how we understand what Revelation might say to the twenty-first century. When we get to Revelation, chapter 5, we will read of the most important vision of the entire book. No one is found powerful enough to open the scroll that holds the fulfillment of history. So, John weeps. Then he is told someone powerful enough has at last been found, so don't weep. But what he sees is a slain and resurrected *Lamb*—the symbol for a very different kind of power.

Revelation challenges us to accept Lamb-power as actual power, the fundamental power of history, the kind of power that runs *with* the grain of the universe. However, lambs don't kill and dominate and instill fear and justify violence in the name of a "realistic" need for peace and order. Lambs don't violently punish their enemies. Yet they provide the image for Revelation's portrayal of the power that matters most.

The book *A Force More Powerful*, by Jack Duvall and Peter Ackerman, tells story after story of the effectiveness of a kind of Lamb-power that challenges forces of domination during the twentieth century. The salt marchers under Gandhi's leadership, the people of Denmark who staged public hymn sings to defy Nazi occupation and smuggled almost every Jew in Denmark to safety, the steadfastly nonviolent union workers in Poland who patiently transformed their country from a satellite in the Soviet Communist bloc to a resilient democracy. These stories, which continue to be enacted in Liberia and Egypt and many other places around the world, overthrow standard understandings of power.[4]

Revelation is not precisely a blueprint for nonviolent political revolution,[5] but it does provide a theology to inspire upside-down notions of politics—if we make the right interpretive choices when we read it. So, we start with a sense that this book contains a revelation that will tell us more *about* the Jesus of the Gospels—not more about a different kind of Jesus who wields a death-dealing sword of judgment in his right hand. The Jesus of the Gospels is one whose "sword" comes out of his mouth. This sword coming from his mouth is kind of a grotesque image if we take it literally. But if we

---

4. Ackerman and Duvall, *Force*. For more on these themes see Engler and Engler, *This*, and Sider, *Nonviolent*.

5. Though note Brian Blount's argument that the key word *hypomene* ("endurance"; 1:9; 2:2, 3, 19; 3:10; 13:10; 14:12) is probably best translated "nonviolent resistance," *Revelation*, 42. See also Bredin, *Jesus*, for an argument that the Jesus of Revelation was, indeed, an "active nonviolent revolutionary."

recognize the symbolism, we may see that the image indicates the path Jesus trod during his life. His power was based on his defenseless witness.

We keep our eyes open for signs that the defenseless Jesus of the Gospels is also the one being revealed in Revelation. And in the opening verses we note a description of Jesus that actually captures the essence of his message—and puts us on notice that the issues of politics, power, and domination are key parts of the revelation. John offers his readers a blessing from God and from Jesus. He describes Jesus using what I call *the pattern of Jesus*: "the faithful witness, the firstborn of the dead, and the ruler of the kings of the earth" (1:5). This is the pattern: Faithful living, to the point of suffering, due to one's resistance to the domination system, even to the point of death. Vindication by God, the witness sustained even through death, with resurrection, sustained hope, and true power. And then the status as ruler of the kings of the earth.

As we reflect on Jesus's identity as "ruler of the kings of the earth," we should always keep in mind we have to do with only *one* Jesus. He has only one way of ruling. He made that clear to his followers: "You know that among the Gentiles those whom they recognize as their rulers lord it over them. But it is not so among you; whoever wishes to become great among you must be your servant" (Mark 10:42–3).

And let's look ahead to how the story in Revelation ends: In new Jerusalem we see a shocking image, given what happens between chapters 6 and 20. The domination system seeks to dominate using the violence of the kings of the earth. However, notice how it all ends up: "The city has no need of sun or moon to shine on it, for the glory of God is its light and its lamp is the Lamb. The nations will walk by its light, and the kings of the earth will bring their glory into it" (21:24). A verse later we are told that "nothing unclean" will enter the city. That is, the Lamb as lamp gives light to the healed and transformed kings of the earth, ruling them with compassion and self-giving love. They are no longer unclean. They no longer operate by the ethics of domination.

Revelation 1 indeed presents, with all its somewhat complicated imagery, an exalted picture of Jesus. But how does this picture speak to us today, as we live in a society that seems to share all too much in common with the beastly society seen in Revelation?

What I think is this: The exaltation of Jesus in Revelation does not so much establish his identity as divinity incarnate. Revelation does link Jesus with God more closely than much of the rest of the New Testament. But why? Not to set the stage for the fourth-century creeds—creeds commissioned by the Roman emperor. Not to establish a doctrinal boundary marker to separate true believers from heretics. Rather, Revelation has a very different agenda. Revelation shows Jesus as exalted in the context of John's book-long critique of top-down, oppressive domination. John shows Lamb-power as the true power of the universe. Even in the face of a sword-wielding empire. Even in the face of terrorism in service of anti-empire retribution. Revelation exalts the Lamb as Lamb, not as warrior. The exalted Lamb is exalted because of his faithful witness to persevering compassion and love.

FOR FURTHER ENGAGEMENT

1. The author suggests we should place the priority on "Jesus Christ" as we read Revelation—more so than on "Revelation (or Apocalypse)" or on "what must soon take place." What do you think he means? Do you tend to agree or disagree?

2. Who are the recipients of this letter (1:4, 11)? Why these churches? What is the meaning of 1:10? How are the "seeing" and the "hearing" described in 1:10–11 to be understood? What strikes you as the most important image in the vision of Christ 1:12–16? How will 1:17–18 influence one's interpretation of the entire book?

3. Do you think John expected history to end soon? Was he wrong? Do you now expect history to end soon? What might end it? Do you think that would be God's will? Why or why not?

4. Can you affirm that Jesus is the "ruler of kings on earth" today? What does that mean to you and how you relate to "kings"?

5. What do you make of John's claim that this book's origins are with God? How much, in reality, does this book reflect *John's* mind? How much do you think it reflects *God's* mind?

6. What do you make of the "liberation" motif (as in 1:5 and elsewhere)? What does it mean to you that Jesus has "freed us from our sins"? Personal only? Church only? Social and political? What did it likely mean to John? What kinds of "sins" did he likely have in mind? (Keep this in mind as the book goes along.)

7. Please note at least one item in this chapter that you found helpful and one that raised a concern or question.

8. The author asserts "chapter 1 tells us that Jesus is very, very powerful." He then suggests that the issue of the nature of Jesus's power is crucial for how we understand and apply Revelation. Reflect on this point.

3

Power in Weakness

[Revelation 2]

Chapters 2 and 3 of Revelation contain messages to seven Christian congregations in cities of the northeastern corner of the Mediterranean. Many
readers of Revelation treat these messages as our last moments of sanity
before we enter into the craziness of Revelation's visions. The messages,
thus, get a lot of attention. However, they are often read in isolation from
the complicated visions that follow. So, we don't usually think of them as the
key to understanding the later visions. I think that's what they are, though.
The seven messages are instructions, in effect, on how to understand the rest
of Revelation.

The first thing to notice when we begin to look at the messages to the
seven Christian congregations of Asia that make up chapters 2 and 3 is that
they are part of the same vision that began in 1:9. At that point, John hears
a "loud voice" telling him to write this book that records what he will see
and "send it to the seven churches, to Ephesus, to Smyrna, to Pergamum, to
Thyatira, to Sardis, and to Laodicea" (1:9–11).

John turns "to see whose voice it was that spoke to me" (1:12), at
which point the first vision of the book begins. John learns that the voice is
Jesus. John first sees many images that, when put together, form a kind of
Christology. Many of these images are then incorporated in the messages
to seven congregations that follow. As we move on to chapter 2, we should
not be misled by the chapter break in our English translation. The original

did not have such breaks, and it would have been clear to the first listeners/ readers that this one vision of Jesus that begins the series that takes up the rest of book includes both the word-pictures describing Jesus in 1:12–20 and the messages that this same Jesus gives to the seven congregations in chapters 2 and 3.

The seven messages thus give us several crucial pieces of data that will help us understand the book as a whole. They include, not least, a picture of Jesus—he whom John announces with the first words of the book to be the subject of the one overall "revelation" of the book. The messages are thus of interest not only for what they tell us about the seven congregations and their environments but also for what they tell us about the giver of the messages. They also, clearly, by their place in the larger narrative of the book, set the agenda for the book as a whole. If we want to understand the later visions, we must always return to these seven messages because they provide the context for the visions that follow.

John leads into the seven messages with his comment at 1:20 that the seven stars Jesus holds in his right hand (1:16) are "the angels of the seven churches." As we read the messages, we see that with each one, Jesus speaks to "the angel of the church" who in some sense mediates the message to the church. Following Walter Wink's discussion in *Unmasking the Powers*[1], I understand the reference to the "angels of the churches" to be a way of personifying each church's inner, spiritual reality. Jesus will speak to each church's essence. Each congregation is in some sense deeply shaped by the social environment of which it is a part. When Jesus speaks to the "angels," he speaks directly to the heart and soul of each congregation.

The collection of the seven congregations does link the message of Revelation with actual congregations in those seven cities in what is now the western part of Turkey. At the same time, it links the message of Revelation to the entirety of the first-century Christian world (the number "seven" symbolizes the bigger Christian movement). The particular and universal join together in these messages—and hence in the book of Revelation as a whole.

REVELATION 2:1–7

> To the angel of the church in Ephesus write: These are the words of him who holds the seven stars in his right hand, who walks among the seven golden lampstands:"I know your works, your

---

1. Wink, *Unmasking*, 69–86.

toil and your patient endurance. I know that you cannot tolerate evildoers; you have tested those who claim to be apostles but are not, and have found them to be false. I also know that you are enduring patiently and bearing up for the sake of my name, and that you have not grown weary. But I have this against you, that you have abandoned the love you had at first. Remember then from what you have fallen; repent, and do the works you did at first. If not, I will come to you and remove your lampstand from its place, unless you repent. Yet this is to your credit: you hate the works of the Nicolaitans, which I also hate. Let anyone who has an ear listen to what the Spirit is saying to the churches. To everyone who conquers, I will give permission to eat from the tree of life that is in the paradise of God."

The first message goes to the congregation in the largest city in the area, though also the city closest geographically to the island of Patmos from which John claims to write. Ephesus was the fourth largest city in the entire Roman Empire at this time (after Rome, Alexandria, and Antioch). It was also an early center of Christianity, featured prominently in the book of Acts and, according to Acts, the apostle Paul's home for several years.

As with the other six messages, the opening words of the message to Ephesus bring in a pertinent piece from chapter 1's vision of Jesus. Here we are told that Jesus "holds the seven stars in his right hand [and] walks among the seven golden lampstands" (2:1, an allusion to 1:16). We have just been told that these lampstands are the seven churches themselves (1:20). So the Ephesus message starts with a strong affirmation of Jesus's presence among these congregations—a presence that surely would be reassuring but also a challenge to sustain faithfulness to Jesus's way.

John's Jesus praises this congregation for not "tolerating evildoers" (2:2) and for "hating the works of the Nicolaitans" (2:6). The congregation has refused to countenance "those who claim to be apostles but are not" (2:2). It works hard and exercises "patient endurance." Revelation mentions "patient endurance" (or, "nonviolent resistance"[2]) numerous times as a central calling for followers of the Lamb (in imitation of him).

The seven messages as a whole challenge John's audience to sustain their commitment to Jesus's path of nonviolent resistance and to resist the empire's hegemony. How might their commitment to resist be sustained? Through "patient endurance," recognizing that saying no to empire will likely result in hardship and even conflict. "Follow the Lamb wherever he goes"—i.e., remain clear-eyed about the true bases of Rome's claims for

2. The translation favored by Blount, *Revelation*, 42.

divine blessing, band together in communities of resistance, "conquer" through self-giving love rather than joining Rome's dominating ways.

We may assume, as will be echoed in later messages, that the Nicolaitans and "evildoers" here are those who advocate accommodation with Rome. Such accommodation, John believes, undermines the heart of the gospel. John's Jesus speaks positively about the congregation's nonviolent resistance to Rome. However, he also sharply expresses a concern as well. "You have abandoned the love you had at first" (2:4). This problem is so bad, that Jesus threatens to "remove your lampstand from its place" unless the problem is resolved. Given that the "lampstand" is actually the church itself, it would appear that the very existence of this congregation is at stake.

Unfortunately for our purposes, it remains unclear to what exactly Jesus's "abandoned the love you had at first" refers. We may find it tempting (and attractive) to think of the phrase as a reference to interhuman love, with the implication that as the Ephesians focused on resistance to Rome, they lost the dynamics of compassion, mutual affection, and a welcoming spirit. But the allusion could just as well suggest a loss of passion and freshness in (and love for) their commitment to the vision of restorative justice and wide-ranging shalom that they received when they first embraced Jesus and his way. So, we don't actually receive a lot of clear guidance from this message concerning what problems to avoid. The book as a whole does not develop the motif of "love" in a direct way.

Maybe at most we can say that, given the centrality of Jesus the Lamb to the message of Revelation and given the centrality in Jesus's life and teachings of wholehearted and passionate love of God and neighbor, a call to love fellow congregants (and everyone else) and to life-shaping commitment to Jesus's way should be assumed. And that the stern warning to the Ephesians stands as a reminder of this assumption—related both to love for other people and love for the path Jesus calls us to follow.

As do the other six messages, the message to Ephesus concludes with a call to "conquer." This call points to one of the central motifs in the book. Revelation portrays reality as highly conflictual, a struggle within which one must seek victory. However, the nature of the victory depends upon the means one uses to engage the struggle. For those aligned with the empire, the means are violence and domination. For those aligned with the Lamb, "patient endurance" (i.e., "nonviolent resistance") is the means. When John's Jesus makes promises to "everyone who conquers," he promises that as with Jesus, "faithful witness" leads to vindication.

Each message has a distinctive promise for the conquerors that points ahead to the later visions of Revelation. Here, the promise is "permission to eat from the tree of life that is in the paradise of God," an allusion to the vision of the new Jerusalem where the "tree of life" produces abundant fruit (22:2). Note, too, that this same tree in Rev 22 also produces leaves that are for "the healing of the nations." So, even though Revelation sets up a sharp contrast between the Lamb's realm and the beast's realm, in the end it hopes for those human beings (and their cultures) that are aligned with the beast to find healing—reinforcing the call to sustain love.

REVELATION 2:8–11

> And to the angel of the church in Smyrna write: These are the words of the first and the last, who was dead and came to life: "I know your affliction and your poverty, even though you are rich. I know the slander on the part of those who say that they are Jews and are not but are a synagogue of Satan. Do not fear what you are about to suffer. Beware, the devil is about to throw some of you into prison so that you may be tested, and for ten days you will have affliction. Be faithful until death, and I will give you the crown of life. Let anyone who has an ear listen to what the Spirit is saying to the churches. Whoever conquers will not be harmed by the second death."

The city of Smyrna, an important seaport, was about forty miles from Ephesus. It was notable for constructing the first temple devoted to the goddess Roma about three hundred years prior to the time of Revelation. By the end of the first century CE, Smyrna stood as a major center of the practice of emperor worship. So, as in probably each of these seven cities, the practice of worship of the biblical God bumped directly against its main competitor, worship of the Roman emperor (i.e., worship of the empire itself).

The initial descriptor of Jesus at the beginning of the second message speaks directly to the Smyrnan's situation. This descriptor, "The first and last, who was dead and came to life" (2:8, alluding to 1:18), reminds readers again of the pattern of Jesus: faithful witness, crucifixion, resurrection, ruler of the kings of the earth (1:5). To link together "Smyrna" and "death" is to speak to the basic challenge facing Jesus's followers. What is at stake is whether one will witness to the path of self-giving love even when it requires witnessing *against* the violence and oppressions of the "great" empire.

This message indicates that the Smyrnans understand what is at stake and have made their choice to follow the Lamb's path. They do this even though, in the context of the city of Smyrna's embrace of the empire's way, their choice means "affliction and poverty" (2:9). What may be the most significant contribution of the message to the Smyrnans to the overall picture of the seven messages is what is *not* said within it. Smyrna (as will also be the case in the message to the similar congregation in Philadelphia) receives no criticism whatsoever. Thus, this congregation serves as a model for what Jesus has in mind for all congregations.

We are not given much information about the Smyrnans' faithfulness—presumably they recognized that the lure of cooperation with emperor worship must be resisted. Their material poverty may itself be a reflection of their faithful choices. It may follow from their disdain for the quest for comfort and material gain through involvement in the work of merchants that draws John's condemnation in Rev 18. However, such poverty does not mask their genuine wealth (in the present!) in things that matter most.

The Smyrnans face the possibility of imprisonment at the hands of "the devil"—perhaps even the possibility of death. When they "conquer," though, and remain on the path of nonviolent resistance, they will receive "the crown of life" (2:10) and "will not be harmed by the second death" (2:11). The "second death" motif points toward the vision of the final judgment (20:11–15) in which those who have lived faithfully and whose names are in "the book of life" avoid the "lake of fire" and enter new Jerusalem.

The message to Smyrna brings into focus the emphasis of the book as a whole. When people fear "poverty and affliction," they are tempted to accommodate the empire. John sees such compromise as idolatrous. It echoes the terrible problems the ancient Hebrews had with foreign gods that pushed them away from faithfulness to Torah. Idolatry invariably leads to injustice and violence (see Amos, Hosea, and Micah). John exposes the terribly violent underbelly of the Roman Empire that belied its claims to be the bringers of peace (the "Pax Romana"). He challenges his audience to break free from the cycle of idolatry leading to injustice and death (see also Rom 1:18–31 for Paul's parallel concern). John's Jesus wants to drive home to the Smyrnans that their choice to turn from such idolatry puts them on the path of life. They are rich now in the wealth that matters to God and are promised the crown of life.

We might easily misunderstand who the Smyrnans' enemies are here. If we remember that Smyrna was a center for emperor worship, and if we keep in mind that later Revelation links the empire directly with Satan (i.e., the "dragon"), and if we also understand that Judaism and Christianity did not at this point exist as separate religions (in fact, John surely understood himself to be a Jew), then the reference to those who "say that they are Jews and are not but are a synagogue of Satan" will make more sense. The very next message, to the congregation at Pergamum, refers to the recipients living "where Satan's throne is" (2:13). Pergamum was also a center for emperor worship, being the home of a temple to Caesar and an enormous altar to Zeus (the ancient Greek high god who by now had been incorporated into the Roman Empire religion).

So, we best understand "synagogue of Satan" in terms of "Satan's throne." Jesus alludes to conflicts between the Lamb's followers in Smyrna, who rejected any acceptance of empire religion, with others who claimed to be Christians but who did participate in that religion. True "Jews," in John's mind, reject accommodation—and those who do not simply are not "Jews" (i.e., worshipers of the true God of the Bible). John does not reject Judaism itself or link it with Satan. His opponents were not members of the Jewish religion in contradistinction with those who were members of the Christian religion. Rather, his opponents are those who see biblical faith as compatible with "going along" with empire religion.

By presenting the Smyrnan congregation as criticism free, John challenges his entire audience to imitate their model. He subverts conventional wisdom. He challenges the link between faithfulness and material prosperity that accepted cultural accommodation as the necessary path to such prosperity.

REVELATION 2:12–17

And to the angel of the church in Pergamum write: These are the words of him who has the sharp two-edged sword: "I know where you are living, where Satan's throne is. Yet you are holding fast to my name, and you did not deny your faith in me even in the days of Antipas my witness, my faithful one, who was killed among you, where Satan lives. But I have a few things against you: you have some there who hold to the teaching of Balaam, who taught Balak to put a stumbling block before the people of Israel, so that they would eat food sacrificed to idols and practice fornication. So, you also have some who hold to the teaching of the Nicolaitans. Repent then. If not, I will come to you soon and make war against them with the sword of my mouth. Let anyone who has an ear listen to what the Spirit is saying to the churches. To everyone who conquers I will give some of the hidden manna, and I will give a white stone, and on the white stone is written a new name that no one knows except the one who receives it."

Like Ephesus and Smyrna, Pergamum was also an important city that strongly supported empire religion. This prominence put the congregation there in a difficult situation. What was called for, in face of the powerful attraction of accommodation, was discernment. Hence, the message begins with the image of a two-edged sword being held by Jesus, drawn from the beginning vision of Jesus (2:12, alluding to 1:16). The "two-edged sword" connotes discernment, being able to separate truth and falsehood. The vision from chapter 1 (picked up again in chapter 19) emphasizes that this sword comes out of Jesus's mouth. So, the sword is not a literal weapon of bloodletting (again a key contrast with the empire—the empire's swords draw blood and visit violence and death; the Lamb's sword is his teaching, his message of self-giving love).

Jesus commends the Pergamum believers for their perseverance ("you are holding fast to my name") even in the face of suffering (the one named martyr in all of Revelation, Antipas, was killed in Pergamum by the empire [2:13]). Jesus repeats twice in this one verse that Pergamum is where "Satan" is present—an allusion to the centrality of empire religion in this community. The congregation, though, struggles to remain true. People within it accept teachings that weaken their resolve to resist the empire. These teachings are called "the teaching of Balaam" and the "teaching of the Nicolaitans." Likely these teachings were the same as each other (interestingly, the name Balaam [Hebrew, from Num 22–24] and the name Nicholas [Greek] mean about the same thing—literally, "conquer the people"[3]). The content of this teaching is not spelled out, but the idea seems to be that they taught that there was nothing wrong with people from the congregation entering fully into the civil religion of Pergamum.

As a rule, the empire religion did not require exclusivity from its adherents. Problems did not arise when people worshiped with the general public in the Roman services but also engaged in their own distinct religious practices. Rome tolerated this kind of pluralism. What caused trouble was when people refused to join in the Roman services in the name of some other faith. This is the kind of trouble John believed his fellow followers of Jesus should be getting into. But they would suffer. Their economic opportunities would be limited. They might even face harsh persecution. John's rivals within the congregations argued that such trouble was unnecessary. They said: We can still worship in our congregation; Rome does not mind that so long as we also join in its services. John's Jesus calls such an accommodation (spiritual) "fornication" (2:14).

John insisted on exclusivity due to his conviction that his readers cannot actually give allegiance to two masters. Inevitably, they will have to choose. The worship of the biblical God requires one to stand against injustice. And

---

3. Johnson, *Discipleship*, 80.

Rome was profoundly unjust. If you accommodate to Rome, your private worship in the Christian congregation actually becomes blasphemous. You worship God while you also accept the injustices of the empire. The problem here parallels the situation in the time of Amos. "Go to Bethel and sin" was Amos's condemnation of those Israelites who attended services claiming to worship God while at the same time exploiting their vulnerable neighbors. Hence, the worship was not an offering to God but a rejection of God. John's Jesus calls upon the congregants in Pergamum to repudiate Balaam and the Nicolaitans—or else face "war." Note that this "war" will be fought with the sword that comes from Jesus's mouth. It will not be a bloody battle, but a "battle" fought based on the proclamation of the word of God in Jesus's life and teaching, what Eugene Boring calls a "war" of convictions.[4]

The reward for the conquerors is nourishment from "some of the hidden manna" (likely a metaphor for God's messianic banquet that welcomes the partiers into the new Jerusalem, see 19:1–10) and the gift of a white stone upon which is written the recipient's name (see 19:12 for a similar reference in relation to Jesus; the stone seems to be a kind of "ticket" that admits its bearer into the new Jerusalem).

REVELATION 2:18–29

And to the angel of the church in Thyatira write: These are the words of the Son of God, who has eyes like a flame of fire, and whose feet are like burnished bronze: "I know your works—your love, faith, service, and patient endurance. I know that your last works are greater than the first. But I have this against you: you tolerate that woman Jezebel, who calls herself a prophet and is teaching and beguiling my servants to practice fornication and to eat food sacrificed to idols. I gave her time to repent, but she refuses to repent of her fornication. Beware, I am throwing her on a bed, and those who commit adultery with her I am throwing into great distress, unless they repent of her doings; and I will strike her children dead. And all the churches will know that I am the one who searches minds and hearts, and I will give to each of you as your works deserve. But to the rest of you in Thyatira, who do not hold this teaching, who have not learned what some call 'the deep things of Satan,' to you I say, I do not lay on you any other burden; only hold fast to what you have until I come. To everyone who conquers and continues to do my works

4. Boring, Revelation, 90–91.

to the end, I will give authority over the nations to rule them with an iron rod, as when clay pots are shattered—even as I also received authority from my Father. To the one who conquers I will also give the morning star. Let anyone who has an ear listen to what the Spirit is saying to the churches."

The fourth message goes to the congregation in Thyatira, a city especially noted for its industry, commerce, and an unusual number of trade guilds. The images of Jesus that John repeated here refer to his "eyes like a flame of fire" and his feet "like burnished bronze" (2:18, alluding to 1:14–15). These seem to be allusions to his power and his awe-inspiring presence. Here, too, the Jesus figure has authority and is *present*—both in comfort and in confrontation. Whichever, he must be taken seriously.

The Thyatiran congregation's strengths echo those of the Ephesian congregation ("faith, service, and patient endurance," 2:19) with the added affirmation of their "love" and, crucially, that their "last works are greater than the first." So, unlike Ephesus, they are not losing their "first love" but are still growing in it. However, also unlike the Ephesians, who do not tolerate the Nicolaitans and their acceptance of Roman religion (2:6), the Thyratirans do tolerate that kind of theology and ethics. The symbol for them is their acceptance of "that woman Jezebel" (2:20). Almost certainly, "Jezebel" is not the prophet's actual name. Jezebel is a figure of condemnation in the Bible. Married to Israel's king Ahab, she was a Canaanite who influenced Ahab—and with him, the broader nation—to turn to other gods (1 Kgs 16:31–33). Jesus uses this label to evoke that same kind of condemnation toward the Thyatiran prophet.

Jesus sees the problems as a contemporary manifestation of what happened in the day of the historical Jezebel: "practicing fornication and eating food sacrificed to idols" (2:21). As with the first Jezebel, now the people in the community of faith are being lured into fitting in with empire religion—leading to spiritual adultery and acceptance of imperial ethics. In the case of ancient Israel, the paradigmatic expression of Jezebel's influence was when Ahab framed and then executed an Israelite whose faithfulness to Torah led him to insist on retaining his land as an inheritance for his descendants (1 Kgs 21).

Ahab led the nation away from a respect for the role of land-as-inheritance. That respect had made it possible for all the people in the community to maintain viable lives. But then they moved toward the acceptance of land-as-possession. That move triggered devastating disparities in wealth between the haves and the have-nots. The disparities joined with exploitation of the vulnerabilities of the have-nots to further enrich the haves. By the time of Amos, the inequality and injustice led the prophet to warn of imminent destruction.

Given Thyatira's role as a regional economic center and noting the condemnation of imperial economics later in Revelation (note especially Rev 18), we may sense that the use of the symbol "Jezebel" may have connoted that accommodation has problematic *economic* ramifications. John's Jesus echoes Amos when he warns of devastating consequences for those who do not repent—i.e., turn back to God's justice.

Part of Jezebel's teachings here include a focus on "the deep things of Satan." Many interpreters see here an allusion to special claims for insight in a Gnostic sense—religious truths only available to insiders. Remembering the other allusions to "Satan" in the messages (and also, the later direct identification of Satan as the "dragon" in chapter 12 and the link between the dragon and the Roman Empire), we might also see here another reminder of the allegation that the Roman Empire is linked inextricably with Satan. The "deep things of Satan" may simply be the claims made by Rome to divine status, i.e., the claim that they have the "right" to kill. They may seem like "deep truths" but are actually only lies of empire.

For those who resist Jezebel's teachings (and hence, resist accommodation to empire) and thereby "conquer," the reward will be to share in Jesus's "rule of the kings of the earth" (2:26–27, see also 1:5), manifested in new Jerusalem. The "rule" can be seen as a kind of shepherding (also a possible translation of *poimonei*, "rule") that ultimately leads to the kings being *healed* (22:4). To "shatter the clay pots" may thus allude to the end of the kings' resistance to the Lamb's rule. When such resistance ends, the kings enter new Jerusalem, where the doors are never shut but also do not admit anything unclean.

The conqueror will also be given "the morning star" (2:28), which is a title given to Jesus at the very end of the book (22:16). That is, the conquerors will be united with Jesus, a powerful promise in face of possible suffering as a result of Jesus-guided nonviolent resistance to the ways of Rome in the present.

POWER IN WEAKNESS

In Revelation, John cares the most about how the people in the churches will navigate life in the Roman Empire. The visions that begin in chapter 4 will in their own creative ways repeat what John conveys here in Rev 2 and 3. They *confront* those who too easily find themselves at ease in Babylon (that is, in the empire) and they *comfort* those who have followed the way of the Lamb and have suffered as a consequence.

We might get some wrong impressions from a quick reading of these seven messages. We might think that when Jesus condemns "fornication" he focuses on sex. We might think the reference to the "synagogue of Satan" alludes to Judaism. And we might think that what's at stake here are doctrinal beliefs. Not exactly.

"Fornication" is an old prophetic metaphor for when the community of faith in the Old Testament turned from the ways of Torah—when people trusted in idols, wealthy people exploited the vulnerable, and when the community trusted in weapons of war. To "commit fornication" in this figurative way is to forget the call to justice, to compassion, and to care for those in need—to forget that true worship is to do justice, love kindness, and walk humbly with God (Mic 6:8).

The reference in the message to Smyrna seems to pit Christians against Jews. But that is not actually the case. John and other Christians thought of themselves as Jews. The conflict here is not between Christians and non-Christians but between two different visions being the people of God. It has to do with their attitude toward the empire. The charge—and John puts some sharp words into Jesus's mouth in these messages—of being a "synagogue of Satan" has to do with being too close to the empire, which is linked elsewhere in Revelation with the dragon, the great snake, that is, Satan (Rev 12:9).

The city of Pergamum, we are told, is where "Satan's throne" is—Satan's throne being a major regional center for emperor worship. In John's view, the Roman Empire acts for evil in the world and not as a representative of the true God. Partly, the empire sought to separate believers from God (to use Paul's language in Rom 8:38–39). It did that in many ways, but probably most fundamentally by its ideology of power as domination. Rome was ruthless; nations and peoples who did not go along were crushed—witness the thousands of Jews who were crucified by the empire before and after Jesus's execution.

These seven messages most of all care about the politics of empire versus the politics of the kingdom of God, the politics of Babylon versus the politics of new Jerusalem. To which politics will those in the churches commit themselves? Certainly, "politics" are religious commitments, but not religion as doctrinal belief or ritual so much as religion linked inextricably with social ethics. As Elisabeth Schüssler Fiorenza notes, the key political question in Revelation is how do believers navigate empire?[5]

---

5. Schüssler Fiorenza, *Revelation*, 57.

John cares deeply about the powerful currents in his culture that push believers to forget Jesus's way of being in the world. The empire gives the message that it does represent the gods and that because of this its power must be feared and accepted as definitive. The villains in the messages to the seven churches, though, are not the beast and dragon, the false prophet and Babylon. No, the villains are people in the churches who advocate cooperation with empire.

The characters from the Old Testament, Balaam and Jezebel, notoriously persuaded those in Israel to forget the ways of Torah and to turn instead toward domination. One telling story, from 1 Kgs 21, shows Jezebel, an outsider to Israel not bound to Torah, persuading her husband, Israel's King Ahab, to seize a vineyard he wants simply because he has the power to. As we learn, though, this vineyard was part of the inheritance system that was meant to protect future generations from landlessness and poverty—core concerns of Torah. Jezebel's influence turned Ahab away from justice, away from shalom.

John sees cooperation with empire happening in these seven churches, too. Leaders, teachers, influential people claim that the faith community should work in harmony with the wishes of the empire. Followers of Jesus, these leaders claimed, could go to the public religious services, do business, gain wealth and status, identify with the values of the empire—and then come back to their churches for a time of private worship. Rome says that's fine—we in the congregations, say the leaders, should accept the double life too.

So, John shows in Revelation what actually goes on when followers of Jesus forget. When you accommodate to your culture, he says, you actually accommodate to the beast, the dragon, even Satan himself. In a later vision, he will state starkly why this is a problem. At the end of a list of all the fine things that Rome produces and that are apparently being enjoyed by followers of Balaam and Jezebel in the churches comes a jarring reminder: the merchants also traffic in slaves—and human lives (18:13). And in Rome will be found "the blood of prophets and of saints, and of all who have been slaughtered on earth" (18:24).

With the negative part of John's agenda, he thus confronts those who accommodate, who keep the message of the gospel to the private corners of their lives, or who find the comfort and security that getting along with Rome promises. Rome built its "peace" on the bones of "all who have been slaughtered on earth." Such accommodation is not genuine peace, but systemic violence of the most unjust and oppressive kind. However, John's *bigger* agenda is positive. John conveys a message of hope and encouragement. Resist the beast, refuse to accommodate, keep the gospel central to all elements of your lives—and you will celebrate with the Lamb and with the multitudes who follow him.

The seven messages contain threats, some strong threats. More importantly, they contain promises. As we see, a key motif throughout Revelation is the call to "conquer," to be victorious (the Greek word here for "victory" is *niké*). The call to "conquer" like Jesus did stands at the heart of Revelation. John portrays two fundamental ways to conquer. Conquer through overwhelming force or conquer through persistent love. One causes the other to suffer; the second is what Gandhi called self-suffering.

The seven messages promise that those who conquer in the same way as Jesus, through persistent love and self-suffering, will be vindicated. The conquerors from Ephesus will "eat from the tree of life that is in the paradise of God" (2:7), an allusion to the tree of life in the new Jerusalem in chapters 21 and 22 that will heal the nations. The conquerors from Smyrna will "not be harmed by the second death," an allusion to the embrace into eternal life by God at the great white throne of judgment in chapter 20. The conquerors from Pergamum will be given manna and a white stone that gives them entry into the new Jerusalem. And the conquerors from Thyatira will be given the morning star, an allusion to the final reference in the book of Revelation to Jesus, who is called the morning star (22:16).

The message to the church at Smyrna captures Revelation's notion of power quite clearly. "I know your affliction and your poverty, even though you are rich" (2:9). You are weak but actually you are powerful. The corollary point is that the empire that seems so almighty and hence attractive to the Jezebels and Balaams, actually is *weak* in its apparent strength.

The political philosopher Hannah Arendt wrote about how violence actually is powerless. "Power and violence are opposites," she wrote. "Where the one rules absolutely, the other is absent. Therefore, to speak of nonviolent power is actually redundant." Arendt held that power is created not when some people coerce others but when they willingly take action together in support of common purposes. She stated, "while violence can destroy power, it can never become a substitute for it." Then she added a sentence that perfectly captures the experience of the United States in the world this past generation: "From this results the by no means infrequent political combination of force and powerlessness, an array of impotent forces that spend themselves often spectacularly and vehemently but in utter futility."[6]

The problem with some of John's readers is that some influential congregational leaders bought the claims of empire (that it is truly powerful) and argued that Christians should accommodate to those claims. Later on,

---

6. Quotes from Schell, *Unconquerable*, 216–31.

in Rev 13, John will see visions that illustrate just how impressive Rome's power seemed. However, the visions will reveal that that power is not life-giving power as claimed by Rome (and by those in the churches who wanted to be at home in the empire). Rather, it is satanic power, the power of domination and death. But still, such power seems overwhelming. "Who is like the beast and who can stand against it?"

Here we find one of the big challenges with the message of Revelation. Does this portrayal of empire as beast apply to our context in today's America? How much does the challenge about accommodation to empire apply to American Christians? Where may we find communities of creative resistance such as the church in Smyrna that was, because of its nonviolent resistance in the way of the Lamb, "rich" even amidst its affliction and poverty?

Certainly, some elements of American Christianity are all too similar to the civil religion of the Roman Empire. Both bless wars and militarism and the economic exploitation of the periphery of the empire that further enriches the wealthy core. Maybe Christianity as a religion has become so linked with empire, at least in our society, that we will need look outside the organized church to find Smyrnan-like resistance in our day—places that cultivate suspicion of coercive power, that embrace cooperative power, and that provide human-scale alternatives to profit-driven corporate economics.

I thought a bit about this, and came up with a few, partly whimsical, examples of resistance. The alternative TV news show Democracy Now over against, say, CBS or Fox News. The Friendly City Food Co-op over against, say, Walmart or Food Lion. The Dogfish Head Brewery over against, say, Budweiser. Park View Federal Credit Union over against, say, Bank of America. A family-run taco stand over against, say, Taco Bell. Kathleen Temple Tailor over against, say, Target. The War Resisters League over against the Pentagon.

The message of Revelation is that we "conquer" with cooperative power, not coercive power. When we can embrace that message, I can see us move in two directions at the same time. One direction is to work within the churches to call our tradition back to its biblical roots—that those who confess Jesus would seek, in his name, to embody his way of creative nonviolent resistance to the ways of empire. The second direction is happily to join with all others of good will outside the churches who seek life, who find true power in joining together in myriad ways to resist, to celebrate, and to encourage.

FOR FURTHER ENGAGEMENT

1. The author notes that the Smyrnan congregation (2:8–11) is "criticism free." Reflect on the implications of that comment. Why is that congregation not criticized? What lessons might its positive portrayal have for how we think of church?

2. Compare the four letters in chapter 2. What is commended and criticized in each church? Do all have both good and bad points? How is Christ described at the beginning of each letter? Compare with 1:12–20. How does each description relate to the content of the letter? How is John's pastoral concern reflected in the letters?

3. Jesus is portrayed as intimately acquainted with, and concerned for, the specific churches. What implications may this picture of Jesus have had for John? How might awareness of this picture shape our interpretation of the rest of Revelation?

4. How literal were Jesus's threats to the churches? What do you think the purposes of the threats were?

5. What do you suppose was at stake in the controversies with the Nicolaitans, Balaamites, and Jezebelians? Do we have similar controversies today (that is, struggles between radical purists and cultural conformists)? What do you think might be analogous today to eating meat sacrificed to idols?

6. The author suggests "the seven messages are instructions, in effect, on how to understand the rest of Revelation." Does this make sense? How important will it be to read Revelation as if the seven messages in chapters 2–3 are integrally connected with the visions in chapters 4–22?

7. The author suggests that it misreads these messages to the congregations of Asia to think that "what's at stake here are religious beliefs." What do you think he means? Do you agree?

4

Weakness in Power

[Revelation 3]

We may read Revelation as a book of conflicts—the beast vs. the Lamb, the Holy Spirit vs. the false prophet, Babylon vs. new Jerusalem. The question is: Who is more powerful? Which is actually the question: What kind of power is more powerful—the power to conquer through domination or the power to conquer through self-giving love? On this question hangs the fate of the earth, we could say. Certainly, for John the writer of Revelation, on this question hangs the fate of the churches.

The seven messages that make up chapters 2 and 3, the first of Revelation's many visions, set the book's agenda. In the previous chapter, I wrote about "power in weakness"—and focused on how the little church in Smyrna, besieged, suffering persecution, with little visible power, actually was praised above all the other churches and proclaimed to be *rich* indeed. In this chapter, I will reflect on "weakness in power"—and focus on how the big church in Laodicea, wealthy, comfortable, lacking in nothing, actually was condemned above all the other churches and proclaimed to be "wretched, pitiable, poor, blind, and naked."

These seven messages to churches in Rev 2 and 3 emphasize just how much the Roman Empire is *everywhere* in the world of this book. Each of the seven cities was a center for devotion to the empire—shrines, temples, and monuments. The various strengths and weaknesses in the congregations to which the messages speak relate to ways in which congregations accommodate to or resist the empire in which they find themselves.

REVELATION 3:1–6

> And to the angel of the church in Sardis write: These are the words of him who has the seven spirits of God and the seven stars: "I know your works; you have a name of being alive, but you are dead. Wake up, and strengthen what remains and is on the point of death, for I have not found your works perfect in the sight of my God. Remember then what you received and heard; obey it, and repent. If you do not wake up, I will come like a thief, and you will not know at what hour I will come to you. Yet you have still a few persons in Sardis who have not soiled their clothes; they will walk with me, dressed in white, for they are worthy. If you conquer, you will be clothed like them in white robes, and I will not blot your name out of the book of life; I will confess your name before my Father and before his angels. Let anyone who has an ear listen to what the Spirit is saying to the churches."

In the message to the congregation in the city of Sardis, we have one of the more negatively critical of the messages. As with the other messages, this one touches on characteristics of the city itself—implying that the congregation there reflects its environment, mostly in problematic ways. The city of Sardis had the appearance of being invulnerable, safe from outside attack. However, in fact, several times in the past its boundaries had been penetrated by Sardis's enemies, leading to disaster for the city. Likewise with the congregation. John's Jesus makes an extraordinarily cutting remark: "You have a name of being alive, but you are dead" (3:1).

The introductory comment, where Jesus is described, states that he "has the seven spirits of God and the seven stars" (3:1). These two images go back to earlier in the vision where "the one like the Son of Man" holds seven stars in his right hand (1:16). These seven stars, we are then told, "are the angels of the seven churches" (1:19). At the beginning of Revelation, "the seven spirits who are before 'the One's throne" (1:4) seem to be a picture of the Spirit of God that proceeds from the throne as the presence of God throughout all creation.

Given the problems with the congregation in Sardis, this picture of Jesus communicates his presence with the congregation—in this case actually a warning as much as a comfort. He sees through the illusion of life that the congregation seems to be cultivating. He knows that the faith and commitment of this congregation are not life giving. By virtue of his having the "seven spirits" (i.e., the Spirit of life), Jesus offers the Sardians liberation from their false piety and death-fostering cultural conformity. But they must choose to "wake up!" (3:2). And they must choose to understand the actual message of the gospel—devotion to the Lamb as the true king and savior. Too easily, the Sardians center their identity as a congregation on the quest for comfort in and accommodation to empire.

The city of Sardis was home to numerous worship centers for Roman imperial religion and its various auxiliary religious movements. Most notably, Sardis hosted an impressive temple dedicated to its patron goddess, Artemis—thought to have been Zeus's daughter, but by this time a servant to the Roman emperor.

The congregation in Sardis, regardless of its reputation (apparently among other Christians in the area) for "being alive," had few virtues worthy of commendation according to this message. Only "a few persons in Sardis . . . have not soiled their clothes." That is, only a few have remained steadfast to the way of the Lamb in face of pressure to adapt to the imperial way. These faithful few "will walk with [Jesus], dressed in white" (3:4).

The basic picture of Sardis, though, is of distance from the Lamb. Unlike the three previous congregations in this series who received sharp criticism (Ephesus, Pergamum, and Thyatira), Sardis does not have a strong witness that stands in tension with the problematic ways of Balaam, et al.—only "a few" remaining "unsoiled" by conformity with the imperial situation. The ultimate disaster, their name being "blotted from the book of life" (3:5) can only be averted by the Sardis Christians' wakefulness, turning from the empire, listening to the Spirit, and "conquering" through persistent love and compassion. As we will see even more forcefully presented in the message to the congregation at Laodicea, it appears that one of the major challenges for the communities of the Lamb is simply remaining focused and committed to active faithfulness. That is, the dangers are those of passivity, easy conformity, and imperviousness to the challenges of following the Lamb's way.

Certainly, as John passionately seeks to convey throughout Revelation, a conflict of life-and-death proportions is happening. But one of the big challenges is simply that self-proclaimed followers of Jesus recognize that the conflict is happening. It is an issue of sight. It is an issue of hearing. It is an issue of awareness. The community at Sardis sinks into separation from the Lamb and is being blotted from the book of life mainly by not listening, by sustaining its comfort and passivity. Nonetheless, Jesus is present even in this morally listless congregation: "Let anyone who has an ear listen to what the Spirit is saying to the churches" (3:6).

REVELATION 3:7–13

> And to the angel of the church in Philadelphia write: These are the words of the holy one, the true one, who has the key of David, who opens and no one will shut, who shuts and no one opens: "I know your works. Look, I have set before you an open door, which no one is able to shut. I know that you have but little power, and yet you have kept my word and have not denied my name. I will make those of the synagogue of Satan who say that they are Jews and are not, but are lying—I will make them come and bow down before your feet, and they will learn that I have loved you. Because you have kept my word of patient endurance, I will keep you from the hour of trial that is coming on the whole world to test the inhabitants of the earth. I am coming soon; hold fast to what you have, so that no one may seize your crown. If you conquer, I will make you a pillar in the temple of my God; you will never go out of it. I will write on you the name of my God, and the name of the city of my God, the new Jerusalem that comes down from my God out of heaven, and my own new name. Let anyone who has an ear listen to what the Spirit is saying to the churches."

The congregation in Philadelphia, in contrast to the congregation in Sardis (and to the congregation in Laodicea, in the message that follows) lives on the cutting edge of faithfulness, being tested and found true.

The initial picture in this message, that Jesus holds "the key of David" (3:7) alludes to the earlier image of the "one like the Son of Man" having "the keys of Death and of Hades" (1:18). Since, as we will learn, the congregation in Philadelphia is small and fragile in human terms, facing the wrath of the beast and remaining true, this opening image is meant to be one of assurance. The Jesus they seek to follow, even when it is costly to do so, is actually the one who holds the key to true life. His verdict holds away, regardless of present appearances on the ground in Philadelphia.

Allusions to Jesus holding the key to Death and Hades, the key of David, foreshadow the drama in chapter 5 when John feels despair and grief at the prospect that no one could be found to open the scroll that proceeds from the one on the throne. But we are already told that Jesus holds the "key"—likely a parallel to his ability to open the scroll. We learn throughout the book of Revelation that Jesus comes to hold the "key" and to open the "scroll" due to his "patient endurance" (or, "nonviolent resistance") that the Philadelphians are called to imitate.

In contrast to the community in Sardis, which has the appearance of being alive but according to Jesus in reality is dead, with Philadelphia the confounding of appearances works the other way. "I know you have but little power," but your works are solid and faithful (3:8).

As with the congregation in Smyrna, in Philadelphia it appears that the Lamb's followers are besieged and face a great deal of oppression and danger. When Jesus praises them (they "have not denied my name," 3:8), he does not simply mean, it is great you let it be known you are my followers. More so, he means, in claiming "my name" you recognize that you must say no to the emperor's name. You recognize an either/or choice of loyalties at stake. This perspective contrasts with many of the people in the churches of Asia Minor who seem to believe that their faith in Jesus and their collaboration with the empire can be a both/and choice.

Also, as with the congregation in Smyrna, in Philadelphia the opponents are Christians who are too eager to fit in with the empire. They are called "the synagogue of Satan." They "say they are Jews" with the implication that they actually are not. We need to recognize that, as noted above, Christianity was not yet separate from Judaism.[1] Hence, the Christians John wrote to *wanted* to be known as Jews. So, John's Jesus says, actually, that these are false believers (in reality, false *Christians*).

Jesus here promises the faithful ones who in this rare case make up the entirety of the congregation that their perseverance will be rewarded with security in their connection with God even in the face of terrible traumas (3:10). He points ahead to what is to come in Revelation with the promise that the Philadelphians will be "a pillar in the temple of my God" (3:12). The reference to new Jerusalem here suggests that this "temple" is actually new Jerusalem itself, which will host God's presence and will not have a literal temple in it because the city itself will resemble the holy of holies and God and the Lamb are themselves the true temple and always present (21:22).

REVELATION 3:14–22

> And to the angel of the church in Laodicea write: The words
> of the Amen, the faithful and true witness, the origin of God's
> creation: "I know your works; you are neither cold nor hot. I

1. According to Daniel Boyarin, the "separation" did not actually become solidified until the fourth century. See Boyarin, *Border*.

wish that you were either cold or hot. So, because you are lukewarm, and neither cold nor hot, I am about to spit you out of
my mouth. For you say, 'I am rich, I have prospered, and I need
nothing.' You do not realize that you are wretched, pitiable, poor,
blind, and naked. Therefore I counsel you to buy from me gold
refined by fire so that you may be rich; and white robes to clothe
you and to keep the shame of your nakedness from being seen;
and salve to anoint your eyes so that you may see. I reprove and
discipline those whom I love. Be earnest, therefore, and repent.
Listen! I am standing at the door, knocking; if you hear my voice
and open the door, I will come in to you and eat with you, and
you with me. To the one who conquers I will give a place with
me on my throne, just as I myself conquered and sat down with
my Father on his throne. Let anyone who has an ear listen to
what the Spirit is saying to the churches."

The seventh and final message provides a focus for John's concerns with
the entire group of churches. The sad state of the Laodicean congregation
stands as a warning to all of John's readers. The message starts with an implied contrast between Jesus ("faithful and true witness," 3:14, alluding to
1:5) and a congregation that is unfaithful and without a witness. Famously,
the reference to the faith of the Laodiceans ("neither hot nor cold") alludes
to the water that came to the city through a viaduct and arrived too warm to
drink and too cold to use for cooking or washing. The "neither hot not cold"
refers to being useless—that is, without a witness.

The big problem is that in their prosperity and comfort, the people
in this congregation think they have arrived; they have all they need ("You
say, 'I am rich, I have prospered, and I need nothing," 3:17). Nothing could
be further from the truth, according to Jesus: "You are wretched, pitiable,
poor, blind, and naked." As it turns out much later in the book, this indictment will tightly link the Laodicean congregation with the empire itself. In
chapter 18, using the metaphors of the empire as Babylon and Babylon as
the "great harlot," chillingly similar words are voiced: "I rule as a queen; I
am no widow, and I will never see grief'" (18:7). John sees a great reversal
in chapter 18 as Babylon is brought low and its self-satisfied boasts prove
utterly empty—parallel to the reversal in the message to the Laodicean
congregation.

Part of the horror of John's critique of the Laodicean congregation is
that Rev 17–18 will unveil the true nature of the empire. Rome may seem attractive to many of John's readers in the seven churches (or, more precisely,
in five of the seven churches, Smyrna and Philadelphia aside). This seeming

benefactor, John's visions will assert, shockingly is "drunk with the blood of the saints and the blood of the witnesses to Jesus" (17:6).

In the spirit of the Old Testament prophets, though, Jesus here intends not to condemn in order to reject and punish, but to critique in order to warn and hopefully bring healing. There is a way out of the Laodiceans' spiral of comfort complicit with death. "I counsel you to buy from me gold refined by fire so that you may be rich" (3:18). The riches Jesus has in mind are the rewards promised to the "conquerors" throughout the messages. The empire's riches are but the dust of death. True riches are available for those who trust in the Lamb and follow his path.

The city of Laodicea was a center both for textile production and medical supplies. These were the source of much of the city's wealth. So, when Jesus promises to provide "white robes . . . to keep the shame of our nakedness from being seen" and "salve to anoint your eyes so that you may see" (3:18), he speaks directly to a contrast between trusting in the commerce of the empire over against trusting in the way of Jesus. To reinforce his redemptive intent in the sharp confrontation, Jesus promises, "I reprove and discipline those whom I love" (3:19) and promises a place "on my throne" to the conquerors (3:21).

Clearly, the words in this seventh message have the specificities of Laodicea in mind—as do each of the other six messages in relation to their locations. However, it is no coincidence that this message concludes the series. The fate of this congregation, its "wretchedness" before Jesus, stands as a warning to all the other communities as well. This is what happens when comfort in Babylon takes precedence over conquering with the Lamb.

WEAKNESS IN POWER

If the message to Smyrna, as well as the one to Philadelphia, underscore one of the fundamental messages of Revelation—the power of Lamb-like weakness—that the series of seven messages ends with Laodicea makes an equally strong point: Revelation's critique of the weakness of beast-like power.

With Laodicea, what we see is that the congregation has, in a genuine sense, actually *become Rome*. It has absorbed the values of empire so totally that there is no longer any resistance. The Laodicean Christians simply parrot the language of the empire. In this sense, Laodicea anticipates what will be true for *most* Christians in later generations. When the soldiers of the Emperor Constantine march to battle the "pagans" in the fourth century, they are led by banners picturing the cross. What had been a symbol of Rome's hatred of the way of Jesus, the symbol of crucifixion, the empire's violence against God's own son, became a symbol for God's blessing on the violence of empire. And *today*, so many American churches have right up front in their worship spaces a powerful symbol of imperial violence—the American flag.

How does the Laodicean church understand itself? "I am rich, I have prospered, and I need nothing" (3:17). How does the Roman Empire, in Revelation shown as a great harlot, understand itself? "I rule as a queen; I am no widow, and I will never see grief" (17:7). In both cases, smug affirmations of self-sufficiency and autonomy are turned upside down. The powerful are shown to be weak. What is it that empire seeks with its power of domination, of wealth, and of the infinite destructiveness through military hardware? "To need nothing. To never see grief."

Empire convinces people to consent to its rule with the promise that those who go along will need nothing, they will never see grief. Power as security. Power as control. Power as certainty. Big promises. But empire must crack down, hard, on those who challenge its claims. Why? Because such challenges might reveal that the empire's "power" actually is weakness.

One example of how the power of domination is revealed to be weakness is a story James Scott tells in his book, *Seeing Like a State*.[2] By the late eighteenth century, the scientific revolution was in full sway. It found expression in humans relating to the natural world; for example, how people related to the forests of Western Europe. People in power came to focus almost entirely on the economic value of forests—the commercial products that could be extracted from the forests, possible tax revenues, ways forests could be exploited to yield profits. "Forests" were no longer thought of as homes to a whole variety of life-forms living in age-old harmony. The vocabulary changed. "Nature" became "natural resources," with an emphasis on usefulness for human exploitation. Trees that were understood to have economic value became known as "timber," while those without such value were labeled "trash trees" or "underbrush."

"Scientific forestry" emerged at this time and deeply influenced the landscape of Western Europe. In the late 1700s, foresters remade Germany's forests. They sought a more easily quantified forest through careful cultivation. They cleared the underbrush, reduced the numbers of species (often to monoculture), and did planting simultaneously and in straight rows on large tracts. Eventually, the old-growth forests were transformed into truly "scientific forests," neat and tidy monocultural, even-aged forests.

The initial results from remaking Germany's forests were spectacular. On an aesthetic level, the regularity and neatness of the appearance of the

2. Scott, *Seeing*, 5–21.

new forests resonated deeply with the values of modern Europe. At first, the new forests provided economic rewards as well. The Norway spruce became the tree of choice due to its hardiness, rapid growth, and valuable wood.

It took time for the effects of this type of forestry to become apparent. Only after the planting of the second rotation of the spruce did the problems become clear. The first generation had grown well because they benefited from the rich soil left by the old-growth forest in all its diversity. However, after that deposit of nutrients had been exhausted, the output of the forest shrank dramatically. A new German term was coined—*Waldsterben* (forest death)—to describe the effects. Weakness in power . . . we aren't always as much in control as we think.

Jesus here in Rev 3 is fairly ruthless in his treatment of the Laodicean congregation. It is a *useless* church, he says. Imagine being thirsty and taking a deep draught of what you expect to be a refreshing beverage. But it's lukewarm, kind of like old bath water. "Blecchh!" You have to spit it out. "What is this stuff?"

This message reflects quite a bit of knowledge about the city of Laodicea. It had to pipe its water from a long distance away and when the water arrived it was lukewarm. It had to be heated or cooled to be usable. Laodicea was known for several particular characteristics. It was wealthy, much more than surrounding cities. Its wealth came in part from its textile industry, and in part because it was a medical center that trained physicians and produced a widely used treatment for eye problems. Presumably, the people in the congregation themselves directly benefitted from Laodicean wealth. So, when it comes to the warnings in the message, John's Jesus could not have been more cutting. You claim to need nothing, he sneers, but in reality, you are wretched and pitiable. You are poor. You are naked. You can't see.

The power you hoard and depend on—power that allows you to rest comfortably in the secure arms of the Pax Romana, in the secure arms of the domination system that empire creates—is *nothing*. In fact, it's *worse* than nothing. Because you believe the lies of the false prophet. You cannot, by brute force and coercion create genuine security and hope. All you can create is an illusion—like the illusion in Germany's Black Forest that through "scientific forestry" they could create an economic gravy train without end. It didn't last long—nor did Rome's "griefless" domination—nor did the self-sufficiency of the Laodicean congregation.

We see this same dynamic firsthand in the United States. After World War II, the US could say, "I am rich, I have prospered, and I need nothing." Unlike the other great powers whose economies were devastated, ours prospered. And we stood on the moral high ground as the great democracy that had stopped the terrible tyrants of Germany and Japan. But the US did not use this power, prosperity, and prestige to move toward a world order based on peace and cooperation. We set out right away on a project of domination. We were wealthy and powerful enough to retain our dominant status for a generation or so. But things have been spiraling out of control for some time. We don't seem to be able to free ourselves from the tenacious hold of militarism even as the military-industrial complex moves the entire nation to disaster.[3]

Revelation shows plenty of hostility toward the beast. It urgently challenges its readers to turn from weakness in power toward power in weakness, from the coercive conquest modeled by Babylon to the conquest through healing love modeled by new Jerusalem. Revelation's urgency is genuine and must be embraced. Still, Revelation is not without hope even for the kings of the earth—as we will see later in the book. More importantly, though, as the letter to Laodicea itself tells us, and as we will see when we move on to Revelation chapters 4 and 5, the book holds out hope for the Laodiceans of the world. John's agenda is to heal more than to condemn.

Let's look at the sharp critique in the message. Laodicea was known for its wealth, its production of textiles, and its medical treatments, including especially eye treatments. So, the message emphasizes to the church its *poverty*, its *nakedness*, and its *blindness*. But why make these pointed criticisms? Not mainly to score rhetorical points. Not mainly to condemn.

The message does challenge the Laodicean self-sufficiency, naming it in terms of false confidence in wealth, in textile production, in medical care. But John wants to make clear the Lamb's offer. Jesus makes available for "purchase" "gold refined by fire" that will give the Laodiceans authentic wealth. He makes available "white robes" that will genuinely clothe those who put them on. He makes available "salve to anoint your eyes" that will provide genuine sight.

The next vision of the book, in chapters 4 and 5, follows directly from this message to the Laodiceans. The danger for all the congregations is that they would become indistinguishable from their surrounding culture. In the US, the danger has been that Christianity becomes inextricably identified with the American empire. Then, it seems that the only way to oppose the empire is to reject Christian faith. What a terrible tragedy. Not least because so many American Christians affirm conquest by coercion rather than conquest by love and compassion. Not least because in rejecting Christianity, many people of goodwill fail to learn from the message of Revelation about the genuine power that shapes the universe.

3. See Grimsrud, *Good*.

However, the seven messages end with the message to Laodicea's call to open the door to a different notion of power and hope and security and wealth. We can embrace these metaphors from the message to Laodicea: Use the eye salve that provides genuine sight; it will allow you to recognize that empire equals death and that to resist empire leads to life. And open the door to the one who embodies this life. As we will see in the next vision, that is the one whose self-sacrifice and nonviolent resistance leads to resurrection and celebration.

So, this, then, is where we are so far in Revelation's story. This first vision in chapters 1–3 warns not to accept the worldview of empire and not to twist Christian faith to fit with that worldview. Such choices lead to death. With the warning comes witness that faithfulness is possible. Genuine wealth is available to those who resist the empire story and embrace a different kind of story, the Lamb's story. Our next vision goes deeper into true power and shows the One on the throne and the Lamb to be already worshiped for bringing healing and giving life. Then will we turn to the other, more notorious, visions that deconstruct empire as a way of life. But the affirmation of hope and blessing precedes the visions of chaos. The message of weakness in power ultimately is *secondary* to the message of power in weakness.

FOR FURTHER ENGAGEMENT

1. One of the main issues that the seven messages are concerned about seems to be that of the followers of Jesus accommodating too easily to their social and political environment in the Roman Empire (or resisting the call to accommodate and suffering as a consequence). Do you agree? Explain. Reflect on this issue of accommodation as it applies to our context today.

2. What implications for modern-day churches do the values expressed in the messages in chapter 3 have? For instance, a church with a reputation for "being alive" is described as actually "being dead" (Sardis). A weak, persecuted church is praised the highest (Philadelphia). A prosperous, "successful" church is condemned (Laodicea).

3. What might persecution in our context actually look like? Should the church in general in North America be persecuted more? If so, what kinds of activities would lead to that persecution? When it happens, why are Christians persecuted today? Do you think that there are "legitimate" and "illegitimate" causes of persecution?

4. The author comments of Sardis, "There is a conflict going on of life-and-death proportions. But one of the biggest challenges is simply that self-proclaimed followers of Jesus recognize that the conflict is happening." How applicable is this thought to Christians now? What might be some significant "conflict" in our context that we are not recognizing adequately?

5. How comforting is the affirmation to the Philadelphia congregation that though "you have but little power," you will "be made a pillar in the temple of my God"? Explain.

6. What does the author mean when he uses the phrase "weakness in power" to describe characterize the Laodicean congregation? What would you say the big problem with that congregation was in Jesus's eyes?

7. The church in Sardis is labeled as "dead." What do you think such "deadness" is about? Does the difference between "alive" and "dead" has to do with being committed to Christ or not? What would "being committed to Christ" entail?

8. Though Jesus calls the Laodiceans miserable, pitiable, poor, blind, and naked, he wants to share a meal with them. Reflect on what that intention might mean.

5

What is God Like?

[Revelation 4–5]

The call to "conquer" unifies all seven messages in chapters 2 and 3. Each congregation faces its own unique challenges, but each also receives the same call from John's Jesus: Sustain your highest loyalty to the way of the gospel and resist demands from the Roman Empire for such loyalty. Each of those messages concludes with a promise of a place with the Lamb and his God for those who "conquer."

The call to "conquer" calls readers to Jesus's way of persevering love. Chapters 4 and 5 next provide bases for taking this call with the utmost seriousness and with the utmost hope.

REVELATION 4:1–11

After this I looked, and there in heaven a door stood open! And the first voice, which I had heard speaking to me like a trumpet, said, "Come up here, and I will show you what must take place after this." At once I was in the spirit, and there in heaven stood a throne, with one seated on the throne! And the one seated there looks like jasper and carnelian, and around the throne is a rainbow that looks like an emerald. Around the throne are twenty-four thrones, and seated on the thrones are twenty-four elders, dressed in white robes, with golden crowns on their heads. Coming from the throne are flashes of lightning, and rumblings and peals of thunder, and in front of the throne burn seven flaming torches, which are the seven spirits of God; and in front of the throne there is something like a sea of glass, like crystal. Around the throne, and on each side of the throne, are four living creatures, full of eyes in front and behind: the first living creature like a lion, the second living creature like an ox, the third living creature with a face like a human face, and the fourth living creature like a flying eagle. And the four living creatures, each of them with six wings, are full of eyes all around and inside. Day and night without ceasing they sing, "Holy, holy, holy, the Lord God the Almighty, who was and is and is to come." And whenever the living creatures give glory and honor and thanks to the one who is seated on the throne, who lives forever and ever, the twenty-four elders fall before the one who is seated on the throne and worship the one who lives forever and ever; they cast their crowns before the throne, singing, "You are worthy, our Lord and God, to receive glory and honor and power, for you created all things, and by your will they existed and were created."

After the seven messages, John looks and sees an "open door" in heaven (4:1). He crosses the threshold and sees a throne. Revelation never describes the physical appearance of the One seated on the throne—actually a confirmation that this is Israel's God, Maker of heaven and earth. From the start, the Hebrews never created images of God. God cannot be reduced to a human picture. Revelation uses the image of thrones often—generally as symbols of power and authority. Satan (2:13), the dragon (13:2), and the beast (16:10) each have thrones. So, the throne here in chapter 4 stands in contrast to those thrones. Which throne will be the one given precedence? The vision here asserts that the God of Jesus is the true God—in contrast to the claims of Caesar. This God's throne is supreme.

So, John gets a vision of God in this moment of transition in the story. He moves from Revelation's direct address to its readers in chapters 1–3 to the terrible visions that will follow beginning in chapter 6. The vision of God in chapter 4 intends both to ground the challenges to John's audience in the reality and character of the One on the throne who calls them forward and to remind the audience that the visions to come, terrible as they may seem, do not negate the healing intentions of this One.

The single vision that makes up chapters 4 and 5 portrays a worship service that has one main message: God is present in the Lamb who brings healing to the world. The vision begins with worship and praise from the twenty-four elders (4:4), proceeds to the four living creatures (4:8), then focuses on the core content—the triumph of the Lamb (5:6–8). It then moves on to more worship, including from the four living creatures and the twenty-four elders, concluding as the service began, with the elders (5:9–14).

Several of the elements of the initial throne vision in chapter 4 help us understand what is to come in Revelation. A rainbow surrounds the throne (4:3), a reference back to the covenant made with Noah in Gen 9 and God's promise not to destroy the earth again. This reminder of God's redemptive intent will be important when we move into the plague visions starting in chapter 6.

The twenty-four elders (4:4) represent the people of God. The image echoes that of 1 Chr 24 where twenty-four divisions of priests were each headed by a "chief" or "elder." These had to be present in the temple at the great festivals. The "seven torches of fire" that are the "seven spirits of God" (4:5) picture God's active presence in the world, something usually spoken of as the Holy Spirit. The reference recalls Zechariah, where the prophet sees seven lamps and hears that they are "the eyes of the Lord, that range through the whole earth" (Zech 4:10).

Elsewhere in Revelation, we read of the "sea of glass" (4:6) as the reservoir of evil out of which arises the monster (13:1) and as the barrier that the redeemed must cross in a new exodus if they are to win access to the promised land (15:2–3). In the new heaven and earth the sea is no more (21:1). In Revelation, the sea, whether on earth or in heaven, belongs to the old order and within that order it stands for that which opposes God's will. Here in chapter 4, it serves as a reminder that God's work in the rest of the book is to get rid of the sea.

This scene sets a tone of joy and celebration, not of the anger and impending judgment we would expect if punishment and destruction were Revelation's agenda. The One on the throne, it would appear, is a healer, not a punisher. All of creation joins in *praise* of the One on the throne—not a likely response should God be about to embark on the spree of destruction many see in the plague visions.

This part of the vision makes the key points that God is indeed present, God enlivens creation, and God is worthy to be praised by all. The true significance of this throne room theophany in the overall message of Revelation will only become clear, though, as we move on to the second part of the "worship service" in chapter 5, the most important chapter in the book of Revelation.

REVELATION 5:1–5

> Then I saw in the right hand of the one seated on the throne a
> scroll written on the inside and on the back, sealed with seven
> seals; and I saw a mighty angel proclaiming with a loud voice,
> "Who is worthy to open the scroll and break its seals?" And no
> one in heaven or on earth or under the earth was able to open
> the scroll or to look into it. And I began to weep bitterly because
> no one was found worthy to open the scroll or to look into it.
> Then one of the elders said to me, "Do not weep. See, the Lion of
> the tribe of Judah, the Root of David, has conquered, so that he
> can open the scroll and its seven seals."

John sees a "scroll" in the right hand of the One on the throne (5:1). That
the scroll is in God's "right hand" emphasizes its weightiness as does the fact
that it is secured with seven seals ("seven" is the number of completeness).
Though we are not told directly, we surely are to understand the contents
of this scroll to be the fulfillment of God's work with creation, a message of
final and complete healing.

Someone must be found to open the scroll and bring the message to its
fruition. To John's bitter frustration, given his longing that the healing come,
"no one in heaven or on earth or under the earth was able to open the scroll
or look into it" (5:3). We can only speculate why this is the case. One idea,
though, is that everyone misunderstands the way the scroll is to be opened.
Everyone looked for the power of domination as the power to bring history
to its conclusion. John's vision may thus make a point similar to the point
Paul makes in 1 Cor 2. Paul refers to the "wisdom" of the age that fails to
see in the persevering love of Jesus the revelation of the deepest and most
profound truths of the universe (1 Cor 2:7).

No one is found and John weeps bitterly (5:4). Then he is told to weep
no more because one has indeed been found. The drama here underscores
the utter uniqueness of the one who is found. It is as if the entire universe
has been scoured, and only *one* is found. Only *one* can open the scroll. The
angel tells John, in effect, that a king, great and powerful enough to break
open the scroll has made an appearance. It is "the Lion of the tribe of Judah,
the Root of David," a great conqueror who can open the scroll. "The Lion
of the tribe of Judah" alludes to one of the first messianic prophecies in the
Bible, Gen 49:9–10. We know from other Jewish literature of New Testament times that the lion was used to indicate the conquering Messiah (e.g.,
see 4 Ezra [2 Esdras 11:37; 12:31]), even though the metaphor is not found

elsewhere in the New Testament. The reference in Genesis alludes to one who wielded the scepter as a dominating king.

The "Root of David" alludes to Isa 11:1. Isaiah likens the royal family of David, the son of Jesse, to a tree that had fallen, but from whose roots had sprung a new tree to restore the kingly rule of David. The verses that follow in Isa 11 give a vivid prophecy of the promised triumphant messianic king.

The language in Rev 5:5 has great dramatic effect. John of course already knows the identity of the victor. However, the drama is important. Many did expect that the deliverer would indeed be an all-powerful king like King David of old. This king would be the long hoped-for Messiah, the one who would "redeem Israel" (as two of Jesus's disciples described to the incognito Jesus on the road to Emmaus shortly after his death, Luke 24:21). This expectation is what John *hears*. One has been found, a great king, a mighty warrior, perhaps anticipating Constantine the Great or Charlemagne, or maybe Franklin Roosevelt or Douglas MacArthur: the great warriors for Christian empire. However, the fact that only *one* has been found should tip us off that this one is different than what most of us expect.

REVELATION 5:6–10

> Then I saw between the throne and the four living creatures and among the elders a Lamb standing as if it had been slaughtered, having seven horns and seven eyes, which are the seven spirits of God sent out into all the earth. He went and took the scroll from the right hand of the one who was seated on the throne. When he had taken the scroll, the four living creatures and the twenty-four elders fell before the Lamb, each holding a harp and golden bowls full of incense, which are the prayers of the saints. They sing a new song: "You are worthy to take the scroll and to open its seals, for you were slaughtered and by your blood you ransomed for God saints from every tribe and language and people and nation; you have made them to be a kingdom and priests serving our God, and they will reign on earth."

What John actually sees reorients the way we understand the vision of the One on the throne in chapter 4. John sees something that redefines his entire world. What John sees interprets what he hears. What John sees makes clear the meaning of victory. What John sees transforms our very understanding of God and the universe. What John sees tells us why it was so difficult to find the right one who actually could open the scroll.

"I saw between the throne and the four living creatures and among the elders a Lamb standing as if it had been slaughtered [who] went and took the scroll from the right hand of the One . . . on the throne" (5:6–7). What John sees, though, is not actually different from what he hears. It is just that the mighty king who has the power to open the scroll and bring the story of humanity to its healing end is the gentle, compassionate, consistently loving, self-sacrificial Jesus. He conquers by persevering on the path of love, all the way to the cross and beyond. The uniqueness here has mostly to do with the method of the victory. Our need to transform our sense of victory is radical.

The *Lamb*, slaughtered (crucified) and yet standing (resurrected), walks over and takes the scroll. As Revelation continues, we will learn that indeed the Lamb does have the power to open the scroll, and by the end of Revelation, the power to bring healing to God's creation. And, as Revelation continues, we will continually be reminded of our need to undergo a genuine revolution in how we conceive power, victory, and the character of God. We must notice just how profound the exaltation of the slain and raised Lamb is here. The vision of Rev 5 may represent the strongest affirmation of Jesus's link with God in the entire New Testament. The Lamb stands right next to the throne. He is not one of the worshipers but actually himself becomes the object of worship. What follows in chapter 5 in relation to the Lamb almost exactly echoes what John reports in chapter 4 about the One on the throne.

So, we have a profound affirmation of the "godness" of the Lamb. This affirmation directly follows from the self-emptying of the Lamb (similarly to how Paul in Phil 2 portrays Jesus—the Mighty One who lives as a servant). The One whose persevering love leads to a cross embodies God as nothing else does. Hence, the most important revelation is not that Jesus is divine. The most important revelation is what this affirmation tells us about God. Jesus's uniqueness as such is not the point here but Jesus's way of embodying how God "conquers."

We understand the One on the throne most clearly in terms of the persevering love of the Lamb. The vision in chapters 4 and 5 thus becomes a radical and transformative vision of God. We see God here, indeed, God on the cross. This God brings victory and transformation and healing to creation through self-giving love.

REVELATION 5:11–14

> Then I looked, and I heard the voice of many angels surround-
> ing the throne and the living creatures and the elders; they

numbered myriads of myriads and thousands of thousands, singing with full voice, "Worthy is the Lamb that was slaughtered to receive power and wealth and wisdom and might and honor and glory and blessing!" Then I heard every creature in heaven and on earth and under the earth and in the sea, and all that is in them, singing, "To the one seated on the throne and to the Lamb be blessing and honor and glory and might forever and ever!" And the four living creatures said, "Amen!" And the elders fell down and worshiped.

The worship service culminates with an ever-widening set of affirmations: "Worthy is the Lamb that was slaughtered to receive power and wealth and wisdom and might and honor and glory and blessing!" (5:12). The worship ripples wider and wider, including praise from every tribe and nation, then from angels beyond count, and then—amazingly—from "every creature in heaven and on earth and under the earth and in the sea" (5:13).

Of course, this is confessional hyperbole, a deliberate exaggeration. Still, John wants to drive home the point with every bit of rhetorical force he can muster that Jesus, the epitome of peaceable embodied convictions, shows us the character of God and the means of victory. And this revelation of what God is like and how God works gains the strongest imaginable endorsement from creation itself. So, the slain and raised Lamb not only reveals God's character, he reveals the character of God's created universe by the response he generates from "every creature" when he takes the scroll.

As will be re-emphasized in the visions to follow, in the life, death, and resurrection of Jesus the end *has* come. The victory that determines the outcome of human history has been won. There will be no other battle. There need be no other victory—other than actions and commitments that reinforce the victory already won and that conquer in precisely the same way (faithful witness to the very end, confirmed by God's nonviolent vindication through resurrection).

This vision determines the meaning of the rest of Revelation. As we turn to the terrible plague visions beginning in chapter 6, we will be challenged to keep the basic message of Revelation 4 and 5 in mind (that the message that God is most accurately revealed in the Lamb and that the Lamb's victory via cross and resurrection is what determines the outcome of the story). The vision could not be clearer, however. So, it challenges us to read what follows very carefully—and in light of the way of the Lamb. As we will see, such a reading is indeed possible; it is, in fact, the best reading.

John could not be more straightforward: *Only* as the embodiment of persevering love can Jesus open the scroll. What makes him unique is not a general claim to divinity but the manifestation of a particular kind of divinity. The struggle throughout Revelation focuses on two distinct types of "conquering"—through domination or through persevering love. "Every creature" worships the Lamb because he embodies the true moral character of the universe.

WHAT IS GOD LIKE?

When we take up the book of Revelation, just like with any other religious text, so much of what we see depends on what we are looking for. The date of the rapture and the identity of the antichrist (à la the Left Behind books[1])? Or the lunatic ravings of a hallucinating first-century fanatic? That's what D. H. Lawrence thought.[2] Or, words of encouragement in face of a vicious authoritarian state? South African theologian Allan Boesak said so thirty-some years ago.[3] Or a challenge to American imperialism as the great American prophet of the 1960s and seventies William Stringfellow claimed.[4]

And what *kind of God* do we expect to find "revealed" in Revelation? We tend to try to find what will reinforce our existing beliefs. We don't always look kindly toward images and ideas that threaten what we think we know. I'm reminded of one of my favorite quotes, from the social thinker John Kenneth Galbraith: "Faced with the choice between changing one's minds and proving that there is no need to do so, almost everyone gets busy on the proof."[5]

My sense is that most people read Revelation with the assumption that its God is violent and judgmental. One of the pivotal moments in my own theological journey came forty or so years ago when a couple of friends had a formal debate in our church about pacifism. The one arguing against pacifism drew heavily on violent judgment in Revelation. He used this judgment to support his belief that sometimes God is violent and thus may, at times, want us to be violent too. That statement challenged me to study Revelation for myself.

The assumptions about God and violent judgment in Revelation can lead some Christians to be happy. A few years after that debate, I visited some folks from my old hometown church. This was during Ronald Reagan's acceleration of the arms race that heightened fears of a nuclear war. One friend smiled and talked about how great it was to know that God would

1. The first of many is LaHaye and Jenkins, *Left*.
2. Lawrence, *Apocalypse*.
3. Boesak, *Comfort*.
4. Stringfellow, *Ethic*.
5. Galbraith, *Economics*, 50.

be behind such a war—punishing the godless Communists and bringing in paradise for born-again Christians.

There are others who also might agree with the God-as-violent-judge reading of Revelation—but for these such a picture of God is a good reason to *reject* Christianity altogether. If violent judgment is what the Christian God is like, forget about it.[6]

Well, we do have other options for how we think of God—even in relation to Revelation. Rev 4–5 gives us some challenging images. As we look at Revelation, what do kind of God do we expect to see? Revelation chapters 4 and 5 together contain one vision. One vision, we could say, of a worship service. The movement from the elders to the four living creatures and then back emphasizes the point in the middle. If we want to learn about God from this vision, we must center our attention on the high point, in the middle part of the worship service. In the middle is the shocking revelation that the Lamb defines God's self-revelation.

But let's first back up a bit before focusing on the Lamb. The first vision of Revelation, given in the last part of chapter 1 and chapters 2 and 3, tells us what Revelation cares about. John writes to help seven congregations navigate life in the Roman Empire. These were actual congregations. Each existed in a city devoted to the empire. In each city, followers of Jesus had their loyalty severely tested.

The messages number precisely seven (seven signifies wholeness, fullness). The number indicates that these messages are for a broader audience than only those original seven congregations. But we will find the meaning of the messages mostly in their original context. In a nutshell, the messages challenge Jesus's followers to maintain their commitment to his way of self-giving love even in face of temptations to give loyalty to an empire based on domination and peace through force. The next vision, of what John sees when the door to heaven is opened (4:1), provides a foundation for the book's call for its readers to "conquer" the violence of empire through suffering love. It portrays a notion of power in weakness that exposes the weakness of power.

The first scene of the heavenly vision that begins at 4:1 centers on the One on the throne. However, the vision never physically describes this character, in keeping with how the Bible refers to God. The surroundings make the identity clear: the throne, the worship by all creation. This vision of power echoes the claims for the god-emperor of Rome. But there is no hint here of anger or judgment, only joy and celebration. The One on the throne is the true God, comparable to the emperor but profoundly different.

6. See Kirsch, *History*.

That is, the true God and the emperor are rivals. You cannot divide your loyalty between the two, Revelation insists.

When read as a whole, the most remarkable element of this vision is the way in which the One on the throne and the Lamb are shown together. Both receive the same worship. And it is only the Lamb who can open the One on the throne's scroll. This vision does support the Christian affirmation of Jesus's divinity. Jesus, the Lamb, stands on the same level as the One on the throne. However, with tragic and ironic consequences, Christians have tended to misunderstand this affirmation. They link Jesus with the One on the throne in a way that all too often makes Jesus a kind of supernatural "Christ" separate from the vulnerability and peaceableness of the Lamb image.

Fairly quickly in history, the loss of Jesus's vulnerable humanity led to terrible problems. Jesus's cross, for example, became a symbol for the violence and militarism of empire—the very empire that had executed him. The Roman Empire became Christianized, or, we could more accurately say, Christianity became imperial-ized. Church members became the empire's best soldiers. The conflict of loyalties central to Revelation was decisively settled in favor of the empire.

Jesus's professed divinity became a way for Christians to ignore the political meaning of his self-giving love that resisted empire and led to his execution. Christians seemed to forget that Jesus directly rejected the way the world's empires do politics: "Their leaders are tyrants" (Mark 10:41). They focused instead on defining what matters most about him in terms of doctrines, not his life and teaching (note, for example, how the Apostles' Creed skips from Jesus's virgin birth to his death).

The link between the exalted Christ and empire has continued to our day—as seen, for example, in the attempt in the 1980s to name a Trident submarine, a key element of the American nuclear arsenal, as the *Corpus Christi* (the "body of Christ"). After protest, the name of the sub was changed to *The City of Corpus Christi*. However, that many American Christians were comfortable with so naming a death-dealing instrument of imperial domination reflects their tendency to define Jesus's divinity in terms of God's coercive power, rather than defining God's divinity in terms of Jesus's vulnerable love.

I think there is a different—and much better—way to read the vision that makes up Rev 4 and 5. It need not be seen as an instance of linking the divine Christ with an all-powerful and coercive divine Father. Again, let's focus on the high point of the worship service. The service begins and ends with praise; in between, we could say, comes the content. We can imagine these two verses, Rev 5:5-6, as the center of a calm pool of water. Then we drop a sizeable rock into this center and watch the waves ripple out. These verses effect a revolution of expectations and understandings of power and victory that can spread and reorient the way we read the whole of Revelation, that reorient the way we read the New Testament and all the rest of the Bible, that reorient the way we understand life in God's creation itself, and that reorient our lives from accommodation with empire to resistance.

The most fundamental expression of God's power is the self-giving love of the Lamb. This love cannot be conquered even by the empire's crucifixion. Whatever we can imagine as the empire's mightiest expression of coercive power cannot defeat this vulnerable Lamb. To realize that the executed Lamb embodies God's power transforms how we understand the One on the throne. It will also change how we understand the later visions in Revelation, visions that seem to be filled with judgment and blood and destruction.

A crucial part of the vision in Rev 4 and 5 follows from the Lamb taking the scroll. All animate creation praises him—the elders, the living creatures, thousands of angels, and ultimately every creature in heaven and on earth and under earth and in the sea. And we must notice: the praise is for what *already* has happened: "You *have* liberated for God saints from every tribe and language and people and nation" (5:9).

That the reason for the praise is what has already happened is central to John's exhortations in the seven messages in chapters 2 and 3. He calls his listeners to conquer, not in the sense that they have to find a way to defeat empire—but in the sense that they have to find a way to live in harmony with the Lamb, to embrace a way of life that already stands in contrast to empire and offers life to all who join with it.

History is full of moments when what we could call "the already-ness" of the Lamb's victory over empire has found expression. Though they always seem all too fleeting, these moments do remind us of the true character of God's power, constantly at work in our world—even if it so often seems hidden.[7] The story of the great Czech prophet Vaclav Havel illustrates one such moment. Dissidents to the Soviet Empire realized they could not (and should not) resist violent domination with their own violence. Instead, they simply sought to create space for being human, to (as Havel put it) "live in truth."[8] And a revolution did happen, the "Velvet Revolution"—and the empire fell. This is the spirit our more recent "Occupy" and "Black Lives Matter" movements also seek to embody.

7. See the stories told in Ackerman and Duvall, *Force*.
8. Havel, "Power of the Powerless," 125–214.

According to Revelation, the way of empire has already failed. It revealed itself to be a tool for evil when it slaughtered the Lamb. And it revealed itself actually to be unable to defeat the Lamb's love when God brought the Lamb back to his feet through resurrection and empowered him to stand. To realize this, to realize that only the Lamb's way gains the praise of creation itself, is to realize that one need not give in to the empire's demand for loyalty. One need not accept the empire's call to take up arms. One need not sell one's soul for the sake of corporate profit and empowerment.

So, what *is* God like?

Let me supplement the Rev 4 and 5 vision with a verse from John's Gospel: "No one has ever seen God. It is God the only Son, who is close to the Father's heart, who has made him known" (John 1:18). And with a text from the first letter of John: "God is love. God's love was revealed among us in this way: God sent his only Son into the world so that we might live through him . . . . No one has ever seen God, [but] if we love one another, God lives in us, and God's love is perfected in us" (1 John 4).

FOR FURTHER ENGAGEMENT

1. The author argues that Rev 4–5 contains the most important vision in the book. He sees it being so important because it links the One on the throne very closely with the Lamb. He summarizes the message in this way: "The most fundamental expression of God's power is the self-giving love of the Lamb." Reflect on this argument—its strengths and weaknesses. Do you tend to agree with what he says here? Explain.

2. What do you make of the description of God in 4:3? What imagery is associated with the throne in this paragraph? What do you think it means?

3. Can you relate to the worship of God in 4:8–11? Do you visualize God as a being on a mighty throne? What value, if any, do you see in this imagery?

4. Why do you think the symbol of a "lamb" is used here of Jesus? What is the significance of this particular image do you think? Is it an effective symbol? Explain.

5. Does it make sense to you that a slain lamb could determine the outcome of history? How would you explain this affirmation to a non-Christian? Does this have any implications for how we think of the Christian life?

6. Some have stated that the true understanding of divine omnipotence here is that of infinite love and not unlimited coercion. Do you agree? Or does that idea go counter to your assumptions regarding God's almighty power? What are the implications of how we think of this question for how we think of God's role in our world and in our lives?

7. The author suggests that the tone of the worship vision in chapter 4 is "joy and celebration"—and makes that point that that tone supports the notion that God is best not seen as a punitive judge in the visions to follow. What do you think of that idea?

8. Reflect on the possible implications of the author's affirmation that "the slain and raised Lamb . . . reveals the character of God's universe."

6

An Angry Lamb?

[Revelation 6]

We have seen that in the vision reported in Rev 4–5, John enters the door into heaven and describes what he saw. First, it was a vision of the throne room—which turned out to be a vision that reassures readers of God's ongoing presence, worthy of continued worship from all creation. This reassurance forms a bookend with the vision of the new Jerusalem at the end of the book. That final vision brings back the image of the "One on the throne" (21:5) being worthy of the praise and adoration that is central in chapter 4.

It is essential that we keep together these two references to the One on the throne's mercy and healing love—and power. Those references must remain in our awareness as we reflect on the visions that come between the throne room and the new Jerusalem in chapters 6–20. In some ultimate sense, we may see that these visions of destruction serve the purposes of the One on the throne's healing power.

To emphasize that the intentions of the God of Revelation are to heal and redeem, the vision of the throne room continues on in chapter 5 to portray the power of the Lamb. This power shows itself in the faithful witness and crucifixion of the Lamb that, followed by resurrection and vindication, allows him to take the scroll. Because of this power, the Lamb receives the same worship from the entire animate creation as the One on the throne. The power of the Lamb leads to liberation from the powers of sin and evil for people "from every tribe and language and people and nation" (5:9).

And these liberated people form a nation of their own that stands in resistance to the nation ruled by the beast.

So, with the context set—God as ruler, the Lamb as liberator, the nation of Lamb-followers established—we turn to a new set of visions beginning at 6:1. These visions begin the process within the broader vision of chapters 4–5 and 21–22 where the One on the throne establishes new Jerusalem.

REVELATION 6:1–8

> Then I saw the Lamb open one of the seven seals, and I heard one of the four living creatures call out, as with a voice of thunder, "Come!" I looked, and there was a white horse! Its rider had a bow; a crown was given to him, and he came out conquering and to conquer. When he opened the second seal, I heard the second living creature call out, "Come!" And out came another horse, bright red; its rider was permitted to take peace from the earth, so that people would slaughter one another; and he was given a great sword. When he opened the third seal, I heard the third living creature call out, "Come!" I looked, and there was a black horse! Its rider held a pair of scales in his hand, and I heard what seemed to be a voice in the midst of the four living creatures saying, "A quart of wheat for a day's pay, and three quarts of barley for a day's pay, but do not damage the olive oil and the wine!" When he opened the fourth seal, I heard the voice of the fourth living creature call out, "Come!" I looked and there was a pale green horse! Its rider's name was Death, and Hades followed with him; they were given authority over a fourth of the earth, to kill with sword, famine, and pestilence, and by the wild animals of the earth.

Revelation never tells us exactly what the "scroll" is, the scroll that the one on the throne turned over to the slain and risen Lamb (5:7). The way chapter 5 presents this scene infers (once we read the entirety of Revelation) that the scroll contains the message to be fulfilled with the coming down of the new Jerusalem. The visions of chapters 6 through 20 convey the process of the scroll being opened so the healing message may come to fruition.

The first step will be to break open the seven seals that keep the scroll closed (6:1). No one had been found to break those seals and open the scroll—hence John's bitter weeping in 5:4. Finally, the one who may open arrives, in a genuine sense a mighty king (5:5), but a king who conquers through persevering love (5:6). Now, with 6:1, this conquering Lamb begins his work.

What follows must be interpreted carefully. Remember first of all that the Lamb referred to in chapter 6 is the same Lamb we met in chapter 5. This is a Lamb of persevering love (that is, the "Jesus Christ" the book of Revelation reveals, 1:1). Whatever the Lamb does should be understood in light of this persevering love. It is because of the Lamb's faithful witness even to the point of death that he is given the scroll (5:7) and widely worshiped. The vision of worship concludes with the four living creatures (5:14). Immediately following, in chapter 6, this same Lamb and these same four living creatures are involved with the seal visions—there is full continuity between chapters 5 and 6.

All that the Lamb does at this point (6:1) is break the seals on the scroll. The actual contents of the scroll itself are not yet revealed—the contents, we could say, that come from the One on the throne and are directly linked with the will of that One. The events that accompany the breaking of the seals cannot be tied directly with the content of the scroll because that content has not yet been revealed.

The seal-breaking events envisioned in chapter 6, therefore, need not be seen as the direct expression of God's will. In fact, what we know of God from chapters 4 and 5 indicates that the terrible events described in chapter 6 are actually contrary to the will of God and the Lamb. A forthcoming vision in chapter 12 will indicate that the terrible traumas that befall the earth beginning with 6:1 are in fact the consequences of the dragon (Satan) "making war" on God's children (12:17).

The events associated with the breaking of the seals, like the events later associated with the blowing of the trumpets (chapters 8 and 9) and the pouring out from the bowls (chapters 15 and 16), actually (though dramatically stated) represent the ongoing events of human history. John links the tragic events of human history with the breaking of the seals. In doing so, he tells us that with the life, death, and resurrection of Jesus, the Lamb, we may accurately understand the dragon's violence, domination, injustice, and destruction, so often expressed through the dragon's minions—the empires and the kings of the earth—in light of the life, death, and resurrection of Jesus the Lamb.

By having the Lamb open the scroll, John metaphorically helps us see the Lamb in the world we live in right now. These are not visions of a future catastrophe a punitive God visits on rebellious creation. Rather they are visions of the world in which we presently live. Think about all the terrible tragedies in human history—especially the seemingly continual wars, and the accompanying disease and hunger. We don't have to look to the future to see the four riders. They are in the past and in the present.

Who are these four riders? The interpretation of the first rider (6:2) is controversial. Some say that because the horse is white it must indicate the "conquering" gospel. Others see the first rider as evil, representing wars of conquest. The basis for the latter interpretation is that it is consistent with the other seals and with the other series of seven plagues that come later in the book, the trumpets and the bowls. This second interpretation seems more likely. When taken together, the four riders represent war and its attendant evils: violence, strife, famine, and disease. The white horse signifies triumphant warfare. The rider goes forth victoriously on a career of conquest.

Revelation uses "conquer" eleven times to allude to conquest by faithful witness (once in each of the seven messages of chapters 2 and 3, in 5:5 of the Lamb, and in 12:11 and 15:2 of the faithful servants). Three times it refers to conquest by violence (here, in 11:7 where the beast kills the two witnesses, and in 13:7 where the beast wages wars against and "conquers" the saints). In these various "conquering" passages, the Lamb and his followers conquer by *receiving* violence; the dragon and the evil powers by *causing* violence.

The language in 6:1–8 suggests that the first rider represents an army invading other countries from the outside (the rider is "bent on conquest"). The second rider represents a general confusion of strife including perhaps civil war or revolution ("that people should slay one another"). These two signs follow the pattern of Jesus's apocalyptic discourse in Mark 13, Matthew 24, and Luke 21, where we read of "wars and rumors of wars" (i.e., wars near and far): "Nation will rise against nation and kingdom against kingdom." The breaking of the second seal extends and intensifies the strife so that all peace is taken from the earth. The red horse probably signifies slaughter, bloodshed. We should note that the only other time in Revelation that the word for "red" here is used is at 12:3 in reference to the "fiery red satanic dragon."

The third rider's horse is appropriately "black," for he introduces famine. The "balance" implies that food will have to be weighed out and rationed with care (cf. Lev 26:26; Ezek 4:16). The price of wheat and barley indicates that they are scarce. It is not clear why some necessities are to be spared: "Do not harm oil and wine."

The last rider, Death, with its accomplice, Hades, stalking behind him, gathers the results of the work of the previous three. John's readers knew that war was commonly followed by pestilence, famine, and wild beasts that multiplied without check. They were also aware of Ezek 21:14: "Prophesy, therefore, son of man; clap your hands and let the sword come down twice, yea thrice; the sword for those to be slain; it is the sword for the great slaughter, which encompasses them."

The first four seals do not portray a sequence of events, but different aspects of Roman power: the expansionistic military success of the Roman Empire, the inner strife and war that was undermining the worldwide Pax Romana, the concomitant inflation that deprived especially the poor of their essential food sustenance, local rebellions, and finally pestilence, death, and widespread hunger. Such brokenness was the bitter fruit of Rome's wars of conquest. Certainly, these phenomena cannot be limited only to Rome. They have happened many times since.

When the "four living creatures" call out "Come!" with the breaking of each of the first four seals, they do not assert that God directly sends forth war and famine and death. Rather, they more simply command John's attention. Each creature cries out and each time John "looks." What John sees, finally, is "Death and Hades . . . were given authority over a fourth of the earth, to kill with sword, famine, and pestilence, and by the wild animals of the earth" (6:8).

The passive tense ("was given") that avoids naming the source of the authority Death and Hades receive points to the *indirectness* of God's involvement in these events. The ambiguity here seems intentional. Death and Hades in some sense get their authority from the dragon. The dragon is the one who desires the destruction of "a fourth of the earth." Yet, John cannot allow that to be the last word. The dragon is not the final authority. The fate of the earth is not destruction but healing. And so, somehow, the wars and famines do not operate outside of God's providential involvement to bring history to its healing end (remember, the story of this healing makes up the content of the scroll itself).

The role of the Lamb, then, in these initial plague visions is not to be the source of war and famine, but to signal that the dragon-inspired destruction will not defeat or negate the victory of the Lamb's healing work. The lesson to be learned from the Lamb's presence here is to follow his way of preserving love even in the face of war and famine.

A key number in Revelation, not yet mentioned but, as we will see, highly significant in relation to the plague visions, is the number three and a half years and variations forty-two months or 1,260 days. It contrasts with seven years (the time of wholeness). The three and a half years refer to the time of the present—our time of brokenness. We will read in later visions that the plagues last these three and a half years. The plagues characterize the time before the establishment of new Jerusalem. The plagues characterize the brokenness of the world we live in.

That the Lamb opens the scrolls does not mean the Lamb causes the violence and destruction. The Lamb's presence tells us that we are to understand the various expressions of hurt and damage in our world from the Lamb's perspective. The passive voice—"a crown was given" (6:2); "its rider was permitted" (6:4); "they were given" (6:8)—that makes the source of the plagues ambiguous makes it possible that the source actually could be the dragon. Chapter 12, with its picture of the dragon's war on the earth, will imply this.

Whether we think of the dragon as the actual source of the plagues or not, at the least the passive voice creates distance between God and the plagues. If God, in some mysterious providential way, is involved in the plagues, God does not intervene directly. God does not reach down directly to make the plagues happen. Many other wills shape these dynamics—especially the wills of those who oppose God.

REVELATION 6:9–11

> When he opened the fifth seal, I saw under the altar the souls of those who had been slaughtered for the word of God and for the testimony they had given; they cried out with a loud voice, "Sovereign Lord, holy and true, how long will it be before you judge and avenge our blood on the inhabitants of the earth?" They were each given a white robe and told to rest a little longer, until the number would be complete both of their fellow servants and of their brothers and sisters, who were soon to be killed as they themselves had been killed.

Throughout the book of Revelation, the pattern of Jesus (faithful witness, death at the hands of the powers, and vindication through resurrection) stands both as the fundamental path the Lamb himself followed that provides the book's decisive victory and as the fundamental path the followers of the Lamb take as well. More than has commonly been recognized, Revelation is a call to discipleship.

The opening of the fifth seal reminds John's readers again of this pattern. With the breaking of this seal, John sees the faithful witnesses who had followed the Lamb's path to the bitter end and now await their vindication. One step in the vindication is that they received "white robes" (throughout Revelation a symbol for lives conformed to the pattern of Jesus).

We should remember again the character of the one the faithful witnesses imitated—that is, the one whose response to his own killers was, "Lord, forgive them." It is difficult to imagine Jesus seeking revenge against his enemies. He called for and practiced love and forgiveness (even seventy times seven: Matt 18:21–22). So, it seems counterintuitive to imagine that the faithful witnesses here call for punishment and revenge. If they sought such in their own lives, they would not have received white robes. Rather, the better understanding of their cry comes with a more literal translation of the word rendered in the NRSV as "avenge" (6:9).

Interpreters often write as if somehow God and the Lamb change character between chapter 5 and chapter 6. Both seem all of a sudden to become crusading avengers. Interpreters also assume that the primitive vengeance is fueled in part by the cries of the martyrs "under the altar" mentioned at 6:9. The martyrs cry out, "Sovereign Lord, holy and true, how long will it be before you judge and avenge our blood on the inhabitants of the earth" (6:9). Is this a cry for punitive justice?

The key word is translated "avenge." However, this word, more literally, could be translated "bring justice." The root of the word, *edikeis*, is *–dik*, which is the root of other words often translated by "just" or "justice." The cry from the witnesses, thus, may be understood as a cry for justice, not simply a cry for revenge. "How long will it be before you bring justice in response to the violence of the inhabitants of the earth?" Such a cry could be understood, then, actually as a call for healing not a call for punishment. How long until the contents of the scroll are revealed when new Jerusalem comes down and the inhabitants of the earth are healed of their warist violence?

Our understanding of what *edikeis* means at 6:9 should be shaped by our more general understanding of what "justice" means in the Bible. Biblical justice is not about vengeance. Biblical justice is about restoring relationships; healing that which has been damaged.[1] So maybe what the martyrs actually cry out is this: "How long before you heal creation; how long before you transform the inhabitants of the earth?" Because, notice two more things here. First, each of the martyrs was given "a white robe" (6:11). The white robes throughout Revelation are the garments worn by those who follow the Lamb wherever he goes. And what was the Lamb's attitude toward those who took his life? "Forgive them." Does it not stand to reason that those who are closest to Jesus, to the point that they receive the reward of the white robe, would share his views about the treatment of offenders?

Then, second, after their call for justice, the martyrs are told to remain patient. This "three and a half years" of struggle we live in will continue for a while longer. Then God will answer your pleas. The witnesses are told to continue to rest, with the assurance that indeed vindication and healing are

---

1. See Marshall, *Beyond*, and *Little*.

coming. We have to read to the end of Revelation to get a clear answer as to what this "vindication" will entail.

The new Jerusalem does "come down" (chapters 21–22) and at that point the nations (whose citizens are the "inhabitants of the earth," the people the rest of the book portrays as God's human enemies) find *healing*. They are healed by the leaves of the tree of life that straddles the river of the water of life (22:1–2). Even the "kings of the earth" (the human rulers who led the "inhabitants" in their murderous ways) find healing.

In the meantime, for God's own purposes, history continues. As an inevitable part of history, those who follow the Lamb's path of resistance, resistance to the ways of the beast, will continue to suffer the consequences. "The number" of martyrs is yet to be "completed" (6:11). This indeterminacy may allude to the need for sustained resistance that will lead to martyrdom during this "three and a half years" between Rev 5 and Rev 21. It is not likely that God has a set-in-concrete number of martyrs that must be achieved before the end.

REVELATION 6:12–17

> When he opened the sixth seal, I looked, and there came a great earthquake; the sun became black as sackcloth, the full moon became like blood, and the stars of the sky fell to the earth as the fig tree drops its winter fruit when shaken by a gale. The sky vanished like a scroll rolling itself up, and every mountain and island was removed from its place. Then the kings of the earth and the magnates and the generals and the rich and the power-ful, and everyone, slave and free, hid in the caves and among the rocks of the mountains, calling to the mountains and rocks, "Fall on us and hide us from the face of the one seated on the throne and from the wrath of the Lamb; for the great day of their wrath has come, and who is able to stand?"

The opening of the sixth seal reveals a terrible, all-encompassing earth-quake, powerful enough even to knock the stars out of the sky (6:13). The earthquake image echoes numerous Old Testament prophets (e.g., Isa 13:10; Ezek 32:7–8; Joel 2:30–31; Amos 8:9; Zeph 1:15). The "earthquake" reflects terrible chaos and judgment—but the story continues later in Revelation and life does not end. The earthquake does not end the story; it is clearly metaphorical.

In the vision of the great earthquake, John condemns the corruption of the nations and empires. He portrays these nations and empires as the agents of the dragon that plague humanity with wars, famine, and pestilence. All the dynamics of death fueled by the dragon are summed up in this vision of judgment. Their seemingly inexorable domination will not stand. That the earthquake image is a political image rather than a literal vision of an earthquake may be seen in who the list of those who flee in terror emphasizes: "the kings of the earth and the magnates and the generals and the rich and the powerful" (6:15). The earthquake, that is, actually reflects God's condemnation of the ways of empire that victimize and violate so many people and reveal empire's hostility toward God.

The earthquake vision concludes with an extraordinarily paradoxical image. The great ones are hiding in terror from "the wrath of the Lamb." What in the world? I suppose it is possible for a real-life lamb to get angry, but vicious anger is not what we associate with lambs. Nor is it what we associate with Jesus, the Lamb. Is there another way to understand "wrath" than simply punitive anger?

Yes, we may understand "wrath" differently. It does not necessarily mean punitive anger. The use of "wrath" here may be another way that John emphasizes the indirectness of the involvement of God in these horrible events of human self-destruction and catastrophe (events, remember, that are characteristic of all eras of human history). "Wrath," as used throughout the Bible, often tends to have the connotation more of "God gave them up" (Rom 1:24) or "God left them to the dynamics of cause and effect" than of God's direct and personal punitive anger.[2]

This "earthquake" then, could be seen as the destructive political consequences unleashed by "the kings of the earth" when they idolize power and domination and exploitation—approaches to governing that inevitably lead to famine and pestilence and war. The role of the Lamb, then, becomes one to reveal the idolatry behind the kings' (mis)rule for what it is. In Revelation 13 we will get a vivid picture of how rulers are idolized ("The whole earth followed the beast," 13:3). The witness of the Lamb means to show that idolatry for what it is—and to turn people *against* the beast.

The story in the Gospels of Jesus's faithful witness (a story that involves confrontation against misused power, both in individual leaders and in systems of domination) tells of the terrible violence against him. This violence was committed by the religious and political structures (who claimed to be God's agents in the world). And the violence led to vindication by God in resurrection (thus exposing the powers-that-be in their rebellion against God). This story actually involves a revelation of the "wrath of the Lamb."

2. See some older writings that develop this sense of wrath: Caird, *Commentary*, and a book that influenced Caird, Hanson, *Wrath*. For a more recent treatment, see Boyd, *Crucifixion*, 778–801.

It is "wrath" in the sense that through his consistent love, Jesus actually challenges the powers-that-be, and he makes clearer than ever before these powers' illegitimacy as God's agents.

The "face of the one seated on the throne and . . . the Lamb" is indeed wrathful toward the kings (6:16–17) because it is unrelenting in its rejection of their ways of domination. The kings are thereby delegitimized, and they simply cannot "stand" (6:17) in the presence of such wrath. The powers of darkness wither in the presence of genuine light. The Lamb utterly opposes the powers of domination that have controlled the "great ones" (Mark 10:42). They try to crush his way, the way of freedom from idolatry. In doing so, they place themselves at the center of God's wrath. The result is their destruction, as Revelation's visions will continue to emphasize. But the destruction of the powers does not necessarily lead to the destruction of their human agents.

Revelation tells us by what means God and the Lamb bring justice. The story ends in new Jerusalem. "The nations will walk by [the light of the glory of God], and the kings of the earth will bring their glory into it" (21:24). Indeed. The justice of God heals even God's greatest human enemies. By what means does this happen? Well, one important part is for those with the white robes to remain patient, to follow the Lamb wherever he goes, and to trust in God's true justice by imitating the Lamb's nonviolent resistance.

But what about the "wrath" here: "the great day of their wrath" (the One and the Lamb)? What does "wrath" mean? "Wrath" in the Bible actually most often means something much more indirect and less personal than anger. In fact, often the word "wrath" is used alone. The English translators add "God's." But the biblical text says "wrath," not "God's wrath." In Romans one, Paul talks about the outworking of "wrath" being that "God gave them (the idolaters) up," not that God directly punished them. Wrath has to do with the processes of life. We tend to become like that which we trust in the most—if we trust in lifeless idols, we become damaged, our hearts are darkened. As we could say, time wounds all heels.

So, we may link the wrath of God and the Lamb with God's respect for human choice. God lets us make our choices and then face the consequences, for better and for worse. Rev 6, then, does not picture an active, punitive, angry God and an angry, vicious Lamb. Rather, Rev 6, through the breaking of the seals, helps readers understand better the world in which we live so we might better follow the Lamb wherever he goes in the way of persevering love.

The sixth seal ends with a powerful question, "Who is able to stand?" in face of the wrath of God and the Lamb (6:17). Instead of the expected seventh seal with its punitive judgment that ends history (under the assumption that the question is rhetorical, and no one actually can "stand"), we will get a very different kind of vision in chapter 7. We will hear of an "uncountable multitude" that *does* stand (7:9).

AN ANGRY LAMB?

Readers of Revelation likely will be disoriented when they come to Revelation chapter 6. It's not too difficult to see in Revelation 1 through 5 a nice message of peace, the Lamb as the way. But then with chapter 6, the plagues begin. The nice part ends.

For many readers, this apparent turn toward judgment seems to come as a relief. This slain Lamb metaphor as the key to history may have its limits. We may be happy to see as we turn to the plagues that the mercy rests on some good, hard wrath of God that gives the wrongdoers of history their due. While God on the throne and the Lamb give us the picture of mercy in chapters 4 and 5, many readers want also to think that God gets angry. A move toward God's anger seems to be the message starting in Rev 6. However, let me suggest something that might seem counterintuitive—or at least contrary to the most obvious reading of Rev 6—or at least contrary to Christianity's teaching about God's anger. I don't think we actually should read these verses as being about God's anger or God's punitive judgment.[3]

The main point of Rev 4 and 5 is to show us God and the Lamb as incredibly merciful. We don't get a physical description of the One on the throne; all we see is the slain and resurrected Lamb, the personification of persevering love. Remember also the agenda of the book of Revelation as a whole. In a sentence: Revelation encourages followers of Jesus to remain faithful to his way as they navigate living in empire.

It is interesting to read interpreters of Revelation, though. Most seem automatically to assume that Rev 6 is about God's punitive judgment, directly visited upon the earth—an assumption made even by many interpreters who take a peaceable approach to Revelation overall.[4] For such interpreters, it's as if the One on the throne, the One who endorses the Lamb's persevering love as the basis for the opening of the scroll, now starts to rip things apart. Even the Lamb himself all of a sudden seems to become angry. But is an *angry* lamb a believable metaphor? I don't really think so. I believe the metaphor in Revelation of the Lamb means to evoke a sense of gentleness not punitive anger, vulnerability not domination.

3. One of the most explicitly anti-God's-punitive-judgment interpretations of Revelation is Eller, *Revealing*.

4. See, for example, Blount, *Revelation*, 135.

In Rev 6, John brings together two truths. First, he affirms that the One on the throne makes, sustains, and heals creation. The scroll that the Lamb took from the One's right hand truly does contain the story of the healing of heaven and earth. This healing will happen through persevering love, expressed most fundamentally in the Lamb's path of faithful witness. But the second truth cannot be avoided: The world we live in remains broken. It remains powerfully alienated. It remains the home of terrible injustices, violence, and domination. People suffer; nature suffers. The need for healing remains all too obvious—as does the influence, even, we could say, the *reign* of the powers of greed and inhumanity. And, these powers, with their distorted view of reality, will perceive God's love as an expression of God's hatred.

How can we understand and affirm God's care for creation and all that is in it, in the face of the brokenness that is so apparent? That is the question Rev 6 (and most of the rest of the book) responds to with these horrific visions of destruction—the so-called plague visions. But does God add to creation's hurt with punishing judgment? How could this be in light of what we learned from Rev 4 and 5? How could this be if truly we see God in Jesus, the Jesus who shows us, above everything else, that God is love?

As it turns out, Revelation has more coherence than many notice. Visions of the slain Lamb as the meaning of history in chapters 5 and 19 bracket the middle part, the plague visions that make up chapters 6 through 18. These plague visions, then, also illumine the *Lamb's* sovereignty, the sovereignty of love. They do *not* contain predictions of God certain, punitive judgment on creation. Rather, they contain insights into what actually is going on in our world right now—and by what means the events in our world right now are to be navigated.

The book has a clear message: Cry out, passionately, for justice—for God's *healing* justice. Follow the Lamb's way; strive for the white robe of love and compassion. A God of love will not set things right through an intervention of brute power that responds to violence with violence, an intervention that would only exacerbate our continuing human cycles of punitive judgment. A God of love will conquer with consistent, persevering love—and call God's people to respond to those plagues with Jesus-like persevering love as part of God's way of conquering.

FOR FURTHER ENGAGEMENT

1. Do you agree with the author's interpretation that the plagues portrayed in chapter 6 are essentially pictures of reality—things that have happened and continue to happen? If so, how can God be using these things for God's purposes and not be their direct author?

2. Reflect on what we are told about the Lamb in chapters 5 and 6. How do the references to the Lamb in chapter 5 relate to those in chapter 6? Are they contradictory?

3. The most common interpretation of the use of "was given" in the four plagues in 6:1–8 is that it is a "divine passive" but means that God is the one who did the giving—that is, that the plagues are God's will. The author suggests, though, that the plagues are not God's (nor the Lamb's) will. "The role of the Lamb in these visions is not to be the source of war and famine but to signal that the dragon-inspired destruction will not defeat or negate the victory of the Lamb's healing work." What do you think?

4. How do you understand 6:9–11? Why are the martyred souls under the altar? Is their cry for "vengeance" a Christian one (6:10)? Why or why not? What do you think is meant by the response in 6:11 to "wait"? Has the number to be killed been completed yet? What might this mean? The author suggests that the word translated "avenge" (6:9) could be understood to mean "bring justice" and be referring not necessarily to punitive judgment but to ultimate healing. Do you find this plausible? Explain.

5. The author offers a less retributive sense of the meaning of "wrath." How would you paraphrase his argument? How would you tend to think of the plagues in relation to God's disposition toward sinful humanity?

6. In the light of your observations of the world, is it actually imaginable that "the kings of the earth and the magnates and the generals and the rich and the powerful" could be terrified of the Lamb (6:12–17)?

7. The author suggests that a punitive reading of Rev 6 stands in tension with the message of Rev 4–5. He asks, "is an *angry* Lamb a believable metaphor?" What do you think?

7

Theology by Numbers

[Revelation 7]

Many people read the book of Revelation as a book that emphasizes God's punitive judgment on the rebellious world. The visions that begin in chapter 6 (especially the three sets of seven plagues in chapters 6, 8–9, and 15–16) are typically seen as visions of destruction coming down from heaven in order to punish wrongdoers and clear the ground for new Jerusalem. I propose a different way to read the book, including a different way to read these plague visions.

As part of my different way of reading Revelation, chapter 7—with its scene of worship and hope—should be seen not as a kind of "digression" or "tangent" from the main story line. Rather, chapter 7 is better read as stating the core message of Revelation: that Jesus the Lamb is Lord and as Lord calls people from throughout the earth to embrace and witness to his ways of mercy and compassion. As people who walk Jesus's path, followers of the Lamb become agents who help heal the rebellious world, ultimately including the human kings of the earth (even as the personified nonhuman powers of oppression and domination are destroyed).

One step as we read chapter 7 as central to the plot of Revelation is to note its connection with the crucial vision of chapter 5. Chapter 5 establishes the Lamb and his path of compassionate witness as the path the One on the throne embraces as the meaning of history. Thus, in a genuine sense, the plagues that are visited on the earth beginning in chapter 6 are the "digression" or "tangent" in relation to the core message of God's healing love. The plagues are subordinate to the healing love; the healing love is not a mere side point to the plagues.

REVELATION 7:1–8

> After this I saw four angels standing at the four corners of the earth, holding back the four winds of the earth so that no wind could blow on earth or sea or against any tree. I saw another angel ascending from the rising of the sun, having the seal of the living God, and he called with a loud voice to the four angels who had been given power to damage earth and sea, saying, "Do not damage the earth or the sea or the trees, until we have marked the servants of our God with a seal on their foreheads." And I heard the number of those who were sealed, one hundred forty-four thousand, sealed out of every tribe of the people of Israel: From the tribe of Judah twelve thousand sealed, from the tribe of Reuben twelve thousand, from the tribe of Gad twelve thousand, from the tribe of Asher twelve thousand, from the tribe of Naphtali twelve thousand, from the tribe of Manasseh twelve thousand, from the tribe of Simeon twelve thousand, from the tribe of Levi twelve thousand, from the tribe of Issachar twelve thousand, from the tribe of Zebulun twelve thousand, from the tribe of Joseph twelve thousand, from the tribe of Benjamin twelve thousand sealed.

Chapter 6 showed the dynamics of what is called "wrath," wrath that characterizes life in history. We will learn later in Revelation that this "life in history" will symbolically be called the "three and a half years" between Jesus's life and death and the final embodiment of new Jerusalem at the end of time. The set of "seal" plagues concludes with the cry: "Who is able to stand" in face of "the wrath of the Lamb" (6:17)? Right away, chapter 7 answers that cry. Many indeed *will* stand (7:9)! Thus, the main point of chapters 6 and 7 when read together is not the destruction or the plagues—rather, the main point is the ability of the Lamb's followers to stand.

The answer to the question about who will "stand" begins right away with symbolic action being taken to show the depth of the "protection" that God's people have in face of the plagues. The "four angels" (7:1) are the counterparts to the "four riders" of 6:1–8. The riders accompany the plagues; the angels accompany God's "sealing" of God's people. This sealing is a sign of God's care, God's protection, God's calling, God's recognition, God's presence.

Zechariah 6:1–8 records a vision of judgment that connects four horses (white, red, black, dappled) with the four winds of heaven. Interestingly, here John refers to the four winds of the *earth*. Perhaps the winds in Revelation, although they are released by divine permission and used as agents of a divine purpose, are in their essential nature earthly—as earthly as those human beings that "dwell on the earth" and the kings of the earth whom they afflict.

There may be "damage" that in some providential sense comes to earth from the sovereign God. But the restraint of the angels, "do not damage" (7:3), indicates that the plagues are not more powerful than God's healing love. In fact, as we will see as we continue in Revelation, the plagues (though originating with the dragon) actually serve God's healing purposes eventually to heal humanity while destroying the personified dynamics of evil (i.e., the "destroyers of the earth"—the dragon, beast, and false prophet).

The title "servants of our God" (7:3) and the act of "sealing" these servants speak to the vocation these people have. God has chosen God's people out of the earth (that is, in the context in which Revelation was written, out from among the Roman Empire). But this calling is anchored in the original election of Abraham, Sarah, and their descendants to bless all the families of the earth (Gen 12:3). Several references in the seven messages of chapters 2 and 3 suggest that the name of God or of the Lamb may be on the seal (see especially 3:13). If so, this seal may be a reference to a believer's identification with God in baptism. The purpose of the "sealing" is not to protect the chosen people from suffering per se but to protect them amidst the suffering. The sealing empowers the servants to remain faithful amidst tribulation. That is, as with Jesus, God promises to be present as they practice nonviolent resistance.

The initial picture of the elect people in chapter 7 seems to confirm that this is a select group, a limited number. We read of (only) twelve sets of 12,000 people, corresponding with the twelve tribes of ancient Israel. The meaning of election has always been vexing. It is a complicated idea in the Old Testament, the New Testament, and in the post-biblical history both of Christianity and Judaism. What does it mean to be God's people? What does it mean to be chosen by God? Is the focus more on what we could call the privileges of election—that we are insiders, we are blessed by God, we are part of the select few over against the godless multitudes out in the world? Or is the focus more on what we could call the vocation of the elect—that we are agents of healing, blessing, and transformation for the entire world?

Starting with this small number of elect who are sorted explicitly into the twelve-tribe ordering of God's people in ancient Israel could be seen to emphasize the privilege aspect. We seem to be introduced to a limited number of people being chosen, the "privileged few." The world is a terrible place, full of plagues—as it must be, right, for God to punish the wrongdoers? But in mercy, God has singled out a few to save, "seal," and carefully number. This could be seen as the faithful remnant that will inherit the cleansed earth after the plagues scour it of the unclean godless masses.

However, based on the vision of Rev 5 we would not expect John's vision to celebrate this kind of privilege. Such a celebration would—in effect—praise the punishment of the masses of non-privileged. Rev 5 actually celebrates the *inclusion* of people from every tribe and language and people and nation (5:9). So, we would not expect that now in chapter 7 we would find a celebration of many being left *outside* the circle of God's redemptive election. And, as we see in the second half of Rev 7, John repeats his creative literary upturning of images from chapter 5 to portray quite an inclusive understanding of election. Revelation presents election as vocation, not privilege, focused.

REVELATION 7:9–17

> After this I looked, and there was a great multitude that no one could count, from every nation, from all tribes and peoples and languages, standing before the throne and before the Lamb, robed in white, with palm branches in their hands. They cried out in a loud voice, saying, "Salvation belongs to our God who is seated on the throne, and to the Lamb!" And all the angels stood around the throne and around the elders and the four living creatures, and they fell on their faces before the throne and worshiped God, singing, "Amen! Blessing and glory and wisdom and thanksgiving and honor and power and might be to our God forever and ever! Amen." Then one of the elders addressed me, saying, "Who are these, robed in white, and where have they come from?" I said to him, "Sir, you are the one that knows." Then he said to me, "These are they who have come out of the great ordeal; they have washed their robes and made them white in the blood of the Lamb. For this reason, they are before the throne of God, and worship him day and night within his temple, and the one who is seated on the throne will shelter them. They will hunger no more, and thirst no more; the sun will not strike them, nor any scorching heat; for the Lamb at the

center of the throne will be their shepherd, and he will guide
them to springs of the water of life, and God will wipe away
every tear from their eyes."

Our interpretation of Rev 7:9–17 must take into account the message of
chapter 5. As we saw above, Rev 5, the book's most important chapter, made
a brilliant rhetorical move. We read of a terrible crisis. While the One on the
throne has a scroll that, when read, will bring ultimate healing and salvation
to creation, no one can be found to open the scroll. John weeps bitterly. But
then he is comforted; someone has been found. And then, John hears about
this great victor—the promised great warrior king, messiah, conqueror, a
Lion. But what John actually sees is a resurrected slain Lamb.

The Lamb *is* the conqueror. What John heard was accurate. But he
conquers through self-giving, persevering love—not by domination and
violence. It is as the incarnation of love that the Lamb then is celebrated by
"myriads of myriads and thousands of thousands." He is declared worthy
"to receive power and wealth and wisdom and might and honor and glory
and blessing" (5:11–12). The true meaning of the symbolism in chapter 5
is found by combining both what John hears and what John sees, but the
decisive meaning is found in what he sees. A Lion who is actually a Lamb;
the Lamb conquers, but through love.

John sets his readers up for a certain kind of understanding of God's
redemptive power in chapter 5. The kingly imagery of 5:5 that follows
from what John *hears* ("Lion of the tribe of Judah") gives an expectation
of a coercive, all-powerful warrior who would be the one who could open
the scroll that had appeared to be unopenable. John, though, turns such an
understanding on its head. What he *sees* revealed as the way God exercises
kingly power in Rev 5 is actually the persevering love of the Lamb. John sees
the slain Lamb standing, the powerlessness of self-sacrifice. God vindicates
the kingliness of the Lamb's weakness—and all of creation celebrates the
Lamb's victory.

Something similar happens here in chapter 7. What John sees reinter-
prets what he hears. One of the standard symbols of Revelation, the number
144,000, so often seen to be a symbol of limited salvation and restrictive
election, gets turned on its head. The actual meaning of 144,000 is not a
limited salvation but an abundant salvation. The 144,000 are revealed here
to be a multitude beyond counting.

However, the expansive visions of both chapters 5 and 7 do not repudiate the specificity of Israel's election. The visions portray election as
a vocation to bless all the families of the earth (recalling Gen 12:3). As a
consequence, they emphasize the vocation of the "saints" to "be a kingdom

and priests serving our God and [reigning] on earth" (5:10). The task given to those who celebrate the Lamb's victory is to help the whole earth be transformed in light of the Lamb's way of being (with the ultimate goal, we will see in Rev 21–22, to heal the nations and transform the kings of the earth).

In chapter 5 John saw a vision of the identity of this Messiah and its God-blessed method of conquering. What John saw in chapter 7 is another amazing vision: "a great multitude that no one could count, from all tribes and peoples and languages, standing before the throne and before the Lamb, robed in white" (7:9). That is, the restoration of the twelve tribes of Israel as a kingdom looks exactly like what Abraham and Sarah had been promised way back at the very beginning—their descendants would bless all the families of the earth (Gen 12:3). The 144,000 and the great multitude are the same thing (just as the Lion of Judah and the slain Lamb are the same thing). The multitude is the restored kingdom, but not a limited group of those specially elected to the exclusion of most other people. Rather, the restored kingdom is made up of everyone who wants to be there, from all peoples.

Just as the vision of the slain Lamb leads to extraordinary worship in chapter 5, so too does the vision of the countless multitude, echoing the same words of praise: "Blessing and glory and wisdom and thanksgiving and honor and power and might be to our God forever and ever!" (7:12). The symbol of 144,000, then, is anything but a symbol of scarcity. It is a symbol of abundance that leads to celebration. It is to be understood in terms of the countless multitude.

The number 144,000 breaks down into a number of abundance. We start with the twelve tribes, named here in chapter 7. But then we multiply that by another twelve (which we should understand to symbolize the twelve apostles, based on a later vision from the new Jerusalem, 21:14). These two sets of twelve are inclusive of all people of faith in both Testaments. Then we multiply again by 1,000—a number in the ancient world that would have seemed much, much bigger in John's time than it does today. In fact, the number 1,000 in general symbolizes a huge, huge amount, pretty much beyond measure.

So, we may easily see how the 144,000 could equal "countless multitude." Still, John's vision anchors this celebration of the multitudes' salvation in the story of Israel. God called this particular people to know God and to share God's mercy with the rest of the world—and this mission is precisely what this vision here celebrates. This number has military connotations—as in a mustered army (cf. Num 31:14, 48; Deut 1:15; 1 Sam 8:12; 22:7; 2 Sam

18:14). In Revelation, the "army's" mission is to defeat the powers of evil (cf. Rev 12:10–11).

So, John sees the 144,000 as a countless multitude, "from every nation, from all tribes and peoples and languages" (the same language used of the worship of the Lamb in 5:9–10 and the naming of those the Lamb has redeemed; that is, the people in chapter 5 and in chapter 7 are identical). Just as the slain and risen Lamb provides the definitive interpretation of what "king" means in Rev 5, so the multitude from every nation shows what the "144,000" means—an image that conveys the abundance of God's healing love. The "sealing" of 7:3 is not for a tiny remnant but for countless multitudes.

We are told that the multitude wears "white robes" (7:9). White robes are a symbol throughout Revelation for those who follow the Lamb's path of faithful witness. The symbol certainly indicates the possibility of death in service to God's healing work, but most of all simply indicates the willingness to follow the path of nonviolent resistance. The "white robes" signify active discipleship, nonviolent resistance to empire, resistance toward the kings of the earth—but in ways that allow for the transformation of those kings. They signify an army that fights, but with the weapons of the Spirit, with the sword of the testimony of Jesus and not the sword of human warfare.

The multitude embodies the inextricable link between the Lamb's way and the One on the throne (7:10), another reiteration of the confession that stands at the heart of the vision that takes up chapters 4 and 5. And, as in chapter 5, the multitude is joined by the angels and the four living creatures, and their song is virtually the same as well (7:12 compared with 5:12).

We learn more about the multitude: "These are they who have come out of the great ordeal; they have washed their robes and made them white in the blood of the Lamb" (7:14). This metaphor ("washed . . . white in the blood") carries great theological and ethical weight. The point is not for-giveness of sins that follows from belief in Jesus's death as a substitution-ary atonement (as in, "he died so that we don't have to"). Rather, the point is about the call to discipleship. "Washed" here signifies active imitation. The "great ordeal" most likely alludes not so much to physical death as to the conflict of loyalties that lies at the center of Revelation. It is an ongoing struggle to say no to the beast's domination, a *costly* struggle in everyday life. John does not have in mind some future cataclysmic event (the futuristic "great tribulation") but rather the "ordeal" of faithful living throughout the "three and a half years" of human history between Jesus's ascension and the end of time.

Jesus's followers gain their "white robes" by living how he lived. "Blood," throughout Revelation, works as a master metaphor that signifies Jesus's path of preserving love taken all the way, even in face of harsh opposition from the powers. The robes are "made white" by following the Lamb in life, not by belief in certain doctrines or the practice of certain rituals. The faithful ones have "washed" and "made white" their robes. Theirs is an active, not merely a passive role. By their faithfulness they join their self-sacrifice to that of the Lamb. The victors gain their victories by passing through great tribulation, not by detouring around it. They are able to do this only because of what the Lamb has done for them in giving himself to be slain. Verse 14 refers to surviving the ordeal, not escaping. This "washing" involves both identifying with the Lamb *and* actively opposing the beast.

The fruits of the persevering love (that may well involve suffering since it involves resistance to the beast and the beast's demands for loyalty) are a litany of safety, hope, and joy. "For this reason" (that is, due to following Jesus in faithful witness), the multitude will worship God and the Lamb (7:15—another reference to the close link between the One on the throne and the Lamb). They worship without pause "within [God's] temple" (which, we will learn, is simply a way of talking about all of creation—see Rev 21–22). No hunger, no thirst, no scorching heat, no tears. Images of comfort and security meant to steel the resolve of readers to keep the Lamb as their "shepherd" (7:16–17). This reference to shepherd here offers comfort and conveys a sense of partnership in faithful witness. We should let the sense of "shepherd" here shape our understanding of the references in Revelation to the Lamb "ruling" with a "rod of iron" (12:5; 19:15). This is "rule" as servanthood (see Mark 10:42–45; also, Isa 53).

In all that follows in Revelation, John's readers are never to forget that the victory is a victory over all that can seduce and contaminate. The threat of physical death is not what makes the great ordeal so serious. Rather, the most dangerous thing about the ordeal is the serious conflict of loyalties. In the conflict, followers of the Lamb may be in genuine doubt as to where precisely their duties lie, unless they remain clear about the central affirmation of their faith—that the whole truth of the One on the throne may be found in the Lamb.

THEOLOGY BY NUMBERS

Numbers are significant throughout Revelation. It is full of numbers. If you pick it up and start to read it, you may feel like it is a kind of impenetrable code. Journalist Jonathan Kirsch, in his book *A History of the End of the World*, writes that "the book of Revelation is regarded by secular readers—and even by progressive Christians—as a biblical oddity at best and, at worst, a kind of petri dish for the breeding of dangerous religious eccentricity."[1]

Revelation's frequent number symbolisms seem to play into this dangerous religious eccentricity. What are the numbers in Revelation? And what do they mean? Clearly, the numbers have symbolic meaning. But there are different kinds of symbols. We may break symbols into two broad categories: specific symbols and general symbols.[2] With specific symbols, one particular meaning is meant by the symbol. For example, note the American flag. The thirteen stripes symbolize the original thirteen colonies and the fifty stars symbolize the current fifty states. With general symbols, the meanings are much broader, more dynamic and subjective. Think again of the American flag—what does the flag itself symbolize? Many things, significantly different things for different people: democracy, religious freedom, the destination for many of our ancestors fleeing trouble—and, empire, war-making, global domination, hypocrisy.

Right after September 11, 2001, a friend of mine who taught at a Mennonite college put a picture of the American flag on his office door. You can imagine that this led to some questions at his peace church school. The meaning of that symbol for my friend changed within weeks and he soon took the picture down. From a statement of solidarity with victims and rescue workers, the flag came soon to symbolize revenge and a new war of aggression against Afghanistan.

I believe that the numbers seven and six hundred sixty-six are two examples of general symbols. Seven pertains to wholeness in a broad sense, applied in different ways in different settings; and six hundred sixty-six has to do with a general sense of humanity resisting the wholeness of God's shalom (the "six" meaning just short of the "seven," intensified by being repeated three times). So, six hundred sixty-six does not refer to a specific person. On the other hand, I believe that 144,000 is a specific symbol. It has one particular meaning. And it is one of Revelation's most important numbers. In fact, the way one interprets the 144,000 will say a lot about one's reading of the book as a whole.

Certainly, others have different views on these numbers. Some who believe Revelation is giving us a blueprint of predictions about the future think that the 144,000 here is a group of Jewish converts to Christianity during the seven-year great tribulation that will follow after the rapture—the

---

1. Kirsch, *History,* 3.
2. Kraybill, *Upside-Down,* 26–27.

new converts will evangelize those "left behind."[3] The Jehovah's Witnesses in their early years about one hundred years ago thought that once they gained 144,000 members the end of the world would come. As the group got bigger and the end failed to materialize, they have had to revise their theology. Now the 144,000 are faithful believers who will be resurrected as spirit beings to provide leadership for the rest of those who make it to heaven.[4] There's one New Age group that teaches that a spiritual master from Venus brought 144,000 souls with him to earth to bring spiritual transformation to those enlightened enough to respond.[5]

Many people tend, then, to see the 144,000 as a limited number, a form of scarcity. Only the few, the proud, and the brave are chosen for this small group of the faithful. But the symbolism in Revelation seven is actually about abundance. The symbolism offers a kind of open invitation—a celebration, even, of God's generosity.

To understand Revelation rightly, we must read it as a narrative, beginning at the beginning, and keeping what has come before in mind as we work through the book. So, when we get to chapter seven, we have an important precedent to help us understand what is being pictured here. What does chapter 7's celebration mean in the book of Revelation? More directly, what does the vision of abundant salvation and celebration mean here in chapter 7? Because, we must not forget, this vision occurs in the midst of the terrible *plague* visions that begin in chapter 6 with the breaking of the seals of the great scroll and continue on in chapters 8 through 10.

Here we come to one of the important forks in the road. To what ends do we interpret Revelation, to what ends do we interpret the Bible, and to what ends do we interpret God and life in our world? We read in chapter 6 of the first six seal plagues: wars, famine, pestilence, and cries for vengeance. And then we have an interlude before getting back to the breaking of the seventh seal in chapter 8. The breaking of that seal actually turns out to be a direct link to seven more plagues connected with the sounding of trumpets that then a few chapters later lead to another plague series linked with the pouring out of "bowls of wrath."

Do we read the worship vision as a side point in the context of the fundamental reality of plagues? Or do we read the plague vision as a side point in the context of the fundamental reality of worship and celebration? Which best defines the message of Revelation—and which best defines our

3. See Rossing, *Rapture.*

4. See Penton, *Apocalypse.*

5. See Wikipedia, "144,000." https://en.wikipedia.org/wiki/144,000.

understanding of reality? Plague or celebration? Scarcity or abundance? Do we laugh to keep from crying—or do we laugh out of genuine joy?

I believe Revelation is about genuine joy. The book is a revelation of Jesus Christ, as it says in the first verse, not a revelation of plagues. It starts with a present-tense statement about Jesus. He is the faithful witness, the firstborn of the dead, and the ruler of the kings of the earth. He loves us, has freed us from our sins, and made us a kingdom. This Jesus, later in chapter 1 and in the messages of chapters 2 and 3, is present among the churches.

Then chapter 5 gives us the key vision of the Lamb's witness and the present-tense celebration of all creation. The book continues with plagues, to be sure, but always there are visions of worship and strong statements like the words in chapter 11: "We give you thanks, Lord God Almighty, who are and who were, for you have taken your great power and begun to reign" (11:17). These worship visions reach their culmination in the vision of new Jerusalem at the end of the book where full healing comes—even to God's human enemies the kings of the earth. Revelation contains not a hint of doubt—the Lamb that was slain stands, and those who would follow him (countless multitudes from all nations) celebrate in the present tense.

The celebration of the Lamb's way of conquest reflects what is most real for our *present* reality. The plagues are also real, but they are but a passing phenomenon. Don't live in fear of them. Don't become fatalistic. Don't think the plagues portray the way things most fundamentally are and the way things must be. Celebrate the Lamb, now—and, now, follow him wherever he goes. This call to celebrate, to worship as if the way of the Lamb is the fundamental reality, is what might be the most difficult part of Revelation's message for us to embrace.

A secular Jewish philosopher named Phillip Hallie helped us understand this challenge.[6] Hallie was a soldier in the American army that fought the Germans in Western Europe during World War II. He believed that was necessary and remained proud of his service. But he always felt uneasy about the incredible violence and destruction of that war—and its legacy of an accelerated spiral of violence that led to more violence.

As a philosopher, he became intrigued with human cruelty—or we could say, he had a horrible fascination with human cruelty. So, he studied it as a philosophical inquiry, focusing on the terrors of the 1930s and 1940s in Germany and surrounding areas. And he became increasingly calloused, it seemed. It's as if he wanted to assure himself of the necessity of his own warism and found himself increasingly burdened by despair. Cruelty leads to ever more cruelty. Then he ran across a strange story that made him weep.

6. Hallie, *Lest.*

He tried to pooh-pooh his reaction, until he realized he couldn't get the story out of his mind.

So, he sought to learn more about a small group of people in Le Chambon, a rural mountain village in southern France. They risked their lives to save thousands of Jewish refugees who found their way to their remote area. Hallie ultimately wrote his book, *Lest Innocent Blood Be Shed*, about this case of goodness. In the terms of Revelation, this was a case of people of faith following the Lamb wherever he goes in the midst of the terrible plagues of war.

Hallie challenges his readers to think: What was the more fundamental reality here. Was it the reality of the fog of war, the kill-or-be-killed dynamic of such a conflict, the husbanding of extraordinary resources to use violence to defeat evildoers? Or was it the reality of those weaponless villagers, taking huge, life-threatening risks, to offer refuge to strangers, refuge to people who could not possibly hope to repay their rescuers? Which was more real?

Let's return to Revelation's images. What kind of action will be most at home in new Jerusalem? What kind of action best reflects the way that the Lamb works as ruler of the kings of the earth? What kind of action most clearly corresponds to the way things truly are? So, in the end, Phillip Hallie's story reminds us of this lesson: Even in the midst of the worst the beast can do, genuine worship of the One on the throne and of the Lamb happens and reflects true reality—embodied worship that remains extraordinarily powerful on behalf of life.

FOR FURTHER ENGAGEMENT

1. The author argues that Rev 7 presents "the core message of Revelation: that Jesus the Lamb is Lord and as Lord calls people from throughout the earth to embrace and witness to his ways of mercy and compassion." How would approaching Revelation thus shape how one would interpret the relationship between the plagues of Rev 6 and the worship of Rev 7? What do you think of this effort to read the plagues in light of the worship?

2. What is meant by the "sealing" in 7:3–8? Who are sealed? Why? Is the number and distribution of the sealing significant? What appears to be its purpose?

3. Who do you think the 144,000 are? Are you part of them? If so, what does that imply about how you should live today?

4. Do you think we should seek to *avoid* tribulation or seek to go through it? Which kinds of tribulation should we avoid? Which should we embrace? What enables people faithfully to go through tribulation? What elements make up John's kind of tribulation: Natural "evils" that "happen" to us? Or suffering we bring on ourselves by working to overcome evil in the world?

5. The author suggests, "the restraint of the angels, 'do not damage,' indicates that the plagues are not more powerful than God's healing love." When you consider the plagues in Revelation and the traumas afflicting the earth today, do you find that assertion believable? Explain.

6. In your own words, restate the author's argument concerning the relationship between the "144,000" and the "countless multitude" in Rev 7. What is your view?

7. The author suggests that the reference to the faithful ones having "washed" and "made white" their robes indicates that "theirs is an active, not merely a passive role . . . that involves both identifying with the Lamb *and* actively opposing the beast." Imagine preaching a sermon on this theme. What would be a couple of your main points?

8

How Not to Inspire Repentance

[Revelation 8, 9, and 10]

From Rev 4–7 we have learned several crucial things about the agenda of the book and its theological center. The One on the throne is confessed as Master of the universe, but the kind of power that best expresses this mastery is the power of persevering love. The Lamb is worshiped due to how the Lamb resists empire nonviolently even to the point of death. The Lamb's resistance frees the multitude from the powers so these people might offer worship before the One on the throne and the Lamb (7:9), worship that finds its ultimate expression when these people follow the Lamb wherever he goes (14:4).

In between the two parallel visions of the Lamb in chapter 5 and the multitude in chapter 7, we have the first of the book's three sets of sevenfold plagues described. These plagues, we learn, are not direct acts by God to punish rebellious creation. Rather, they reflect a creative assertion that though the world we live in is full of wars and rumors of war, God's will for healing remains active. Revelation as a whole tells how this healing *will* come.

So, now with chapter 8 we turn to a second set of seven plagues, and their level of destruction expands from one-quarter to one-third destruction. Nevertheless, keeping in mind the visions of healing in chapter 7, I believe we must read the plague visions in light of the affirmations Revelation has already made about God's intentions, God's power, the promise of God's victory, and—importantly—the means by which the victory is achieved.

What we *don't* have here, contrary to many interpreters, is a picture of God Godself unleashing terrible destruction in order to coerce people to repentance. The plagues in chapter 8, though, cannot be understood apart from what follows in chapters 9 and 10.

REVELATION 8:1–5

> When the Lamb opened the seventh seal, there was silence in heaven for about half an hour. And I saw the seven angels who stand before God, and seven trumpets were given to them. Another angel with a golden censer came and stood at the altar; he was given a great quantity of incense to offer with the prayers of all the saints on the golden altar that is before the throne. And the smoke of the incense, with the prayers of the saints, rose before God from the hand of the angel. Then the angel took the censer and filled it with fire from the altar and threw it on the earth; and there were peals of thunder, rumblings, flashes of lightning, and an earthquake.

When the Lamb opens the seventh seal (8:1), the first plague series segues into the second series. The scroll's content itself will not be revealed until the plague dynamic is fully spent. That will not happen until chapter 20's final judgment when Death and Hades join the dragon, beast, and false prophet in the lake of fire. So, the first set of plagues (the seals) leads directly to the second set (the trumpets). The plagues of the seventh seal are actually made up of the trumpet plagues that follow and are described in chapters 8 and 9.

The plague visions give us a picture of present reality. This "present reality" will later be characterized as the "three and a half years" of historical existence between chapter 5's life, death, and resurrection of Jesus and chapters 21 and 22's new Jerusalem. The plagues do vary a bit from series to series, most notably in their destructive reach, but the variations are best seen not as chronological so much as rhetorical. The several plague series each essentially show the same reality as the others but the intensification of their destruction points to a sense of urgency. John's readers must respond creatively and redemptively to the brokenness caused by the dragon and his minions. The need to continue to resist the dragon's lure and demands remains ever more urgent.

As with the Lamb opening the seals in chapters 6 and 7, so here the image of the "seven angels who stand before God" and are ready to sound the trumpets that will bring in the next set of plagues points to a close connection between God and the plagues. So, we need to remember chapters 5 and

7. Then we will read what follows in light of those chapters and their picture of the intimate and inextricable link between the Lamb's way of self-giving love and the victorious power that the One on the throne exercises. The victory is won through persevering love, not through violence and coercion.

Why are the angels here amidst the plagues? As with the Lamb's presence at the opening of the seals, the angels' proximity shows (or "proves") that while the plagues are caused by the dragon and his minions, the dragon is not able to defeat God's purposes for creation. God does not directly cause the plagues, but God is present amidst the fallout of the plagues to bring about healing. As we saw in chapters 5 and 7 (and will see more of in future chapters), the violence and bloodshedding of the powers nonetheless conclude with the Lamb's victory.

Revelation 8 alludes to this process of blood shedding that leads to victory when we encounter "another angel" who is given incense "with the prayers of all the saints on the golden altar that is before the throne" (8:3). These are the same "saints" mentioned in 6:9–11 whose witness unto death resulted in their being given "white robes" (pointing to the "multitude" in chapter 7 who are also given "white robes"). So, the prayers here in 8:3 remind us that faithful witness (even to the death) leads to vindication, the dynamic that characterizes the pattern of Jesus and the vocation of his followers.

When the angel throws the censer with the incense "on the earth," what results are "peals of thunder, rumblings, flashes of lightning, and an earthquake" (8:5). These are all signs of the powerful work the One on the throne undertakes to transform creation—not through punitive judgment though, but through the healing engendered by the faithful witness of the multitude. With the coming of the trumpet plagues, that faithful witness is more important than ever. This is a challenge to John's readers: You likely will face hard times in your resistance to the empire. Hold fast, your willingness to stay with Jesus and follow his way will be used by God as God brings new Jerusalem down to the earth.

REVELATION 8:6–13

Now the seven angels who had the seven trumpets made ready to blow them. The first angel blew his trumpet, and there came hail and fire, mixed with blood, and they were hurled to the earth; and a third of the earth was burned up, and a third of the trees were burned up, and all green grass was burned up. The second angel blew his trumpet, and something like a great

mountain, burning with fire, was thrown into the sea. A third of
the sea became blood, a third of the living creatures in the sea
died, and a third of the ships were destroyed. The third angel
blew his trumpet, and a great star fell from heaven, blazing like
a torch, and it fell on a third of the rivers and on the springs of
water. The name of the star is Wormwood. A third of the waters
became wormwood, and many died from the water, because it
was made bitter. The fourth angel blew his trumpet, and a third
of the sun was struck, and a third of the moon, and a third of
the stars, so that a third of their light was darkened; a third of
the day was kept from shining, and likewise the night. Then I
looked, and I heard an eagle crying with a loud voice as it flew
in midheaven, "Woe, woe, woe to the inhabitants of the earth, at
the blasts of the other trumpets that the three angels are about
to blow!"

Trumpets—which typically in the Bible sound to offer warning—announce
another series of plagues to be visited on the earth. The first four (8:7–12)
echo the first four of the seal plagues from chapter 6. They are similar, but
these plagues are even more destructive than the first set. With the seals,
the damage was to one-fourth of the earth—Death and Hades "were given
authority over a fourth, to kill with the sword, famine, and pestilence, and
by the wild animals of the earth" (6:8). With the trumpet plagues, "a *third*
of the earth was burned up [and] all the green grass was burned up" (8:7,
emphasis added). Not only does the scope increase from one-quarter to
one-third, the level of destruction within the fraction designated is greater.
Death and Hades were "given authority" over one-quarter, implying that
not every life within that one-quarter was ended. But with the trumpets,
everything within the one-third is "burned up" and one-third "of the living
creatures in the sea died" (8:9).

In fact, the level of destruction in these plagues is too great to be believed. We should note as well that after these plagues are described, life on
earth more or less returns to normal. John makes a rhetorical, not predictive, point. He conveys a growing sense of urgency. As people disregard the
message about the Lamb, things are only going to get worse and worse for
them—so to turn away from the beast and toward the Lamb is *required*,
right now. However, John does not predict an inevitable chronological progression of human life getting worse and worse leading to the rapture and
Armageddon. Rather, he simply creatively voices an intensifying challenge
to his readers to take this message seriously and to turn toward God.

Note the lack of named agency in these plagues. In the account of these
first four trumpet plagues, we read: "were hurled," "was burned up," "was

thrown," "were destroyed," and so on. But who specifically hurled, burned, threw, destroyed, etc.? We are not told. Since the "seven angels" are the ones who sound the trumpets, we should understand God to be involved. The lack of direct attribution of these acts to God, though, should give us pause before we accept the standard interpretation and understand these plagues as direct acts of God's punitive judgment.

That the God of Revelation or the God of the broader biblical story (who is the God of Jesus the Lamb) would do such punitive judging simply does not make sense. Why would the God of Jesus act in that way? We should also remember that Revelation links the Lamb with the One on the throne more closely than any other place in the New Testament. And Revelation also makes clear the modus operandi of the Lamb—persevering love all the way down. We should assume that this persevering love is also the modus operandi of the One on the throne.

The significance of the "was" and "were" language of 8:7–12 may best be seen as a way of addressing the paradox of a universe that is governed by a sovereign God whose character and power are *love*. Such a universe shows an openness and respect for human freedom that makes possible a lot of evil and destruction—such as reflected in the admittedly hyperbolic plague visions. But the evil and destruction do not defeat or even operate in complete autonomy from the providential love of the Creator. God is present, even if not interventionist.

Perhaps, then, we may understand the trumpets as signifying the freedom God grants creation (freedom that all too often does result in plagues) as well as giving a sense, in the sweep of Revelation's visions (visions that point toward the overall direction of the biblical story), that God remains the Master of the universe who brings healing and redemption out of the plagues. The rest of the book will fill in the blanks (in visionary fashion) of the workings of God's healing care for creation in relation to the freedom that allows for the plagues.

REVELATION 9:1–6

> And the fifth angel blew his trumpet, and I saw a star that had fallen from heaven to earth, and he was given the key to the shaft of the bottomless pit; he opened the shaft of the bottomless pit, and from the shaft rose smoke like the smoke of a great furnace, and the sun and the air were darkened with the smoke from the shaft. Then from the smoke came locusts on the earth, and they were given authority like the authority of scorpions of the earth.

They were told not to damage the grass of the earth or any green growth or any tree, but only those people who do not have the seal of God on their foreheads. They were allowed to torture them for five months, but not to kill them, and their torture was like the torture of a scorpion when it stings someone. And in those days people will seek death but will not find it; they will long to die, but death will flee from them.

In Rev 9, the unfolding of the vision of the plagues associated with the seven trumpets continues. Chapter 8 echoed the first four of the seal visions in chapter 6, except with much more destruction. We should read these plague visions in light of their being surrounded by visions of redemption and faithfulness. The surrounding visions portray a worship service in chapters 4 and 5 and a redeemed multitude that stands before the Lamb in chapter 7. As well, we will see the faithful witness of God's people in chapters 11 and 12. Emphasizing the redemptive visions will help us keep the plagues in perspective. The plagues are not the fundamental reality. And they are not the work of a vengeful God punishing human wrongdoing.

After the four plagues of chapter 8, there is a brief interlude where a talking eagle cries out in pain in face of what the earth endures with the plagues. The term in 8:13 that is translated "woe" could also be translated as "alas!" and has the connotation of sorrow and empathy more than that it announces God's direct punitive judgment. The eagle cries out three times, pointing to the next two trumpet blasts that will be described in chapter 9 and a third "woe" that is not clearly identified. The seventh trumpet blast (11:15–19) could be the third "woe." Since the focus of the trumpet is the promise that God will "destroy the destroyers of the earth" (11:18), the idea could be that this "woe" will end all the "woes" by doing away with the actual source of the destruction, the dragon and his minions. Beginning with chapter 9, Revelation hints with increasing clarity that the dragon is the direct actor behind the plagues.

The fifth and sixth trumpets do speak of more trauma on earth and give more detail to the picture of this time of the "three and a half years" between Jesus's victory described in Rev 5 and the coming of new Jerusalem in chapter 21. The "star" that John sees that has "fallen from heaven to earth" (9:1) likely is the same entity as the "angel of the bottomless pit (or abyss)" who is the "king" of the terrible "locusts" (9:11). This entity's activity constitutes the fifth trumpet plague (or the first "woe") of 9:1–12. That is, this "star" or "angel" is the dragon himself.

For the first of several times, John mentions the "abyss." Here, in 9:1–2, the fallen "star" opens the "shaft of the abyss" and thick smoke pours forth.

In 9:11, it is the "angel of the abyss." Then, in 17:8 we are told that the beast who the great harlot will ride ascends from the abyss. Finally, in 20:1–3 we read of the dragon being thrown into the abyss and then briefly released. A clue about the meaning of "abyss" and of the "key" the fallen star is given that opens the "shaft of the abyss" comes from early in the book. The vision of Jesus Christ in the second half of chapter 1 contains a series of descriptive characteristics of this one who walks among the "lampstands" (i.e., the seven churches, 1:20). One of the images that the vision mentions is that Jesus has "the keys of Death and Hades" (1:18). Then in 3:7, in the opening statement to the message to the church at Philadelphia (one of the two churches praised without critique), Jesus is described as "the true one, who has the key of David, who opens and no one will shut, who shuts and no one opens." So, we should link the "abyss" closely with Hades.

The sum of these various references does not provide a strongly coherent set of definitions about the abyss, Death and Hades, the beast, the dragon, and Jesus Christ and how they interrelate. However, if we keep all these allusions in mind as we look at 9:1–2, we are helped to understand what John means to convey. One of the main points 9:1–2 makes is to alert readers to the actual dynamics of the "plagues," dynamics that characterize life during this time of present human history in which we live.

The "star" (that is, dragon) is "given the key" that actually belongs to the Lamb (1:18, assuming that the "abyss" is the same as "Death and Hades"). This is not to say that the dragon works for the Lamb or does the Lamb's will. Rather, the handing over of the key is part of the general picture in Revelation that the powers do not defeat God's healing work. Rather, God works alongside the violence of the powers to bring salvation and wholeness. All the terrible things that happen in history (directed by the powers, not by God) do not defeat the purposes of God. Because of God's victory, followers of the Lamb may live in hope and courage. They may follow the Lamb wherever he goes, affirm merciful existence, and resist the ways of empire.

The immediate consequence when the dragon gets the key to the abyss in chapter 9 is unleashing the devastating locusts on the earth. This plague draws on stereotypical ancient fears of massive and destructive infestations of such insects who would eat virtually everything in their paths. More directly, the picture here links with the locust plague from the exodus story. That allusion, like several in Revelation to events from the exodus, can help us see that John's specific visions ultimately serve the overarching vision of Jesus Christ the book contains—a vision of redemption and liberation (like the exodus story).

One interesting twist in Rev 9 is that the plagues are not focused on the followers of the Lamb. Though the followers are spared here (the locusts are told not to damage those who "have the seal of God on their foreheads," 9:4), they will be attacked in later chapters. Here, though, the plagues are focused on those who do *not* belong to the Lamb's community. Due to the effects of the locusts' destruction, "people will seek death but will not find it" (9:6).

REVELATION 9:7–12

> In appearance the locusts were like horses equipped for battle. On their heads were what looked like crowns of gold; their faces were like human faces, their hair like women's hair, and their teeth like lions' teeth; they had scales like iron breastplates, and the noise of their wings was like the noise of many chariots with horses rushing into battle. They have tails like scorpions, with stingers, and in their tails is their power to harm people for five months. They have as king over them the angel of the bottomless pit; his name in Hebrew is Abaddon, and in Greek he is called Apollyon. The first woe has passed. There are still two woes to come.

We then learn more about the locusts. They are not actually real locusts but a metaphor for soldiers and, it seems likely, specifically Roman soldiers. "Their faces were like human faces" (9:7), they are armored and vicious, and they have a king. This king is the "fallen star" of 9:1–2, that is, the dragon. However, these are not simply demonic forces as free-floating evildoers. The name of their king is "Abaddon" (in Hebrew) and "Apollyon" (in Greek). The word means "Destroyer" and could well allude to the Emperor Domitian, who ruled the empire during the last decade of the first century when Revelation was probably written. The dragon and the Roman Empire are thus closely linked.

"Apollyon" may be an allusion to the god Apollo. Domitian claimed to be Apollo incarnate. The locust was used as a symbol for Apollo. So, perhaps here the vision means to bring together emperor worship, the violence of Rome, and the influence of Satan. Later in Revelation what seems obliquely intimated here becomes increasingly explicit. The Roman Empire that so attracts those in the seven churches, an attraction that John's Jesus condemned in chapters 2 and 3's messages, is empowered not by the true God as it claimed but by the powers of evil. What is at stake in the choices about where to place one's loyalty is literally a choice between the God of the Bible and the powers of evil.

Even as they wreak havoc on human life, the locusts have only limited powers of destruction. They cannot hurt those with the seal of God. They cannot "damage the grass of the earth or any green growth or any tree" (9:4). They could not kill those they tortured, and their time for doing their damage was limited to five months (the normal life span of locusts). And all of their activity is said to be "allowed;" they did not act out of their own independent power. Perhaps these limitations are a way to reinforce the claim that the dragon ultimately cannot overpower or defeat the Lamb. In the end, after the dragon gathers his forces for what he mistakenly expects to be a big battle (16:16), he will simply be captured and thrown into the lake of fire (chapters 19 and 20). The ultimate impotence of the dragon in Revelation echoes Satan's impotence in relation to Jesus in the Gospels.

Chapter 9 prepares us for a major, though subtle, shift in emphasis. The chapter builds towards its conclusion, that the "rest of humankind" (those without the seal of God) who are tortured by the scorpions will not repent and turn to God as a result of those tortures (9:21). This failure to effect repentance is itself an indication that the plagues are coming from the dragon, not from God. Chapter 7 already implies widespread repentance. The scorpions' tortures, and the other consequences of the plagues, do not operate apart from God's overarching care for creation, and they certainly do not defeat God. But they themselves do not, nor were they intended to, bring about repentance. What will follow beginning in chapter 10 will show what does actually lead to repentance.

REVELATION 9:13–21

> Then the sixth angel blew his trumpet, and I heard a voice from the four horns of the golden altar before God, saying to the sixth angel who had the trumpet, "Release the four angels who are bound at the great river Euphrates." So the four angels were released, who had been held ready for the hour, the day, the month, and the year, to kill a third of humankind. The number of the troops of cavalry was two hundred million; I heard their number. And this was how I saw the horses in my vision: the riders wore breastplates the color of fire and of sapphire and of sulfur; the heads of the horses were like lions' heads, and fire and smoke and sulfur came out of their mouths. By these three plagues a third of humankind was killed, by the fire and smoke and sulfur coming out of their mouths. For the power of the horses is in their mouths and in their tails; their tails are like serpents, having heads; and with them they inflict harm. The

rest of humankind, who were not killed by these plagues, did not repent of the works of their hands or give up worshiping demons and idols of gold and silver and bronze and stone and wood, which cannot see or hear or walk. And they did not repent of their murders or their sorceries or their fornication or their thefts.

The intensity of the plagues ratchets up even more with the sixth trumpet plague (and second woe). "The four angels who are bound at the great river Euphrates" are released (again the anonymity of the agent behind the plagues) in order "to kill a third of humankind" (9:15). Probably, "the four angels" should be linked with the "four horsemen" of famine, pestilence, and war of chapter 6. Here, we again have horses and riders, along with a cavalry of "two hundred million" (9:16). But this time, the horses themselves are agents of death and destruction on an unimaginable scale.

It would be a mistake to read these images as predictive of some future great war. They are instead simply greatly exaggerated pictures drawing on the present anxieties of John's readers living in the Roman Empire. First-century Romans feared extreme war, war likely due to invasions of their land from the east, "the barbarian hordes" from territories that the Romans had never conquered. John intensifies the levels of death and destruction from one-fourth of the earth to one-third in order to underscore the ongoing urgency of his call to turn from trusting in Rome, a call to trust in the Lamb instead. As we will soon see, John's urgency in part is for the sake of "the inhabitants of the earth" (that is, those without the seal of God). John hopes that they may actually find the way to genuine repentance that is stimulated by the persevering love of the Lamb and his followers.

We should note that most of the damage the "horses" do results from what comes out of their mouths: "fire, smoke, and sulfur." Elsewhere in Revelation, this allusion to violence coming from the mouths of the dragon and its minions is repeated. The victory of the rider of the white horse in chapter 19—that is, Jesus Christ—also results from what comes out of his mouth (19:15,21). Revelation portrays a war of words.

The plagues (and certainly not God's direct hand) will not literally kill one-third of humanity in the hopes of getting the rest to repent. From now on, we will read of plagues that seem to speak of massive death followed by activities indicating that such massive killing did not actually happen. Later, even after a plague of total destruction (16:3), the inhabitants of the earth remain to oppose God and ultimately to repent. The plagues, then, symbolize the ongoing destruction wreaked by the powers of evil (who in human history are disguised as what seem to be agents for good who allegedly establish "peace and order"). The plagues do not promise violent, punitive judgment against stiff-necked humans in rebellion versus God. Rather, they remind readers that the world remains in many ways enslaved by the powers of evil and always in need of the witness to the Lamb's way of healing love.

The plague visions call John's readers to recognize that the empire often acts as a minion of the dragon. And they call readers to persevere as they follow the pattern of Jesus (faithful witness to the point of great suffering with trust in God's vindication and ultimate healing of broken creation). Chapter 9 can easily be misinterpreted as a picture of just how hostile humanity has become toward God. To guard from such a misreading, we should read the chapter in light of what has come before (the worship visions of chapters 4–5, 7) and in light of what will come next (the vision starting in chapter 10 of how actual repentance does happen).

A key aspect of chapter 9 comes at its end, an often-misunderstood picture of the failure of the inhabitants of the earth to repent in 9:20–21: "The rest of humankind, who were not killed by these plagues, did not repent" (9:20). But who could blame them? If the world is a place of God-ordained torment, war, and death, why would people want to trust in the One who is presented as its creator and ruler? What the inhabitants of the earth need is some other picture of God that shows the One who desires their trust to be an agent for human wellbeing. A God worth trusting in will not simply punish and devastate. We will get such a picture in chapters 10–12.

In light of what follows in Revelation, we need to understand this picture of the failure of humankind to repent not mainly as an indictment on human hard-heartedness. It is true that in face of the plagues, humanity turns to idols (note John's powerful evoking of Ps 115's indictment of the dynamics of idolatry in 9:20), and such idolatry only makes things worse. But we should be sympathetic to this turn. Humanity is under siege from the powers of evil, powers who are masters of deception. In their pain, human beings try to find comfort and a sense of security wherever they may find it.

What is needed is a powerful witness to a God of *love*, not a God of retributive violence. Such a witness is precisely what will follow starting in Rev 10. So, the picture of the failure of humanity to repent is more a reminder that retribution will not lead to healing—and that the One on the throne who is so closely connected with the Lamb (chapters 4 and 5) is not the source of the plagues. The One on the throne is the source of a way of being in the world that brings healing even in the face of the plagues, even in the face of the devastation that characterizes so much of life in history.

REVELATION 10:1–7

> And I saw another mighty angel coming down from heaven, wrapped in a cloud, with a rainbow over his head; his face was like the sun, and his legs like pillars of fire. He held a little scroll open in his hand. Setting his right foot on the sea and his left foot on the land, he gave a great shout, like a lion roaring. And when he shouted, the seven thunders sounded. And when the seven thunders had sounded, I was about to write, but I heard a voice from heaven saying, "Seal up what the seven thunders have said, and do not write it down." Then the angel whom I saw standing on the sea and the land raised his right hand to heaven and swore by him who lives forever and ever, who created heaven and what is in it, the earth and what is in it, and the sea and what is in it: "There will be no more delay, but in the days when the seventh angel is to blow his trumpet, the mystery of God will be fulfilled, as he announced to his servants the prophets."

We should understand the plagues not as directly sent and controlled by God but more as a way of describing the ongoing traumas of fallen human existence in history. The plagues picture something that actually (we will learn beginning in chapter 11) has its direct source in the machinations of the dragon but that nevertheless does not defeat God's purposes and, actually, providentially even furthers them. Hence, we may recognize that Rev 9 makes the point that the plagues actually could not hope to bring about repentance and the turning from idols. Indeed, though this is not an explicit point the visions make, we may understand that the plagues tend to exacerbate the problem of humanity trusting in idols.

People trust in idols and as a consequence are pushed by the idols toward "murders, sorceries, fornication, and thefts" (9:21) because they are insecure and traumatized, fearful and in pain. So, if God wants to reverse this dynamic, it will make much more sense for God to take a different tack than punitive violence. And this different tack, already described back in Rev 5 (the interpretive key for the entire book), will be detailed beginning in chapter 10.

John sees "another mighty angel coming down from heaven" (10:1). At first it appears that this angel unleashes another set of plagues, this time a plague of "thunders"—that is, more of the same. However, the story actually turns in a different direction. Initially, we should notice the imagery that is used to describe this "mighty angel." It has a "rainbow over his head" (10:1). This mention of the "rainbow" evokes the picture of the One on the throne back in 4:3. As well, the "rainbow" here evokes the rainbow of Gen 9, where it symbolizes God's *unstrung* bow, a bow that suggests that God will no longer respond to human brokenness with violent warfare but instead with persevering love. This "mighty angel" does *not* appear to be an agent of punitive judgment.

And the "mighty angel" has a "face like the sun" and legs "like pillars of fire" (10:1). The "face like the sun" seems to allude to the vision of Jesus in chapter 1 ("his face was like the sun shining with full force," 1:16). The "legs like pillars of fire" evoke another image from the picture of Jesus in chapter 1: "His feet were like burnished bronze" (1:15; cf. also 2:18). This "mighty angel" is a liberator or savior more than a punitive judge.

Then, to deepen the sense of connection between the mighty angel and Jesus, we are told that the angel "held a little scroll in his hand" (10:2). We can't be certain about the connections here. Is the angel Jesus himself? Perhaps, though it may be more likely that we are simply meant to see a close connection between this messenger and Jesus. The scroll—though here it is "little," and the scroll given to Jesus back in chapter 5 is not described by its size—surely relates to the content of Jesus's scroll. I understand that content to be the ultimate message of Revelation, the fulfillment of human history in new Jerusalem. If it's not the same exact scroll that the Lamb is given in chapter 5, it could be seen as the same kind of scroll with the same kind of content.

Then comes something extraordinary. The angel shouts ("like a lion roaring," evoking the chapter 5 image of Jesus as the "lion of the tribe of Judah" [5:5]) and "the seven thunders sounded." It appears that we are going to have another series of plagues, and John prepares to record them. But then, unexpectedly, "a voice from heaven" orders the message of the seven thunders to be "sealed up" and not written down (10:4). The voice interrupts the process of one set of plagues that lead to another even more intense set and then to another. The plot of the book actually seems to shift here.

We are not told directly why the thunder plagues weren't recorded. However, from the development of the plot here and in the next couple of chapters it could be that this is a subtle way to tell readers that *God's work* in the world is not about the plagues and that God recognizes that the dynamics of healing do not follow the logic of punishment and threatened punishment leading to repentance. What will follow in chapter 11, and will actually succeed in gaining repentance, is another expression of *the pattern of Jesus* (faithful witness, suffering, vindication). So, the thunder plagues are ignored in 10:4 as a way of letting us know that God's work in the world is not about plagues as a response to human sin but rather is about persevering love.

The angel then swears allegiance to the one "who lives forever and ever" (i.e., the One on the throne). The angel's words, "There will be no more delay, but in the days when the seventh angel is to blow his trumpet, the mystery of God will be fulfilled," the mystery and fulfillment that God has announced to the prophets (10:6–7). Do we know what this "mystery" is and what is meant by "fulfilled" here? In light of the entire book of Revelation, plus what follows immediately in the rest of chapter 10 and then in chapter 11, I suggest something a bit different than what is commonly assumed. The "mystery" is the pattern of Jesus, especially insofar as his pattern of persevering love is the means to *conquer*. Such a path is indeed, in Paul's words, "foolishness to the Gentiles [i.e., to the *Romans*]" (1 Cor 1:23). In a world shaped by the beast's ideology of domination, it is indeed a "mystery" how persevering love can conquer. The angel, though, indeed proclaims that God is a healer more than a punisher.

Surely the sense of "fulfillment" here and throughout Revelation has the outcome of new Jerusalem as the completion of the purpose of humanity on earth in mind. But what is the practical meaning of such an affirmation? Not "pie in the sky by and by" at all, but its meaning is to claim that the pattern of Jesus *is* our purpose right now. This is Revelation's call: Know that your purpose is to follow Jesus in the midst of empire, the beast, and the dragon and their minions. The words that follow will confirm this call.

REVELATION 10:8–11

> Then the voice that I had heard from heaven spoke to me again, saying, "Go, take the scroll that is open in the hand of the angel who is standing on the sea and on the land." So, I went to the angel and told him to give me the little scroll; and he said to me, "Take it, and eat; it will be bitter to your stomach, but sweet as honey in your mouth." So, I took the little scroll from the hand of the angel and ate it; it was sweet as honey in my mouth, but when I had eaten it, my stomach was made bitter. Then they said to me, "You must prophesy again about many peoples and nations and languages and kings."

The same voice that told John to "seal up" the story of the thunders speaks to John again, telling him to take the scroll from the mighty angel and eat that scroll. That John can eat the scroll shows this is not precisely the same scroll as the one in chapter 5. However, the message to John about the scroll indicates that it is actually of a type with the Lamb's scroll. John eats it and experiences it as bitter and sweet at the same time (10:10). This enigmatic experience might point both to the "sweetness" of the healing of creation and the "bitterness" of the suffering necessary to bring the healing. The "three and a half years" during which the plagues that wreak so much havoc and mark human history is also a time for celebration and for the experience of God's healing love.

When John takes and eats the scroll, he evokes the story of Ezekiel who had a similar experience (Ezek 2:8–3:3) that marked his initiation into prophetic ministry. John has obviously already been prophesying. But in being told to eat his scroll here, he is reminded of his vocation, a vocation to testify to the way of the Lamb. As well, John eats the scroll in the same scene as the sealing of the thunder plagues following right after the vision of the failure of "the rest of humankind" to repent in face of the plagues. His prophesying will move in a redemptive direction. The presence of the "mighty angel" who evokes Jesus here also is part of the change of direction that this overall vision in chapter 10 presents.

John is profoundly linked with the Lamb of Revelation five here. He "must prophesy again about many peoples and nations and languages and kings" (10:11). But this time, as we will see in chapter 11, the emphasis will be on the actions of God and the Lamb and their followers that actually will evoke repentance. And the phrase "peoples and nations and languages and kings" echoes the language that describes those who worship the Lamb in 5:9 ("from every tribe and language and people and nation") and 7:9 ("from every nation, from all tribes and peoples and languages").

What 10:11 adds to this list is the reference to "kings." However, as we will learn by the end of the book, even the "kings of the earth" will enter new Jerusalem. So, this new focus on prophesying "the voice from heaven" gives John is ultimately to prophesy healing and salvation "for a great multitude that no one could count" (7:9).

HOW NOT TO INSPIRE REPENTANCE

The plague visions in the middle of Revelation challenge interpreters. Since they seem to be initiated by God, how are they to be understood in relation to God's loving intentions for the world? The trumpet plagues in Rev 8 and 9 follow upon the seal plagues in Rev 6. The trumpet plague vision leads to this point, according to most interpreters:

> The rest of humankind, who were not killed by these plagues,
> did not repent of the works of their hands or give up worshiping
> demons and idols of gold and silver and bronze and stone and

wood, which cannot see or hear or walk. And they did not repent
of their sorceries or their fornication or their thefts (9:20–21).

John, it seems, is incredulous. Even after all this judgment, stiff-necked and
rebellious humanity will not repent. Stiff-necked humanity still will not turn
from its idols and turn toward God. As a consequence, the text seems to
imply, God initiates these plagues to inspire sinful, idolatrous, rebellious
human beings to repent and to turn from their idolatries toward God. That
is, these unrepentant human beings are incredibly stubborn. The humans
see one-third of the earth destroyed and they won't turn in faith toward the
destroyer!

Is shock over human refusal to repent indeed what the text means to
convey? Is the point here that God initiates these terrible plagues in order to
get people to repent, and to punish (*justly*) those who remain stiff-necked
and won't repent? If so, those who remain rebellious richly deserve their
fate. The point, then, would be to emphasize just how bad humanity is.
However, if God actually does think punishment will bring repentance
and change, God is not very smart. God, in that case, would be a lot like
the head of the British air force policy toward Germany during World War
II—a man named Arthur Harris, and nicknamed, appropriately, "Bomber"
Harris. Bomber Harris believed that if the British and their Allies bombed
German cities and their civilian populations heavily enough, the residents
would rise up against the Nazis, overthrow them, and embrace the British
as their liberators.

Right. British bombs created a firestorm in Hamburg, the worst infer-
no the world had known up to that point. It incinerated tens of thousands of
children, women, and old people. And they imagined their violence would
make them seem to be liberators? In the event, as you would expect, even
with the evils of the Nazi government, the bombing of German cities turned
out to strengthen the resolve of the German people to stay the course against
their ruthless enemies.[1] Plagues are not likely to lead to love for their source.

Yet the vast majority of the interpreters of Revelation—from the theological right to the theological left—assume that in Revelation God brings
these plagues in order to motivate people to give up their idols and turn
to God.[2] But does this assumption make sense? Why would people repent
and turn toward a God who is such a punisher, one who kills one-third
of humankind to show that killing is wrong? Just as with the bombing of
Hamburg, destruction visited by the plagues is a terribly blunt instrument

1. See Grayling, *Among*.

2. See for example, on the right, Osborne, *Revelation*, 385 and, on the left, Sweet,
Revelation, 157.

of judgment that brings profound collateral damage upon humanity. It kills the young and old, moral and unrighteous, kind and unkind.

Chapters 8 through 10, though, actually show us that God is *not* a God using violent judgment as a means to get human beings to repent. The view of God as the spearheader of punishment simply is not true to the Bible, all things considered. Now, of course the biblical materials do give us powerfully mixed signals. There are images of punishment, though perhaps not as many as we may think. And we have many images of mercy and healing. But holding together each of these views of God at the same time as equally valid does not result in coherent theology. We need to choose which ones provide the interpretive core.

This "revelation of Jesus Christ" chooses Jesus as its core. In the Gospels he reveals God as healer, not punisher (e.g., the prodigal son story). Jesus taught us to be merciful and love our enemies in order to be like God. Jesus quotes Hosea: "I desire mercy, not sacrifice" (Matt 9:12; 12:17). Hosea himself gave one of the clearest capsule pictures of God: Despite the people's unfaithfulness, "I am a holy God and I will come in mercy, not in anger" (Hos 11).

We have good reasons to think that Revelation's message actually is not one where God creates plagues to try to bring about repentance. If God were to do this, it would actually be a lesson in how *not* to inspire repentance. John's overall message is much more sophisticated and profound than the simplistic reward and punishment views that even some of the best interpreters of Revelation hold. We should interpret these plague visions in light of what comes before them and what comes after them in Revelation.

When John insists his book is a revelation of Jesus Christ, he makes it clear that this Jesus Christ is the Lamb. The Lamb is the one whose witness of self-giving love provides the meaning of history. The victory of the Lamb, a victory celebrated as decisive in chapter 5, is the victory of this self-giving love, not the victory of punitive violence. This is the point of Revelation: It reveals Jesus as the Lamb, the meaning of history, the one who equates God with the prodigal son's father, who said be merciful as God is merciful, and who said of his killers, "forgive them, they know not what they do."

What is the outcome of the Lamb's victory? New Jerusalem. Who is in new Jerusalem celebrating with the Lamb and the One on the throne? Certainly, the followers of the Lamb who earn white robes by following the Lamb and his ways. But new Jerusalem also includes the kings of the earth who bring the glory of the nations into this holy place (21:24), a place of wholeness. The kings hide from God in chapter 6, and they are the leaders of the inhabitants of the earth who do not repent in chapter 9. They lead the armies of the beast (16:14). The plagues have created fear and resistance. The plagues actually serve the purposes of the beast. But repentance does come, in the end. The kings of the earth embrace the Lamb. How can this be?

The message in 9:21 about the people not repenting is not so much about stiff-necked humanity (though, tragically, we are). The message, actually, is that plagues are a terrible way to try to get repentance. People don't repent after the plagues. And God does not use them for that purpose. In light of the refusal to repent in chapter 9, what we see over the next several chapters is a creative (and not always easy to understand) series of images. The images show how God actually does work to bring about repentance—by means other than punitive judgment.

In a nutshell, God's means for healing is to continue the Lamb's witness to self-giving love. Right after the statement about the refusal to repent, John sees this "mighty angel" whose presence signals a change in focus. What follows in chapters 11–14 are visions of witness by the Lamb's followers; witness leading to martyrdom. But, ultimately, leading to healing, even for the kings of the earth.

When John is told not to write down the thunder plagues, the story takes a turn. We are reminded that the plagues are not how God brings in new Jerusalem. They do not get repentance. God's healing work is totally different. Instead of reporting the thunders, another series of destructive plagues, John starts to tell of the martyr/witness of the Lamb and his people: The two witnesses of chapter 11. The woman and her offspring of chapter 12. The 144,000 of chapter 14. These are the ones who, through their persevering love, reveal the content of the great scroll. God's coming city of wholeness includes even God's human enemies. These visions, as we will see, are a call to us also to follow the Lamb wherever he goes.

How do we think, then, of the plagues? They express God's impersonal "wrath," not God's personal punitive anger. John responds to questions of the plagues, God's sovereignty, and the power of God's love. The plagues *are* linked with God's work. God does not desert creation, and God brings healing. But in their direct expression, the plagues are the work of evil and serve evil. God's love sees to it that evil does not win—but only through Jesus's way of persevering compassion and mercy that resists the cycle of violence. In the end, mercy wins the day, and evil destroys itself. But the victory of mercy is amidst the terrors of a broken world—the only kind of victory that matters, complicated as that is.

FOR FURTHER ENGAGEMENT

1. The author suggests that the sixth trumpet that leaves one-third of humanity dead (Rev 9:13–21) has the effect of showing that humanity will not be moved to repentance by punitive judgment. "What is needed is a powerful witness to a God of *love*, not a God of retributive violence." How do you think of the issue of how God works among human beings to move them toward repentance and salvation? Based on your reading of Revelation so far, what do you think its basic message is regarding God's response to human brokenness?

2. What is your emotional response in reading the accounts of the seal and trumpet plagues? Anger? Joy? Fear? Bewilderment? Who do you think causes the plagues and who suffers from them? Do you think they are being experienced now in the present? If so, what should our attitude toward them be?

3. The trumpet plagues seem to reflect, to some degree at least, the plagues in the Exodus story. In the Exodus account is the key point the punishment of the Egyptians or the liberation of the Israelites? Is Revelation making the same point?

4. In 9:13–19 John seems to utilize common social fears to drive home his point about the terribleness of the plagues. What common social fears would a modern-day John play on?

5. The author suggests that the "plague visions give us a picture of present reality." Does that make sense to you? Do you think that we are currently living amidst the "plagues" of Revelation? If not, when do you think the plagues happened or will happen? If so, what implications does that belief have for you?

6. What do you think of the author's idea that the visions of seal and trumpet plagues (and the bowl plagues to come) portray a "level of destruction too great to be believed"—that "John makes a rhetorical, not predictive, point"? Does it make the message of Revelation more palatable to think of the plague visions this way? Explain.

7. The author sees the moment where John is told not to write down the thunder plagues (10:4) as a key turning point in Revelation. Summarize and evaluate what you understand to be his theory about this.

8. Commentator Craig Koester argues that the plagues "do not distinguish the God of the Christian community from the gods of the empire." Based only on the plague visions there would be no reason

to give their allegiance to the Christian God. "For that to occur, a different kind of testimony is needed. That is why the path toward final judgment is interrupted in the wake of humanity's refusal to repent— so that John and others can bear witness."[3] How do you respond to Koester's point? If he is correct, how would that affect one's interpretation of these passages?

3. Koester, *Revelation*, 447.

9

Standing by Words

[Revelation 11 and 12]

At the end of Revelation 10, John eats the scroll that the "mighty angel" holds in his right hand, a symbolic act that echoes Ezek 2–3, where the prophet accepts his commission to witness. Here, John is told, after he eats the bittersweet scroll, "you must prophesy again about many peoples and nations and kings" (10:11). So, when we turn to chapter 11, we know that John is "again" presenting insights about the ways of the Lamb in the violent and chaotic world of his readers—a world dominated by the Roman Empire.

REVELATION 11:1–14

> Then I was given a measuring rod like a staff, and I was told, "Come and measure the temple of God and the altar and those who worship there, but do not measure the court outside the temple; leave that out, for it is given over to the nations, and they will trample over the holy city for forty-two months. And I will grant my two witnesses authority to prophesy for one thousand two hundred sixty days, wearing sackcloth." These are the two olive trees and the two lampstands that stand before the Lord of the earth. And if anyone wants to harm them, fire pours from their mouth and consumes their foes; anyone who wants to harm

them must be killed in this manner. They have authority to shut the sky, so that no rain may fall during the days of their prophesying, and they have authority over the waters to turn them into blood, and to strike the earth with every kind of plague, as often as they desire. When they have finished their testimony, the beast that comes up from the bottomless pit will make war on them and conquer them and kill them, and their dead bodies will lie in the street of the great city that is prophetically called Sodom and Egypt, where also their Lord was crucified. For three and a half days members of the peoples and tribes and languages and nations will gaze at their dead bodies and refuse to let them be placed in a tomb; and the inhabitants of the earth will gloat over them and celebrate and exchange presents, because these two prophets had been a torment to the inhabitants of the earth. But after the three and a half days, the breath of life from God entered them, and they stood on their feet, and those who saw them were terrified. Then they heard a loud voice from heaven saying to them, "Come up here!" And they went up to heaven in a cloud while their enemies watched them. At that moment there was a great earthquake, and a tenth of the city fell; seven thousand people were killed in the earthquake, and the rest were terrified and gave glory to the God of heaven. The second woe has passed. The third woe is coming very soon.

John is given a "measuring rod" with which to "measure the temple of God and the altar and those who worship there" (11:1). This measuring seems to symbolize a kind of protection for followers of the Lamb that is not offered to "the court outside the temple," a court that is "given over to the nations" (11:2). It seems doubtful that "protection" means that followers of the Lamb are being promised that they won't suffer. More likely, it's simply a way of affirming the ability of the witnessing community to persevere even in the midst of suffering and trauma. Battered and bruised but not overcome.

Another symbol for this witnessing community is the "two witnesses" (11:3). These witnesses are called "two olive trees" and "two lampstands"—both images used elsewhere in the Bible for communities of faith. They will "prophesy for one thousand two hundred sixty days"—that is, three and a half years (or forty-two months). This is "broken time" (half of the seven years that we could call "whole time"), broken time that in Revelation symbolizes time in history, the time of the plagues, the time remaining before the new Jerusalem comes down.

So, we have a kind of recapitulation of the plague visions (which in various ways show how the nations "trample over the holy city for forty-two months" in the language of 11:2) but with an added dimension. The "two witnesses" are essentially the same actors in this drama as the faithful "con-querors" mentioned in the seven messages in chapters 2 and 3, the followers of the Lamb. That is, these two witnesses carry out the vocation Jesus gives to all his followers to witness to his way amidst the plagues.

The imagery in 11:4–6 is rather violent (the two witnesses "consume" their foes with fire and have the power to strike the earth "with every kind of plague"). Nonetheless, the fire "pours from their *mouths*" (11:5, emphasis added), indicating that their "weapon" is actually simply the word of their testimony. The word indeed might be confrontive, but "fire" is figurative, not literal. The witnesses directly challenge the lies of the dragon, the beast, the false prophet, and the harlot who we will meet in the chapters to come.

The image of the fire coming from the mouths of the two witnesses most of all underscores the significance of speaking truth in the context of great falsehoods. The strategy that John offers his readers in Revelation is essentially a strategy of taking care and taking courage in how they speak. He calls them to challenge the vision of life with which the empire inundates people and to present a viable alternative with their testimony. The alterna-tive to empire must be articulated verbally ("with fire") while of course also finding embodiment in Jesus's followers' lives.

We briefly meet "the beast" for the first time here, as he is the one who "comes up from the bottomless pit" to attack the witnesses and, in the moment, "conquers them and kills them" (11:7). They remain dead for "three and a half days" (11:9,11), likely another allusion to the "broken time" between Jesus's ascension and the descending of the new Jerusalem. John probably intends to underscore the vulnerability of the witnesses and hostility toward them that originates with the evil powers. Like Jesus, they "conquer" not by killing but by being willing to die. They were "a torment to the inhabitants of the earth" (11:10)—but in a way that was not inconsistent with their willingness to die rather than to be conformed to the ways of the beast, based on the "fire" of their testimony.

They are resurrected after the "three and a half days" and are taken "up to heaven" (11:12). Then a "great earthquake" kills seven thousand people (11:13). This "earthquake" is probably best understood to symbolize the entire series of plagues about which we have just read in chapters 6 through 10. The "seven thousand" symbolizes massive deaths—seven (the number of completeness) and one thousand (meaning a huge number). Yet, 90 percent of the people survive.

Remarkably, at this point "the rest were terrified and gave glory to the God of heaven" (11:13). This giving of glory contrasts with the responses of the kings of the earth and others at 9:21 who in the face of intense plagues "did not repent." The difference in the account of chapter 11 is that here we have the two witnesses who offer testimony to the way of the Lamb even in the face of their own deaths. To link this image here with the ultimate presence of the kings of the earth in the new Jerusalem (21:24), we could say that one reason the kings are able to be transformed is due to the witness offered to the point of death by the followers of the Lamb.

REVELATION 11:15–19

> Then the seventh angel blew his trumpet, and there were loud voices in heaven, saying, "The kingdom of the world has become the kingdom of our Lord and of his Messiah, and he will reign forever and ever." Then the twenty-four elders who sit on their thrones before God fell on their faces and worshiped God, singing, "We give you thanks, Lord God Almighty, who are and who were, for you have taken your great power and begun to reign. The nations raged, but your wrath has come, and the time for judging the dead, for rewarding your servants, the prophets and saints and all who fear your name, both small and great, and for destroying those who destroy the earth." Then God's temple in heaven was opened, and the ark of his covenant was seen within his temple; and there were flashes of lightning, rumblings, peals of thunder, an earthquake, and heavy hail.

The sound of the seventh trumpet signals the end (so it would seem) of the story. With this trumpet, the set of seven trumpet plagues is complete. Yet the book of Revelation is actually only halfway through. The story is over, but the book is not. Thus, what follows will go back over the story that has already been told before new Jerusalem comes down at 21:1.

The "loud voices" celebrate the unification of the "kingdom of the world" with "the kingdom of our Lord" (11:15). This joining together is the end point, not that the kingdoms of the world would be eradicated. As we will see, new Jerusalem comes down. The world is transformed and healed; the good creation is redeemed. The vision in 11:15–19 links closely with the vision of the "One on the throne" in chapter 4. The twenty-four elders worship. In some sense, the implied forward look of chapter 4 finds its fulfillment here. We have a number of what we could call "fleshing out" visions to come before 21:1, though.

Verse eighteen prepares us for the final judgment that will be described in chapter 20. Again, though, we have much to see before what this verse speaks of will find further elaboration. Part of our question, thus, is: Why do we need these additional visions that will be described before the end?

One contribution the intervening visions will certainly make is to clarify more who the "destroyers of the earth" are, the destroyers who will ultimately be destroyed. Given that we already have been told of "the inhabitants of the earth" ultimately giving glory to God (11:13) and that we will be told of the presence of even the kings of the earth in new Jerusalem, what we will learn is that the "destroyers of the earth" are not human beings but the spiritual forces of evil (such as the "beast" we briefly met in 11:7). We could say, in less mythological language, that the "destroyers of the earth" are the social systems and prejudices and destructive values that hinder human well-being. The distinction between the powers and their human agents will become important as the further visions of plagues and judgment unfold.

REVELATION 12:1–6

> A great portent appeared in heaven: a woman clothed with the sun, with the moon under her feet, and on her head a crown of twelve stars. She was pregnant and was crying out in birth pangs, in the agony of giving birth. Then another portent appeared in heaven: a great red dragon, with seven heads and ten horns, and seven diadems on his heads. His tail swept down a third of the stars of heaven and threw them to the earth. Then the dragon stood before the woman who was about to bear a child, so that he might devour her child as soon as it was born. And she gave birth to a son, a male child, who is to rule all the nations with a rod of iron. But her child was snatched away and taken to God and to his throne; and the woman fled into the wilderness, where she has a place prepared by God, so that there she can be nourished for one thousand two hundred sixty days.

With chapter 12, John begins a more detailed account that provides a fuller picture of the forces at work in the plagues we have seen and will see more of. It becomes clearer over the next several chapters that the powers of evil are involved in the kinds of events that make up the plagues. It also becomes clearer by what means God wins and implements God's kingdom.

First, "God's temple in heaven" is opened (11:19) as part of the trumpet vision that announces, "the kingdom of the world has become the kingdom of our Lord and of his Messiah" (that is, the One on the throne and the Lamb) and the time has come "for destroying those who destroy the earth" (11:18). This "time has come" should be seen as a plot device, the time within the story Revelation tells where we turn to the "destroyers of the earth" and their fate is realized. Revelation does not set out a chronology for the world's future but exhorts its readers to take part in the work that will destroy the earth's destroyers—who are the powers behind the empires of the world, including the Roman Empire. The "opening" of the temple here signals a change in focus. The second half of the book will culminate with a return to the temple, though we will see in chapters 21 and 22 that John has in mind a radically changed notion of the temple.

Chapter 12 contains a wealth of images and events. Many are cryptic and difficult to understand. As elsewhere in Revelation, we should focus more on the overall sensibility that is being conveyed than to expect to see in each of the images a direct correlation with a particular historical person or event. With all our uncertainty about many of the specifics, the general message here is clear. A new dimension is added to the story with the introduction of the dragon. We are now able better to understand the paradoxes of previous chapters concerning the plagues in relation to the One on the throne, the One so closely linked with the Lamb. God is not the only cosmic actor in this drama.

Shortly after the temple "in heaven" is opened "a great portent appeared in heaven." This will be the first scene in the process where God destroys the destroyers of the earth and brings full liberation to the followers of the Lamb and the rest of creation. It is notable that the first of Revelation's "portents" (i.e., the profound symbolic visions) is of this woman "clothed with the sun" who seems to represent several entities. Most centrally she represents the community of God's people who received and sought to embody Torah and who brought forth God's "Messiah" (11:15) as well as also Jesus's birth mother and the early Christian churches.

Two later "portents" relate to the work the woman initiates of "destroying the destroyers of the earth"—the entry of the dragon as an overt actor in the drama (12:3) and a reference to the "seven angels" whose plagues bring to an end "the wrath of God" (15:1). These three "portents" belong together. The woman along with her offspring "throws down" the dragon. They "conquer him by the blood of the Lamb and by the word of their testimony" (12:11). This conquest will turn out to be the precise means by which the wrath of God, wrath referred to in the account of the third portent, comes to an end.

The woman gives birth to a male child on whom the enmity of the dragon focuses (who is identified a few verses later as "that ancient serpent, who is called the Devil and Satan, the deceiver of the whole world," 12:9). The reason for this enmity (or, maybe better, intense fear) is that this child is destined to "rule all the nations" (12:5). As "ruler," this child is directly linked with the mention in the previous chapter of the "Messiah" who joins with "our Lord" to make the "kingdom of the world" their kingdom (11:15;

remember also the identification of Jesus as "ruler of the kings of the earth" at the beginning of the book, 1:5).

The swirling imagery here reiterates the main claims of the "Revelation of Jesus Christ" that makes up this book. The vocation of God's elect people, Israel, has been to provide the communal context for the implementation of the strategy God will use to destroy the destroyers of the earth and to transform the kingdom of the world into the kingdom of God. Crucially, this "kingdom" is termed the kingdom of the Lord and his Messiah. That is, using the imagery from earlier in Revelation, this is the kingdom of the One on the throne and of the Lamb. As will be re-emphasized in just a few verses, this transformation happens in only one way: The persevering love of the Lamb (i.e., Messiah) is the only means to defeat the dragon.

The dragon has tremendous power (his "tail swept down a third of the stars of heaven and threw them to earth," 12:4), as we recognize if we accept that he is the power behind the terrible plagues we read of in chapters 6 through 10. However, crucially, right away we see that the dragon's power is no match for the power of the One on the throne and the Lamb. We see the limits to the power of the dragon here when we read that though he is poised to "devour her child as soon as it was born" (12:4), in fact the child "was snatched away and taken to God and his throne" (12:5) and the woman escapes to safety.

The woman flees to the "wilderness," another rich if cryptic image. Linking with the exodus story that lurks in the background throughout Revelation, we may see the wilderness as a place of refuge where God's people go after God miraculously "snatched" them from Pharaoh's Egypt. But the wilderness is also a dangerous place. The woman (probably now especially representing God's faithful people) is "nourished" in the wilderness for one thousand two hundred sixty days (or forty-two months or three-and-one-half years). This "nourishing" implies that John has in mind the strengthening of God's people during the dangerous, plague-filled years of human history between Jesus's resurrection and the final transformation of the kingdom of the world into the kingdom of God.

What follows for the rest of the book is the struggle between the woman's child (known to us from earlier in the book as the Lamb) and the dragon (and his minions, the beast, false prophet, Babylon, the great harlot, and their human allies). These are the two main characters of the drama, the dragon and the Lamb. We see from the start of this part of the story, though, a paradox. A seemingly all-powerful dragon and this little child engage in a battle that proves not to be a battle because the dragon actually has no true power in face of the Lamb's refusal to be deceived. And the child (Lamb) will conquer.

Revelation 12 parallels chapters 7 and 11. In chapter 7, John sees "angels" bent on destruction (like the dragon here) and hears that "the servants of our God [will be marked] with a seal on their foreheads" (7:2–3). What follows there is a vision of victory that is won by the Lamb's persevering love and the servants' faithfulness to that love. Likewise, in chapter 11, the "temple" (linked there with those who "worship" in it) is "measured," in contrast to "the court outside the temple" where "the nations . . . will trample over the holy city for forty-two months" (11:1–3). As the chapter continues, we read of the faithfulness of the "two witnesses" (i.e., the people of God) even in face of death. That faithfulness results in God's victory.

Chapter 12 reiterates this same story. God provides protection that allows for faithful witness but also suffering, even death, for the faithful ones. The faithful witness proves to be the means that defeat the dragon. These are creative ways to present what we have seen from the beginning of the book: the pattern of Jesus (faithful life, death, vindication) that results in "a kingdom, priests serving [Jesus's] God and Father" (1:5–6).

REVELATION 12:7–12

> And war broke out in heaven; Michael and his angels fought against the dragon. The dragon and his angels fought back, but they were defeated, and there was no longer any place for them in heaven. The great dragon was thrown down, that ancient serpent, who is called the Devil and Satan, the deceiver of the whole world—he was thrown down to the earth, and his angels were thrown down with him. Then I heard a loud voice in heaven, proclaiming, "Now have come the salvation and the power and the kingdom of our God and the authority of his Messiah, for the accuser of our comrades has been thrown down, who accuses them day and night before our God. But they have conquered him by the blood of the Lamb and by the word of their testimony, for they did not cling to life even in the face of death. Rejoice then, you heavens and those who dwell in them! But woe to the earth and the sea, for the devil has come down to you with great wrath, because he knows that his time is short!"

In 12:7, we read "war broke out in heaven." The forces of God are led by "Michael," the commander of the "angels" who battle the dragon. This appears to refer to the head of the archangels who is mentioned occasionally (and without elaboration) in ancient Jewish and Christian writings. Clearly the point here is not about the identity of the dragon's opponents but about the claim that the dragon has been thrown out of heaven. That is, there is no ongoing battle between two equal cosmic powers, God and Satan. Satan is simply expelled by angels; God's own hand is not even necessary.

As we see reiterated in what is to come in Revelation, though the book presents good and evil at war, this is not a Manichean universe with two equal powers that struggle for dominance. We have to do with *one* ultimate power—the One on the throne. Several times, beginning here, we see the enemy forces simply "defeated" (11:8), "thrown down" (11:9), captured and "thrown alive into the lake of fire" (19:20), and "thrown into the lake of fire" (20:10).

We get a fuller picture of the identity of the dragon in 12:9: "that ancient serpent, who is called Devil and Satan, the deceiver of the whole world." This description points to the key element in *how* the powers that oppose God work—the element of *deception*. The entire "revelation of Jesus Christ" draws its inspiration from the need to challenge the lies the people in John's congregations were told. In a nutshell, the "deception" that bamboozles "the whole world" is about power. Is the greatness of Rome (as paradigm for a whole series of human empires going back at least to ancient Egypt) an expression of true power such that people in John's communities must give the empire their loyalty? Or is true power the way of the Lamb—a way that demands loyalty toward God's kingdom and disloyalty to all idolatrous empires?

Chapter 12 contains one of the most direct statements about power in Revelation. The dragon has deceived many to accept its definition of reality (including many who profess to follow the Lamb—see chapters 2 and 3). However, the "loud voice in heaven" proclaims a different picture of reality. "Salvation," "power," "kingdom," and "authority" are all claims made by human empires, again, paradigmatically by Rome. Revelation asserts that true salvation, power, kingdom, and authority have *instead* to do with God and God's "Messiah" (the Lamb). "The accuser of our comrades," the dragon who is the power behind empires, "has been thrown down" without actually being able to put up a fight (12:10).

And now comes the key point—the central assertion of Revelation, and indeed of biblical faith itself: "They have conquered him by the blood of the Lamb and by the word of their testimony, for they did not cling to life even in the face of death" (12:10). The "they" here presumably refers to the "comrades"—those who "follow the Lamb wherever he goes" (14:4), though God and God's Messiah are probably in mind too. The victory over the dragon is precisely the same victory as the victory of the Lamb, the victory celebrated in chapter 5.

The meaning of "the blood of the Lamb" is not the later satisfaction atonement where Jesus offers a sacrifice that enables God to offer forgiveness—a sacrifice utterly unique to him. Here, rather, the point is Jesus's way of persevering love lived to the death that serves as a model and as empowerment for his followers to do the same thing. "The blood of the Lamb" (the faithful life of Jesus unto the shedding of his blood when the empire executes him) *along with* the faithful "testimony" (or "witness") of his followers are what conquer the dragon. John calls his readers here to be part of this work (remember that each of the seven messages in chapters 2 and 3 concluded with a call to action and a promise to those who conquer).

The point, it seems, is not that things are up for grabs, that the dragon might win a battle with God concerning the ultimate outcome of history. Rather, it's that the dragon, now "thrown down to the earth" (12:9), continues to deceive the inhabitants of the earth and to prevent them from being at home in new Jerusalem. To "conquer" is to trust that the way of persevering love is the truth and that the dragon and his empires make false claims about their own power. We see a bit of a paradox in 12:12. Following the praise of God, the Lamb, and the comrades for conquering the dragon comes a warning to "the earth and the sea" because "the devil has come down to you with great wrath" (12:12). The point seems to be that the victory is won, that faithful imitation of the Lamb conquers, yet this victory is bittersweet (remember the scroll John eats, 10:9–10) because during this historical time (the three and a half years) the struggle continues: worship amidst the plagues.

REVELATION 12:13–18

So, when the dragon saw that he had been thrown down to the earth, he pursued the woman who had given birth to the male child. But the woman was given the two wings of the great eagle, so that she could fly from the serpent into the wilderness, to her place where she is nourished for a time, and times, and half a time. Then from his mouth the serpent poured water like a river after the woman, to sweep her away with the flood. But the earth came to the help of the woman; it opened its mouth and swallowed the river that the dragon had poured from his mouth. Then the dragon was angry with the woman and went off to make war on the rest of her children, those who keep the commandments of God and hold the testimony of Jesus. Then the dragon took his stand on the sand of the seashore.

The final part of Rev 12, like the rest of the chapter, tells a story that does not quite make literal sense but that seems to reiterate the entire book's basic plot. The dragon is "thrown down to the earth" (12:13), defeated by Michael and hence not able to wrest dominion from the One on the throne. But in his rage, he continues to fight and wreak havoc on whomever he can—presumably for the three and a half years.

The dragon pursues the woman, but she is kept safe "for a time, and times, and half a time" (i.e., three and a half times). The place of safety is "the wilderness" (12:14), an allusion to the exodus journey from Egypt to the promised land (and also the place where Jesus encountered Satan and withstood the temptations to give loyalty to Satan rather than to God). The dragon's onslaught includes an attempt to sweep the woman away in a flood. Now, the safety of the woman is assured when "the earth came to the help of the woman," perhaps a reminder of the rainbow in chapter 5 and the sense that the creation ultimately serves the purposes of the creator. The dragon has come down to the earth (12:12), but the earth resists the dragon's agenda (though its inhabitants do take his side, 13:4, 8). Note that the dragon's attack comes from its "mouth"—and the earth's aid comes from its "mouth." The war of words continues.

The final idea here is that the dragon, after the defeat in heaven and the failure to capture the woman, turns its hostility toward "the rest of [the woman's] children, those who keep the commandments of God and hold the testimony of Jesus" (12:17). This allusion seems to confirm that the plagues and tribulations from this middle section of the book are most directly an expression of the dragon's fury—even as they ultimately serve God's purposes. The dragon himself is the source of the famine, pestilence, and war. That is, as we will see in chapter 13, the beast (i.e., the Roman Empire and similar phenomena) and its allies are agents of Satan and not of God as they create a kind of "peace and order" based on violence and domination.

One confusing part of the vision in the latter part of chapter 12 is the precise identity of the woman in relation to the community of God's people. The woman births the Messiah, seemingly an allusion to this community. But in the end, when the dragon can't capture the woman he turns to war on her children, seemingly also an allusion to this community. Perhaps one way to understand these images is to see in them two manifestations of the community's vocation—to be the source of the Messiah (the woman) and also to be the ongoing manifestation of God's shalom work in the world (her children). Of course, precision is not at the top of John's literary concerns.

Chapter 12 ends with a transition. The dragon takes "his stand on the sand of the seashore" (12:18) at the space between the sea and land. It would seem that what John has in mind here is that the sea is the source of the chaos and idolatry that shatters human well-being. What comes out the sea is the dragon's main servant, the great "beast" (13:1). What follows in the next several chapters of Revelation will be another way of thinking about the plagues, with an emphasis on their political expression.

It is important to keep in mind the message that we have gotten so far of the protection of God's people alongside the portrayal of suffering and trauma. The beast will seem extremely powerful and the followers of the Lamb extremely vulnerable—as *is* the case. However, the burden of Revelation is to transform our sense of power and vulnerability. We have been told several times that God's care will be sustained, and that God has already won the victory. The visions in chapters 13 through 20 in various ways ultimately emphasize this same message.

STANDING BY WORDS

Revelation 11 and 12 contain two wondrous stories that, in all their bewildering detail, essentially tell the same story. God indeed works to heal God's good creation, and a crucial role in this work is to be played by the human followers of the Lamb. The role these followers have to play asks of them two things. First, that they embrace the ministry of telling the truth amidst the nations of the world. Second, that they, in embracing this ministry, refuse to be deterred by suffering and even death. This ministry involves *speaking* truth, using meaningful words to testify to the way of the Lamb.[1]

Let's think of these two stories in the context of the bigger story that the book of Revelation tells. The first 5 chapters of Revelation present the agenda of the book—to encourage people who have faith in the Lamb to follow his path while they navigate the treacherous waters of life in the Roman Empire. Revelation starts with an account of the pattern of Jesus—the faithful witness to a way of compassion that resists the injustices of empire. He gave his life in order to free all those who would embrace his revelation of God's mercy. Then Jesus challenges his followers in various congregations. They "conquer" the powers through persevering love, not through accommodation to the ways of empire.

To underscore the core message, we are told in chapter 5 of the triumphant Lamb. His self-giving love opens the path to bring history to a healing conclusion. However, in the time between the Lamb's faithful life, death, and resurrection, and the coming of new Jerusalem (when the contents of

---

1. The section heading, "Standing by words" comes from Wendell Berry, a great truth speaker, *Standing*.

the great scroll the Lamb takes from the One on the throne will be fully revealed), in this time in between, some hard things are going to come.

Beginning in chapter 6, we read of a series of plagues that bring terrible suffering and destruction on an ever-increasing part of creation—both human beings and nature. Initially, we are given the impression that these come from God. However, the portrayal of God's relationship with the plagues is deliberately *vague*. John uses the passive voice ("they were allowed . . . "), and the term "wrath" is common. These literary devices give the sense of a built-in process where negative actions lead to negative consequences. This is God's world, so these consequences in some sense can be seen as from God, but in an indirect, essentially impersonal sense.

Then, in chapter 9, we see where the plagues lead—human beings who live separate from God "still do not repent." So, for the healing to happen, God must intervene beyond simply the negative spiral of sin leading to bad consequences that defines "wrath." In chapter 10 we learn of a "mighty angel" who shares important characteristics with Jesus. Like the Jesus envisioned in chapter 1, the mighty angel has a rainbow over his head, a face like the sun, and legs like pillars of fire. Another series of plagues, the thunders, is readied, but then, unexpectedly, they are shut up. We have a turn in the plot. Instead of a spiral of violent judgment, we will have actions that break the spiral. Significantly, John himself is given a scroll to eat that evokes the great scroll the Lamb took from the One on the throne in chapter 5. Having eaten this scroll, John reports visions in chapters 11 and 12 that are quite different from the plague visions.

These stories in chapters 11 and 12 tell us that the "witnesses" in both chapters were not afraid to suffer. As they speak truth in face of a world bent on domination and on repression of truth, they face consequences. Jesus, though, shows the way. He was the faithful witness (that is, the faithful martyr, the faithful truthteller) who conquers even as he is killed. Jesus as faithful truthteller is also the message of chapter 5. The slain Lamb is the "Lion of the Tribe of Judah" who is able to take the scroll (5:5). Likewise with the people in the congregations addressed in chapters 2 and 3. They were called to "conquer"—not by finding a place at the table of the powerful, not by gathering their own weapons of coercion, and not by waiting for the Lamb to do their killing for them so that they would not have risk suffering themselves.

Rather, in chapter 11, the Lamb's people conquer when they follow the path of truth telling all the way. The beast makes war on them and actually "conquers" them—that is, puts them to death. In this case, as with Jesus, violence by the beast does not end the story. God vindicates these witnesses and raises them from the dead. This faithful witness adds a new dimension to the story. The failure to gain repentance at the end of chapter 9 is followed in chapter 11 with another "earthquake" that leads to 90 percent of the people repenting and giving glory to God (11:13). The decisive element may be seen as the faithful witness that shows the people that God is a God of mercy, not simply punitive judgment.

In the story told in chapter 12 of the woman and her offspring, the statement is made explicitly: "Now have come the salvation and the power and the kingdom of our God and the authority of his Messiah, for the accuser of our comrades has been thrown down. They conquered him by the blood of the Lamb and by the word of their testimony, for they did not cling to life even in the face of death" (12:11). They conquered him by the blood of the Lamb and by the word of their testimony, for they did not cling to life even in the face of death. This is huge. "Our comrades," that is, we human beings who seek to follow the Lamb, have a crucial role to play in God's victory. The establishment of new Jerusalem is an effort of God *and* of human beings. We are not simply passive observers. Revelation as a whole exhorts its readers to faithful truth telling and the willingness to do truth telling all the way to the end. This is how we help conquer the dragon.

So now we are told that God is not our enemy. No matter how we might think of God's indirect and providential oversight of the plagues, we are told here of the actual agents of the plagues. The direct death and destruction that characterizes these 1,260 days of history between Jesus's resurrection and the final coming of the new Jerusalem are the work of the beast making war on the two witnesses and the dragon making war on the woman's offspring. Revelation's next several chapters will make the role—and the fate—of these evil powers much clearer.

The pictures in chapters 11 and 12 are meant to encourage. While you can take for granted for now that the beast and dragon will be active, you must not become fatalistic or nihilistic in face of their deeds. Nor must you become "realistic" and take up their own methods to combat them. God's method for faithful human beings to conquer is the same as it was for God's Son: "Conquer by keeping the commandments and holding the testimony of Jesus" (12:11) whose self-giving love is the force more powerful that actually does conquer the powers of evil. Conquer by *breaking* the spiral of violence, by making healing possible even for God's human enemies.

This is what I think Revelation 11 and 12 have to say to us today: We too live in a time and place, like first-century Rome, where empire as a way of life corrupts language and thereby inflicts damage on persons and communities. So, we need to discern how language destroys meaning, and we need to discern how to speak truth in face of that destruction. How is language being emptied of meaning in our setting? Well, just listen to political ads and speeches during any election year—or read the pundits who in the name of being "even-handed" refuse to provide accountability for overt lies that truly do seem mostly to come from one side of the political spectrum.

Also think of the language of war and militarism. When our bombers kill ten times more civilians than combatants their work is called, antiseptically, "collateral damage." I remember a political cartoon from the first Gulf War in the early 1990s of a weeping mother who holds a small, inert form: "This collateral damage was only eight months old," she cried. Take even the term "national defense." The US changed the name of the War Department to the "Defense Department" right after World War II. This was precisely the moment when the United States transitioned to a permanent war footing and greatly expanded US foreign military presence around the world. The War Department was mainly defensive and temporal. When earlier wars ended (e.g., the Civil War and World War I) the country returned to a quite small military presence. With the Defense Department after 1945, the US took the offensive and stayed engaged. Increasingly, the entire federal government was militarized.

Another set of examples would be the way we use the language of commodification to speak of things we used to use more personal language for. Students become "consumers of a product, education." Forests become "timber harvests."

In Revelation, what is most dangerous about the beast is how it defines reality and the impact of that way of defining. This is why—as we will see in chapter 13—John presents the beast in religious terms. The beast's power, then and now (as Gandhi recognized), depends upon the people who live in its domain giving their consent to its rule. The danger for John's communities of faith was that they would grant this consent and not recognize that the truth of the Lamb and the "truth" of the beast tend to be altogether *different* things. We know from history, and from looking around today, that to resist the beast's way of defining reality, that is, to tell the truth, can be risky business indeed. But John proclaims that the power the beast actually has is far from total. It only seems that way when we accept its definitions. When we don't accept its definitions, it is greatly weakened.

Another debased word in our world today is "realism." Political theory that calls for accommodation to power politics is called "realistic." Just to trace the trajectory in the United States since 1945 shows the claims of the "realists" to be bogus. It was said to be the most "realistic and necessary thing" to go to war in Korea and in Vietnam and continually to accelerate the arms races and to fight terrorism with war upon war—even in the face of disastrous consequences. This "realism" bankrupts our country, economically, environmentally, and morally.

The truth-tellers we should celebrate reject such "realism" and willingly tell the truth all the way, even in face of death. Perhaps our most famous truthteller in this country is Martin Luther King Jr., who has, unfortunately, been somewhat sanitized to serve the dominant narrative of our power elite. So, we tend not to hear about his sharp and oh so direct critique of the war in Vietnam (a critique that cost him President Johnson's support) and his sharp and oh so direct critique of our unjust economic system. Yet he continued on his path even in face of the risks that did end his life.[2]

One of my favorite, though lesser known, American heroes is US Representative Jeanette Rankin of Montana.[3] She was one of the first women elected to Congress and in her first term proceeded to vote against American entry into World War I. She lost her next election. But she refused to go away and, amazingly, over twenty years later was finally elected again—just in time to cast the sole vote against our entry into World War II. That put the final nail in the coffin of her political career. I think only when we take the full measure of how much the "good war" cost our society will we come to appreciate her truth telling as much as we should.

FOR FURTHER ENGAGEMENT

1. The author suggests that 12:11 may be the most important verse in Revelation: "They have conquered him by the blood of the Lamb and by the word of their testimony, for they did not cling to life even in the face of death." In light of what you know about the author's interpretation of Revelation, why is this verse so important? How do you evaluate his interpretation?

2. What do you think is meant by the "war in heaven" (12:7ff)? Is this a reference to a past or a future event?

3. Who do you think "those who dwell on the earth" are in the present day? Are you part of them? What is your attitude toward them?

4. Who are the "destroyers of the earth" in 11:18? How do you think they are destroyed? Do we have any role to play in this? How can it be that this is a "constructive" thing?

5. With regard to Rev 12:3 and later references, what kind of power does the "dragon" (identified as Satan) have in the world? How should we relate to that?

2. See West, *Radical*.
3. Smith, *Jeanette*.

6. When 11:4–6 refers to the two witnesses (likely the Lamb's community) consuming their foes with fire and having the power to strike the earth "with every kind of plague," what do you understand to be going on? What is the significance of the fire pouring "from their mouths"? What do you think of the author's assertion that "their 'weapon' is actually simply the word of their testimony" (p. 2)?

7. What is the significance that the dragon's power, in the author's words, "is no match for the power of the One on the throne and the Lamb"? How does chapter 12 show us that point? What might it mean for us today?

8. The author writes: "In Revelation, what is most important about the beast is how it defines reality and the impact of that way of defining." How do you think the beast defines reality in our world? What are parallels and differences with how Revelation portrays this "defining"?

9. What do you think of this statement: "The conversion of the nations, rather than their destruction, is God's will for the world"? What evidence from the first half of Revelation would support this point?

10. Chapters 11 and 12 both refer to the martyrdom of Christians in a paradoxical way—both as the dragon's victory over them and as the means of their victory over the dragon. Reflect on that paradox.

10

Fighting the Beast

[Revelation 13:1–14:5]

Revelation 12 ended with an ominous image, "the dragon was angry with the woman, and went off to make war on the rest of her children, those who keep the commandments of God and hold the testimony of Jesus" (12:17). What follows will tell of this "war," though we should understand that the "war" is the same phenomenon already portrayed in the plague visions. And, crucially, we also already know the outcome of the war. Revelation does not allow for any doubts about the outcome of the dragon's war. Right away in the book, back at 1:5, John affirms that Jesus is the victorious "ruler of the kings of the earth." Then, the center point of the book, chapter 5, proclaims Jesus as worthy *in the present* "to receive power and wealth and honor and glory and blessing" (5:12) as the victor.

So, whatever the impression we might get from the picture of the dragon's "war," especially in the vision of the mighty beast we see in chapter 13, this is a war that is not really a war. The outcome is not in doubt. And, as we will see, the methods of combat between the dragon's side and those "who told the testimony of Jesus" are quite different, two diametrically opposed approaches to "conquest."

REVELATION 13:1–10

And I saw a beast rising out of the sea, having ten horns and seven heads; and on its horns were ten diadems, and on its heads were blasphemous names. And the beast that I saw was like a leopard, its feet were like a bear's, and its mouth was like a lion's mouth. And the dragon gave it his power and his throne and great authority. One of its heads seemed to have received a death-blow, but its mortal wound had been healed. In amazement the whole earth followed the beast. They worshiped the dragon, for he had given his authority to the beast, and they worshiped the beast, saying, "Who is like the beast, and who can fight against it?" The beast was given a mouth uttering haughty and blasphemous words, and it was allowed to exercise authority for forty-two months. It opened its mouth to utter blasphemies against God, blaspheming his name and his dwelling, that is, those who dwell in heaven. Also, it was allowed to make war on the saints and to conquer them. It was given authority over every tribe and people and language and nation, and all the inhabitants of the earth will worship it, everyone whose name has not been written from the foundation of the world in the book of life of the Lamb that was slaughtered. Let anyone who has an ear listen: If you are to be taken captive, into captivity you go; if you kill with the sword, with the sword you must be killed. Here is a call for the endurance and faith of the saints.

We briefly met the beast back in chapter 11 where the "two witnesses" (essentially the same as those who hold the testimony of Jesus in 12:17) are warred upon, conquered and killed by the beast "that comes up from the bottomless pit" (11:7). This "bottomless pit" is first mentioned at 9:1. There, a "fallen star" goes from heaven to earth, is given a key to the shaft of the bottomless pit, and looses a plague of locusts who torture "those who do not have the seal of God on their foreheads . . . for five months" (9:4–5). These various themes will be developed more in chapter 13. The beast rises "out of the sea" (13:1). The "sea" in Revelation has an ambiguous status. It sits in front of God's throne (4:6) and is the home of creatures beyond count who worship the Lamb (5:13). Yet, here in chapter 13 it is the source of the great beast who terrorizes John's world. The "conquering" people of God stand beside the sea in chapter 15, praising God, and at the conclusion of the book, 21:1, we are told that "the sea was no more" when new Jerusalem comes down.

A couple of ideas in the background in Rev 13 may be, one, that "the sea" evokes the "bottomless pit" of 9:1 out of which tormenting locusts came (similar to the tormenting beast here) and at 11:7 where the beast is explicitly said to come "up from the bottomless pit and make war on" the witnesses to the Lamb. Two, the beast coming out of the sea might also link with the sea monster Leviathan (as in Ezek 29:3; 2 Esd 6:47–52; and 1 En. 60:7–10).

In any case, the beast is terrible and oppressive. Its ten horns and seven heads symbolize the power of domination—the antithesis of the Lamb's power. The images of wild, deadly animals (leopard, bear, lion) evoke Dan 7's portrayal of the great empires of an earlier age. Here, clearly the Roman Empire is in mind, at least as the immediate manifestation. And John makes one of the most important connections in the entire book when he writes that the beast's "power and his throne and great authority" come directly from the dragon (13:3).

John wants to write clearly to his readers. Their temptations to accommodate with the ways of the Roman Empire are actually temptations to accommodate with Satan (the implication is that just as Jesus turned from Satan's temptations early in his career, so should his followers now; note also the allusion to "Satan's throne" in 2:13). To attribute the beast's power and authority to Satan also provides more clarity about the source of the terrible plagues. God may be able to use the plagues (or at least, the plagues are not able to defeat God's purposes), but the plagues themselves come from Satan, not God.

The "blasphemous names" on the head of the beast are the same "names" that Christians give Jesus—such as "lord," "king," and "savior." What makes them "blasphemous" when used of the beast (i.e., the Roman emperor) is that they signify loyalty. The beast demands the loyalty that these "names" connote. But for John, there is only one "lord, king, and savior." To use those titles of any others is to commit blasphemy. Loyalty to the beast/dragon leads to violence and exploitation; loyalty to the Lamb/One on the throne leads to persevering love.

The beast's death and resurrection (13:3) may reflect a current widespread belief that the emperor Nero would return after death (if not in his own person, then in the person of one of his successors). The beast appears to be invulnerable. Its power is inexorable. It cannot be resisted. The whole earth follows the beast with wonder (13:3); each one having seen how the idolized head can yet rise again. And all whose hope is not ultimately in the Lamb's way have no hope except in some human system, to which either expressly or by implication they give the blasphemous name of "god."

The motif of "worship" parallels the motif of "conquest." We have seen that the One on the throne and the Lamb are worshiped by all creation due to the Lamb having "conquered." But in the "real world" of power politics, a different kind of conquering leads to worship from "the whole earth." This worship is given to the beast and, behind the beast, to the dragon (13:4). Christians should remember Jesus's temptation to "worship" Satan—to which Jesus retorted, "It is written, 'worship the Lord your God, and serve only him'" (Luke 4:7). "Worship" in Revelation connotes deep loyalty and allegiance, not simply a weekly religious ritual.

John has raised the stakes about as high as they can go. For his readers to accommodate to the empire's ways and to give the empire their consent is to be party to the blasphemous dynamics of Satan's "war" on the woman's children mentioned at the end of chapter 12. As is clear in Rev 13, such consent itself actually empowers the beast. The "power and authority" that the dragon gives the beast, we will learn, is not intrinsic power that the beast would have no matter how people responded to him. It is power "given him" by people living deceived lives, lives in which they give consent to the beast's claims to be "lord and savior." The questions, "who is like the beast, and who can fight against it?" (13:4), seem in their immediate context to be rhetorical. Given what appears to be the irresistible might of the beast, resistance must surely be futile. But when read in the larger context of the book of Revelation, this saying, "who can fight against it?" actually is a serious question and a call to action. "Who *will* fight against it?" John's answer to the question points to Revelation's message as a whole.

Revelation is an ethical exhortation. Indeed, someone *has* been found who will "fight against the beast" and open the scroll and bring healing to all creation. The appropriate response from John's readers (then and now) to the apparent might of the beast (and to the apparent might of all the great empires in human history) is to take courage, not to quake in fear or despair. The appropriate answer has already been given: The Lamb and his followers fight against the beast. They conquer by the blood of the Lamb and the word of their testimony (12:11). The beast is vicious, though. Whatever it might mean to fight successfully against the beast, it will not mean to fight with the use of greater firepower. Because the beast is "allowed" to exercise its authority for "forty-two months" (13:5), that is, three and a half years, a time period familiar in Revelation, its authoritarian ways will be manifest throughout the time of human history. These authoritarian ways will characterize the entire era.

It's not likely that by this statement about the perennial presence of the beast John offers a counsel of despair. His main intent is not to predict the future or even to guarantee a happy ending. Rather, he means to present a method for resistance to the beast and dragon. To say the beast will always be present is not to say we are doomed for the entirety of human history. It is to say that the need to follow the path of the Lamb, which does provide the means to conquer in the here and now, will always be present. So, by repeating "forty-two months" John simply finds another way to say there is only one victorious way to live (persevering love) and that will always be the case. Accommodation to empire will never be life giving.

The "it was allowed" in relation to the beast is a challenging concept. The beast "was allowed" to "exercise authority for forty-two months" and to "make war on the saints and to conquer them" (13:5–6). Does *God* "allow" this? Or is it more that humanity "allows" it by the consent it gives to empire? Since chapter 13 goes on to address the dynamics of propaganda and the gathering of consent, it seems likely that the "allowing" is done by humanity. And the antidote is to follow the Lamb (14:1–5) who actually does *successfully* fight the beast.

Revelation presents God's sovereignty in a sophisticated way in relation to the violent dynamics of the world in which we live. On the one hand, Revelation is clear: God and the Lamb *conquer*. They are the true Lords over creation. Revelation makes this point made early in chapter 1 and reiterates it throughout the book. On the other hand, the world remains a hurtful and unjust place in so many ways. How do these two elements of reality coexist? The answer lies in the nature of God's power and the method God and the Lamb use to conquer. The world is not spinning out of God's control, with only meaningless corruption and domination. However, God's way of exercising power seems weak and ineffective. Revelation calls for trust that the Lamb's way of being in the world is indeed the answer to the problem of rampant injustice.

John presents God's conquest by telling us that there is a sense in which God does not stop the powers from wreaking their havoc—hence, the Lamb opens the scroll that unlooses the terrible plagues. There is a sense that God does not stop the beast from operating. But the plagues actually are the dragon's doing, not God's. Love cannot work its powerful healing transformation if God totally controls everything. Yet the world is still in the hands of a loving God who works this transformation. John means to reassure his readers that God is not absent or defeated. Even more, though, John challenges his readers to remember that *only* the way of the Lamb is capable of actually conquering the powers.

John pulls no punches when he sketches the extent of the beast's grip: "Authority over every tribe and people and language and nation" (13:7). "All inhabitants of the earth will worship it" (13:8). Note, though, that surely these statements are rhetorical hyperbole, part of the beast's propaganda to gain humanity's consent. We already know that a countless multitude of people from "every nation, from all tribes and peoples and languages" worship the Lamb (5:9–10; 7:9).

Which claim of who actually receives the multitude's worship do we believe? This question points to the sense of "allow" in Rev 13 where human beings, by believing the beast's claim for sovereignty, *allow* the beast to exercise such destructive power. The manufacturing of this consent is the work of the second beast that we meet later in chapter 13. Who "gave" the beast its authority (13:7)? I suggest that "the inhabitants of the earth" themselves give this authority. Interestingly, historians argue that the divinizing of the Roman emperor actually originated with the people and only after recognizing its utility did the emperors themselves begin to claim divine status.

John refers to "all the habitants of the earth" whose names have "not been written from the foundation of the world in the book of life of the Lamb that was slaughtered" (13:8). With this he likely means that the "inhabitants" have rejected Jesus's way of life, trusting in violence instead of persevering love. There is a hint of determinism or predestination here, but as the plot unfolds it will become clear that God's intent is to win those inhabitants over. God does not give up on them; their fate is not sealed. John does not seem to believe that human beings are predetermined to be condemned. The message to the church at Sardis (3:5) makes it appear that the default status for any person is to be *in* the book of life. People can only be taken out should they explicitly reject God. As we will see, once the powers of evil are out of the picture even the worst of "the inhabitants of the earth," the kings, find their way into new Jerusalem—that is, they join the book of life.

The account of the first beast ends with John's exhortation to his readers to refuse to fight the beast using its own methods. "If you kill with the sword, with the sword you must be killed" (13:10). John calls for "endurance" and "faith," not retaliation. He echoes the message from the angels to the martyrs "under the throne" in 6:9–11: Be patient, trust God for justice. This call underscores the contrast present throughout Revelation between the two paths. Conquer through violence, or conquer through love.

REVELATION 13:11–18

> Then I saw another beast that rose out of the earth; it had two horns like a lamb, and it spoke like a dragon. It exercises all the authority of the first beast on its behalf, and it makes the earth and its inhabitants worship the first beast, whose mortal wound had been healed. It performs great signs, even making fire come

down from heaven to earth in the sight of all; and by the signs
that it is allowed to perform on behalf of the beast, it deceives
the inhabitants of earth, telling them to make an image for the
beast that had been wounded by the sword and yet lived; and it
was allowed to give breath to the image of the beast so that the
image of the beast could even speak and cause those who would
not worship the image of the beast to be killed. Also, it causes all,
both small and great, both rich and poor, both free and slave, to
be marked on the right hand or the forehead, so that no one can
buy or sell who does not have the mark, that is, the name of the
beast or the number of its name. This calls for wisdom: let anyone with understanding calculate the number of the beast, for it
is the number of a person. Its number is six hundred sixty-six.

A second beast arises "out of the earth" (13:11) and serves the first beast's
purposes. Perhaps the "out of the earth" signifies that this beast owes its
existence to worldly empires. It arises as their "propaganda minister" who
does the work of "manufacturing consent" through use of imagery, ideology, groupthink, social expectations, spin doctoring, and all the other ways
that the powers that be manipulate the public in order to sustain and expand
their power. This second beast, later named the false prophet (16:13; 19:20;
20:10), serves the first beast and exercises great authority on its behalf. The
picture given here underscores that the beast's "authority" is predicated on
the acquiescence of the people. The job of the false prophet is to whip up
support, shape public opinion, provide the popular ideology, and create my-
thologies that makes people *want* to give their loyalty to the beast.

John again makes it clear that the dragon's power lies behind the false
prophet's and the beast's "authority": This second beast "spoke like a dragon"
(13:11). The power behind state authoritarianism is Satan. John calls for his
readers to exercise discernment as they deal with state power. It is difficult
to see the false prophet for who he actually is because he has "two horns
like a lamb" (13:11). This is, he can look like a benevolent, even religiously
benign, force. The "worship" the false prophet empowers (13:12) could, for
those of John's readers who are tempted to accommodate with empire, seem
quite compatible with being part of the Lamb's communities.

Signs and wonders (13:13–14) can draw a gullible crowd, a crowd that
wants something to believe in and to give its loyalty to. The crowd does not
realize that the power behind the power here is Satan. Nor does the crowd
realize that the worship that is called for is not an expression of loyalty to
God and to genuine peace and wellbeing. Hence, John's claim that the false
prophet *deceives* the crowd (13:14).

The false prophet "was allowed" to do these things, I would suggest, by the consent of the people. We should also see in the background a sense of God's patience with the outworking of the dynamics of history. The effect of this consent is that the beast is "given breath"—that is, the beast is animated, given a kind of life, by the worship it receives. The image of the false prophet doing this work indicates both an awareness of the significance of the crowd giving its consent and a sense of the actual weakness of the beast. The beast and the false prophet rely on the worship from the people for their very existence. Their power rests on the people giving their consent. This worship, in turn, shapes those who give it. The "mark of the beast" (13:16) is a metaphor signifying cultural conformity. Only those who believe in the beast and swear their loyalty to it can fully function in the beast's empire (13:17).

John writes, "this calls for wisdom: let anyone with understanding calculate the number of the beast, for it is the number of a person. Its number is six hundred sixty-six" (13:18). When he gives this number, he almost certainly does not mean it to be some kind of hidden code. Surely all of his readers would have known that the beast signified the Roman Empire and its human god-emperor. John's main point is to call for "wisdom" not secret knowledge about the identity of the beast. Know that behind the signs and wonders of the empire lies the power of Satan. Don't be drawn in to giving the empire the loyalty that belongs only to the Lamb.

The actual number "six hundred sixty-six" seems essentially irrelevant, despite all the energy put into deciphering it in Christian history. In a broad sense, six hundred sixty-six likely mainly signifies the beast and his deceptions. Perhaps one way to calculate the number is to say that it is *six* in triplicate, it is not seven—seven being the number of wholeness and power. The beast claims to be the peacemaker and to have mighty power, but actually falls short of God's peace and God's power, just as six falls short of seven.

REVELATION 14:1–5

> Then I looked, and there was the Lamb, standing on Mount Zion! And with him were one hundred forty-four thousand who had his name and his Father's name written on their foreheads. And I heard a voice from heaven like the sound of many waters and like the sound of loud thunder; the voice I heard was like the sound of harpists playing on their harps, and they sing a new song before the throne and before the four living creatures and before the elders. No one could learn that song except the one hundred forty-four thousand who have been redeemed

from the earth. It is these who have not defiled themselves with
women, for they are virgins; these follow the Lamb wherever he
goes. They have been redeemed from humankind as first fruits
for God and the Lamb, and in their mouth no lie was found;
they are blameless.

The impact of the contrast between the "I saw . . ." of 13:1 and the "then I saw
. . ." of 13:11 with the "then I looked . . ." of 14:1 is lessened by the artificial
chapter division in our Bibles, a division not present in the original text. The
three phrases need to be read together. The third answers the first two. The
vision of 14:1–5 concludes the beast section. What is seen in chapter 13 only
has meaning in Revelation in light of the conclusion in 14:1–5. "I saw" the
two beasts, but then "I looked" and "there was the Lamb" (14:1). This is the
answer to the "who can fight against [the beast]" question of 13:4. The Lamb
stands as the victorious conqueror. The images that follow are full of military
allusions. The "144,000 . . . [that] have not defiled themselves with women"
(14:1, 4) represent a mustered army, ritually pure and ready for battle. And
they are well-trained: "They follow the Lamb wherever he goes" (14:4).

To understand the number 144,000 we need to go back to chapter 7.
As we saw in that chapter we have a crucial "hear one thing, see another"
vision. John *hears* "144,000" (12,000 from each of Israel's twelve tribes, a
metaphor for the people of God). Then he *sees* a countless multitude from
"every nation, from all tribes and peoples and languages" (7:9). That is, the
144,000 defines the multitude as the people of God and the multitude defines the 144,000 as symbolizing a number beyond counting. This meaning
of the 144,000, when applied to what John sees in 14:1, provides a counter
to the sense in chapter 13 of the beast having authority "over every tribe and
people and language and nation" (13:7). The 144,000 shows that the beast
does not actually have this kind of authority.

The two pictures—the multitude in 13:7, the 144,000 in 14:1—are
claims for who will win the battle for the hearts and minds of the world's
peoples. Revelation makes it clear. *Jesus*, not the beast, rules "the kings of
the earth" (1:5). So, don't believe the beast's claims implied in the visions of
chapter 13. The true conqueror is the Lamb, who in face of the beast's violent
way of conquering in chapter 13 nonetheless *stands*. "Mt. Zion" here likely
is synonymous with what will later be called new Jerusalem—the place for
God's healing work in the world.

The imagery of "many waters," "loud thunder," "the sound of harpists,"
"a new song," and "before the throne and before the four living creatures and
before the elders" (14:2–4) points back to the vision of God in chapter 4.
And that vision, as we saw, is part of a vision of a worship service that carries

on into chapter 5. That worship service has as its focal point the victory of the Lamb through persevering love and the resultant praise of the Lamb. So, 14:1–5 means to reiterate the centrality of the Lamb's faithful witness to the work of God to bring healing. These allusions directly counter the notion that the beast has ultimate power.

The statement "no one could learn the song except the 144,000 who have been redeemed from the earth" (14:3) does not refer to a small number. The idea here is not that access to this song is limited to only a few, or even that it is a difficult song to learn. Rather, the idea is that only by following the path of the Lamb—the path of persevering love—can people learn the song. Revelation teaches, on the one hand, that the song can be learned by everyone and will be learned by multitudes beyond counting. Revelation also teaches, on the other hand, that the way to learn this song is quite specific. This specificity is ethical more than doctrinal. It is not confessing a certain doctrine but confessing a certain way of life.

The allusion to non-defilement (14:4) is not meant to be taken literally as a statement about avoiding sex. It echoes prophetic references in the Old Testament that equate sexual acting out with idolatry (e.g., the book of Hosea). There is likely also in mind a sense of the warriors in the Old Testament being made ritually pure before entering into battle (e.g., Deut 23:9–14; 1 Sam 1:25; 2 Sam 11:9–13). What is crucial is to see that this purity and rejection of idolatry simply symbolize "following the Lamb wherever he goes" (14:4). The point, again, is ethical. Follow the path of persevering love as a form of "battle"—conquering as Jesus conquered, a direct contrast here with the beast's way of conquering.

HOW DO WE FIGHT THE BEAST?

As we read about the beast that rises out of the sea in Rev 13, we should remember something important about this obviously highly symbolic character. With whatever it is that is being symbolized, not everyone would see it as beastly. One person's beast might be another person's buddy. It is like my dog, little Sophie. Talk about gentle, sweet, affectionate, and kind. But to our cats, Zorro, Silver, and Ani, Sophie was most certainly *the* beast. Vicious, aggressive, loud, and obnoxious. There would have been people in Revelation's audience with a quite positive view of what John calls the beast. John's agenda, in part, is to challenge his readers to recognize the beast here as a beast. And thus, he challenges us. What is like the beast of Revelation in our world? Does this vision speak to us at all?

One of the things we get from this vision is an overwhelming sense of the beast's power. Almost certainly what John most of all has in mind is the Roman Empire—that had conquered most of John's known world, executed Jesus and many other prophets, destroyed the Jewish temple in Jerusalem, and demanded of its subjects reverence and loyalty bordering on and actually crossing the line into religious worship. The empire, it seemed, brooked no opposition. The beast is set to wreak havoc for forty-two months, a period of time we have seen often in Revelation (sometimes as three and a half years or 1,260 days). These numbers symbolize historical time, the time in the present where we live. If John's vision had ended with chapter 13, it would indeed be a vision of despair. No wonder people in John's churches would also have wanted to give the empire homage and grant it the loyalty it demanded. They likely would have felt that resistance was futile.

However, when we look at the vision in chapter 13 we need to go on to chapter 14 and ultimately to the end of the book. John does *not* mean to counsel despair. Nor does John mean to give comfort to those in his audience who don't think the beast is so beastly. Still, in John's time it would have been hard to find hope. And we struggle with hope as well. I wrote a book on the moral legacy of World War II.[1] I suggest, flowing out of that war, that we may see a strong trajectory over the past seventy-five years of more wars and rumors of wars and preparation for wars—including wars that could end life on earth. Even when we elect presidents who seem inclined to resist that trajectory, they don't. The beast of militarism only roars ever louder.

A bit over one hundred years ago, the great German social thinker Max Weber wrote despairingly about what he called the "iron cage" of technology, of impersonal "progress," of expanding corporate capitalism, that increasingly shrinks and compromises human freedom and self-determination. I think if Weber were around today, he would also add to his iron cage the dynamics of environmental disasters, present and looming in the foreseeable future. Some beast or another seems pretty powerful yet in our day. Still, John does *not* counsel despair. He counsels precisely the opposite. John seeks to empower his audience. He wants his people to be empowered to resist, to bear witness, even (remarkably) to celebrate in the present.

In stories of resistance to various beasts of the twentieth and twenty-first centuries, we see over and over how important a role celebration has played in undermining the domination system.[2] In Denmark during World War II, people gathered for public hymn sings that undermined the attempts by the Nazi occupiers to define their reality. The Black church in

---

1. Grimsrud, *Good.*
2. See Ehrenreich, *Dancing.*

the American South during the civil rights movement provided a place to praise and celebrate and find solidarity and to be reminded that the white so-called Christians did not have the power to define God's will for them. In South Africa, the anti-apartheid movement also found ways for public celebrations as did the opposition to the Pinochet regime in Chile.[3] And many, many others—probably wherever beasts have been and are resisted.

The celebrations scattered throughout Revelation play a similar role. And John promises before the book is over that the witness will be fruitful and the celebrations will not simply be whistling in the dark. They will in fact help lead to the healing of creation, healing of the nations, healing even of the kings of the earth (the human beings most enslaved to the beast). How can this be?

During the vision of chapter 13, the narrator cries out, "who can fight against the beast? Who can resist it? Who can stand against it?" In chapter 14 we get an answer. "Then I looked, and there was the Lamb, *standing* on Mt. Zion!" And standing with the Lamb are the 144,000. The Lambs fights and wins—and with him the 144,000. And they sing. And they celebrate. The apparent overwhelming power of the beast in chapter 13 actually turns out to underscore the victory and celebration of the Lamb and his followers. Things seem so bad; this makes the triumph all the more striking.

The vision of 14:1–5 transforms the meaning of chapter 13. Now we see that the beast scenes do not accurately picture reality. They show only the surface. Who stands against the beast? Who can fight against it? The Lamb and the 144,000. But who is this 144,000? This is one of those numbers in Revelation that has gone down in infamy—along with a number we see in chapter 13, the number 666. The number 666 is the number of the beast; we could say that 144,000 is one of the numbers of the Lamb.

Let's look at the six hundred sixty-six first. It is important to notice the setting. The beast, we could say, is the "anti-Lamb" (even though the actual word antichrist is not used here). With the rise of our "end times" theology in the past one hundred fifty years, many have sought to identify who this character is or will be. The Kaiser during World War I. Mussolini or Hitler during World War II. Nikita Khrushchev during the Cold War. Saddam Hussein. Notice these were all enemies of the United States. As a political progressive, I once thought I had it figured out—a world leader with six letters in each of his names. Know who I mean? Ronald Wilson Reagan. The problem is, each of these people kept dying—and staying dead. The true antichrist might seem to die, but he would recover, miraculously. No one has done this yet.

---

3. See Ackerman and Duvall, *Force*, for summaries of these stories and others.

Of course, I actually see this number much more symbolically and not about a present or future evil world leader. As I wrote above, the number 666 symbolizes something more general—human culture organized to resist God. The six is just short of the number of wholeness (that is, the number seven); three sixes emphasize the failure. This actually is not a very important symbol in the story—the main point is the beast and seeing the beast as beast, not as benefactor, regardless of what number we give it.

The number 144,000 is more important, though. Often it has been seen as a *limited* number; only we who are specially called are in; the rest of you unwashed masses are *out*. Good for us, too bad for you. But the actual meaning of this number is different. Back in chapter 7 we learned what "144,000" refers to. The 144,000 is not a limited number of specially chosen people who stand with the Lamb. The 144,000 is a countless multitude of people from all nations. This worshiping multitude vision counters the picture in chapter 13 of the beast being given authority over "every tribe and people and language and nation" (13:7). The beast's authority actually is an illusion—because the Lamb *can* stand against it. The Lamb can fight against it. So can the Lamb's followers. Celebration and healing are present, not despair and an irresistible iron cage.

The use of 144,000 in chapter 14 has an added dimension. The 144,000 is an army. Organized, actually, to *fight* the beast. But—and this is a huge "but," this is the "but" that determines our view of what the entire book is about—they are organized not to fight with swords but to fight with the same weapons as the Lamb, self-giving love. We need to remember the master vision of the whole book: Rev 5. The Lamb is the one who can open the scroll, not as a mighty warrior but as a self-giving healer. So, then, the meaning of our passage, 13:1—14:5 is a call to resist and a reminder that indeed such resistance does work. And the passage gives us guidance for this fight. How do we fight? Let me note three clues.

First, simply see the beast as beast. Remember, many in John's audience took comfort in dividing their loyalty between the Lamb and the empire. They did not see the empire as beastly. Likewise, many Christians throughout history have willingly joined their nations' call to war and preparation for war. They also divided their loyalties. John's exhortation is to *disbelieve* in empire. Disbelieve in militarism. Disbelieve that might makes right. Don't give consent. Recognize the beastly dimension for what it is and recognize that to affirm the beastly element, to give it a blank check, places everyone in great jeopardy. The message does not mean to assume the worst about every element of one's country. But it is a call to discernment. Twenty-first century America is not totalitarian; but it does all too often cross the line into being beastly in all too many ways. The challenge to followers of the Lamb, I think, is consistently (and constantly) to keep *his* way in mind when we face claims for our loyalty. We can appreciate the *non*-beastly things, but we must not let them lead us to become too comfortable and too complacent with beastly elements.

A second clue is to note that the myth of redemptive violence fuels an ongoing spiral of perceived wrongdoing followed by retaliation followed by more retaliation and more retaliation. When those who resist the wrongdoing take up the sword, only the sword wins. So, this is John's message: Refuse the sword. Break the cycle of violence. "Let anyone who has an ear to hear listen: If you are to be taken captive, into captivity you go; if you kill with the sword, with the sword you must be killed. Here is a call for the endurance and faith of the saints" (13:10). Recognize that retaliation feeds the beast—so break the spiral. You don't resist the beast in its deepest reality with violence. Such "resistance" leads to a victory for the beast, even if it may lead to the overthrow of a particular earthly king. Again, let me invoke World War II. The long-term effect of that war shows that while the specific Nazi and nationalist Japanese sword-bearers were indeed defeated, the sword itself, not genuine peace, ultimately won that war.

The third clue is to band together to sing and follow the Lamb. The 144,000 (the countless multitude) stand with the Lamb. They make a sound like that of many waters, like the sound of harpists playing on their harps, and they learn a new song. They are "redeemed from the earth" to celebrate. Or, we could say, they are freed from the domination of the beast in order to embrace life. And this happens *during* the forty-two months, this happens right now. Every time we celebrate life and healing and resistance and genuine peace, we join in this "new song."

Let me end this chapter with an example of "standing" from the wonderful Harry Potter books. I believe these books tell a powerful story of creative nonviolence and the power of self-giving love that gain victory in the battle against the myth of redemptive violence and empire. The hero, Harry, throughout his first six years at Hogwarts School and in the following year of going underground, resists the evil Lord Voldemort and many other authority figures who try to undermine his resistance. He suffers quite a bit, sometimes feeling quite isolated but never actually wavering. One of his friends, Neville, does always support Harry but through most of the story Neville is pretty inept and lacks self-confidence.

When Harry goes underground and Voldemort takes over control of the school, Neville leads the resistance—with great effectiveness. Harry returns for a final confrontation, not knowing much of what Neville has been doing. When they meet, Neville is beaten, bloody, but absolutely unbowed. Harry is stunned, and impressed, to learn all that Neville and his allies have been doing as they stood up to the oppressive teachers Voldemort had installed. As Neville tells of the resistance and suffering, Harry says, "Blimey, Neville, haven't you taken too many chances?" No, Neville says. "The thing is, it helps when people stand up to them, it gives everyone hope. I used to notice that when you did it, Harry."[4] Stand up to the beast—in all its forms. That gives everyone hope.

FOR FURTHER ENGAGEMENT

1. What are some implications for saying that the dragon's (or, Satan's) power is behind the beast's power? If, as the author writes, it is true for John that his readers' "temptations to accommodate with the Roman Empire are actually temptations to accommodate with Satan," how might that notion apply to present-day followers of Jesus? How parallel are John's Roman Empire and our USA? What do you think might be "satanic" about our culture?

2. How would you compare God's power and Satan's power? Is the difference only that one is stronger? Or are they different kinds of power? How can we discern this today?

3. Do you agree with the author about a "political" reading of Revelation 13? Do the images here have any relevance in the present-day United States? How about present-day Russia or China? The present-day European Union? Is it related to all countries, no countries, or some particularly problematic countries?

4. Do you agree that the only authority the beast has to exercise on earth is that which people themselves give it? If that is so, what are the implications with regard to resisting that authority?

5. Reflect on the implications of "following the Lamb wherever he goes" (14:4) for resisting the beast's demands reflected in chapter 13? Does Jesus's exemplary way of life have any relevance for present-day political life (meaning our present-day relation to and involvement in our nation's political life)? If so, what?

6. What present relevance do you see in the author's description of the second beast? "It arises as their 'propaganda minister' who does the work of 'manufacturing consent' through use of imagery, ideology, groupthink, social expectations, spin doctoring, and all the other ways

4. Rowling, *Harry*, 574.

that the powers that be manipulate the public in order to sustain and extend their power."

7. How persuaded are you by the author's interpretation of 14:1–5? "The Lamb *stands* as the victorious conqueror . . . . The 144,000 defines the multitude as the people of God . . . . Revelation makes it clear Jesus, not the beast, rules 'the kings of the earth' . . . . Follow the path of persevering love as a form of 'battle'—conquering as Jesus conquered." Explain.

8. Where supporters of the empire saw conquest as the basis for Roman legitimacy and invincibility, John makes it a hallmark of Roman tyranny. How comfortable would you be with applying this perspective of John's to the United States? Explain.

9. Americans do not literally "deify" their national leaders, but it does seem that many American Christians tie their patriotism and their faith closely together. Do you see a latter-day "false prophet" at work in this aspect of present-day Christianity? Why or why not?

11

How to Read Revelation

[Revelation 14:6–20]

Chapter 13 concludes with a call to wisdom (13:18). This chapter's picture of the beast and the false prophet dominating the world reflects the perspective many of John's readers would have had. Some would have welcomed the empire's kind of "peace" and sought to accommodate themselves to its ways and protect themselves from the consequences that are alluded to with the beast "making war on the saints" (13:7). Others may have still believed in resisting the beast but would have despaired of fighting "against it" (13:4). So, the call to wisdom is crucial. The beast might simply destroy the witness of the Lamb's assembly—either by crushing the resisters or, more likely, by converting them to an accommodating approach to faith where the beast and the Lamb seemingly coexist.

John wastes no time, though, in countering the temptation to accommodate or despair. Of course, the content in Revelation that leads up to chapter 13 gave powerful reasons not to take that vision as definitive of the actual situation. The Lamb already has been identified as the ruler of the kings of the earth. He is worthy to be worshiped by all creation and the one who brings healing to countless multitudes from all corners of the earth. Chapter 14, then, actually does not provide the antidote to the beast's claims so much as reiterate what has already been asserted—but with new depth. The first section of the chapter actually completes the vision of the beast and false prophet, as we saw above. It asserts that the Lamb and his community

of "144,000" will be able to fight, successfully, against the beast. The chapter
then goes on with several visions of judgment.

REVELATION 14:6–13

Then I saw another angel flying in midheaven, with an eternal
gospel to proclaim to those who live on the earth—to every nation and tribe and language and people. He said in a loud voice,
"Fear God and give him glory, for the hour of his judgment has
come; and worship him who made heaven and earth, the sea
and the springs of water." Then another angel, a second, followed, saying, "Fallen, fallen is Babylon the great! She has made
all nations drink of the wine of the wrath of her fornication."
Then another angel, a third, followed them, crying with a loud
voice, "Those who worship the beast and its image, and receive
a mark on their foreheads or on their hands, they will also drink
the wine of God's wrath, poured unmixed into the cup of his
anger, and they will be tormented with fire and sulfur in the
presence of the holy angels and in the presence of the Lamb.
And the smoke of their torment goes up forever and ever. There
is no rest day or night for those who worship the beast and its
image and for anyone who receives the mark of its name." Here
is a call for the endurance of the saints, those who keep the commandments of God and hold fast to the faith of Jesus. And I
heard a voice from heaven saying, "Write this: Blessed are the
dead who from now on die in the Lord." "Yes," says the Spirit,
"they will rest from their labors, for their deeds follow them."

As with the plagues earlier in the book, we should read the judgment scenes
in Rev 14 in light of the book's overall message. John provides an angle of vision for understanding the true character of the Roman Empire (and other
human empires). The Roman Empire rests on a foundation of violence and
injustice even if there is a modicum of peace and harmony in the experience
of many Romans. John also wants to emphasize the negative consequences
for those of his readers who might give in to the temptation of offer Rome
the kind of allegiance it demands, allegiance that John believes cannot be
compatible with following the Lamb's way.

Most fundamentally, though, John seeks to encourage his readers with
the promise that indeed the Lamb's way is the way of the Creator. Following
this way is the path to life. This promise ultimately is for all human beings
as well as for the rest of creation. Whatever sense of punitive judgment the

visions might give, the point remains that all that happens is somehow subsumed under the overarching reality of God's healing love.

As it will turn out, the "destroyers of the earth" who are to be destroyed are the *spiritual* forces of evil. The structures of systemic violence and ideologies of domination and oppression will be destroyed, not the human beings who might align with those powers. However, John also indicates that human beings who might align with those powers are living in mortal peril. God will not force them to turn toward life. Hence, part of the urgency may be seen in the spiraling intensity of John's visions. This urgency stems from John's sense that those among his readers who are tempted to give their loyalty to empire must turn away, or they might indeed become that which they worship and thereby share the evil powers' fate.

John sees three angels who give one version of the dynamics of judgment, probably the most direct portrayal of these dynamics in Revelation. First, crucially, he sees an angel that proclaims "an eternal gospel . . . to every nation and tribe and language and people" (14:6). And we know from chapter 7 that in fact this gospel is received and embodied throughout the world by an uncounted multitude. We do *not* hear a pro forma "proclamation" that justifies punitive judgment (in the sense that since the people "hear," they can therefore justly be punished). Rather, the angel's proclamation affirms one of Revelation's basic truths: The eternal gospel is proclaimed and is embraced.

The call to worship (14:7) comes from the first angel and follows on the heels of the vision of the victorious Lamb in 14:1–5. This is not worship that is evoked by fear and displays of God's overwhelming might. It is worship evoked by the persevering love of the Lamb and of those who follow the Lamb wherever he goes (14:4). Then John sees a second angel. This angel briefly confirms what the juxtaposition of the vision of the beast with the vision of the triumphant Lamb implies: "Fallen, fallen is Babylon the great! She has made all nations drink of the wine of the wrath of her fornication" (14:8). We will learn more about this assertion in the chapters to come.

Though the statement of its fall is the first mention of "Babylon" in Revelation, we may assume that John's readers would have immediately recognized the reference to one of ancient Israel's worst enemies. Significantly, this first mention proclaims Babylon's fall. It is not invincible after all. Ancient Babylon destroyed the temple and the kingdom of Judah just as the present Roman Empire had done. Both empires may be identified with the beast. Babylon as a metaphor, though, ranges more widely than the historical Rome. "Babylon" likely alludes to any human empire that regularly sheds the blood of prophets (18:24).

That Babylon means the beast is made clear when John asserts that Babylon has made the nations drink the "wine of her fornication." This graphically describes what John referred to in chapter 13 when he wrote of the beast being worshiped by "every tribe and people and language and nation" (13:7). As he already made clear with his reference to the Lamb *standing* (14:1), John asserts that the beast/Babylon does *not* stand. Babylon falls. We will learn much more about that process of "falling" in the chapters to come. Just as the Lamb's ability to "stand" follows from his persevering love to the point of death (5:5), so we will learn that the blood of the saints causes Babylon to fall (17:6).

We best understand the troubling imagery of torment linked with the third angel's cry (14:9–11) as mainly rhetorical, not a literal description of what *will* happen. Given what has come before and what will follow after this, it is impossible to understand "the smoke of [the] torment . . . forever and ever" as the actual fate of all those who worship the beast (14:11). This graphic picture will be described as applying to the spiritual forces of evil that God destroys, the dragon, the beast, and the false prophet (19:20; 20:10). The best way to read 14:9–11 is to see these verses as a hyperbolic warning to John's readers: The consequences will be terrible should you put your ultimate trust in the empire and its values and ways of life.

We will learn more about what is meant by "the wine of God's wrath" in the verses to follow. To understand this image, we will need to recognize the centrality of the shedding of the blood of Jesus and his followers to the process of judgment and salvation (remember the victory of 12:11, won through the blood of the Lamb and the word of his followers' testimony). As well, we should remember that "wrath" in Revelation generally has the sense of the processes of life. Those who live in harmony with God's love become whole, and those who trust in the way of the sword will likewise be transformed into violent, fearful, alienated people.

John intends to draw a contrast between those who are persecuted by the beast because they refuse its mark (13:15) and those who suffer God's wrath because they accept its mark. In light of the message of Revelation as a whole, we should see this contrast as the difference between those who are able to worship and embrace life and those for whom life becomes a burden, a source of fearfulness and self-destruction. The beast "conquers" with violence against those who refuse his mark. The Lamb "conquers" with persevering love that is perceived as something to be afraid of and to avoid by those who accept the beast's mark.

After the three angels speak, John reiterates the point of their messages: "A call for the endurance of the saints, those who keep the commandments of God and hold fast to the faith of Jesus" (14:12). And we should remember that one of the fruits of that endurance will be the healing of the nations and the presence in new Jerusalem of the transformed kings of the earth (21:24). John intends his readers to desire that healing and transformation, not to take delight in the possibility that some of those aligned with the dragon might remain alienated from life to the very end. The fruit of such "endurance"—which is another way of saying, the fruit of following the Lamb wherever he goes and conquering the beast through the means of faithful witness—is blessing and rest (14:13).

REVELATION 14:14–20

> Then I looked, and there was a white cloud, and seated on the cloud was one like the Son of Man, with a golden crown on his head, and a sharp sickle in his hand! Another angel came out of the temple, calling with a loud voice to the one who sat on the cloud, "Use your sickle and reap, for the hour to reap has come, because the harvest of the earth is fully ripe." So the one who sat on the cloud swung his sickle over the earth, and the earth was reaped. Then another angel came out of the temple in heaven, and he too had a sharp sickle. Then another angel came out from the altar, the angel who has authority over fire, and he called with a loud voice to him who had the sharp sickle, "Use your sharp sickle and gather the clusters of the vine of the earth, for its grapes are ripe." So the angel swung his sickle over the earth and gathered the vintage of the earth, and he threw it into the great wine press of the wrath of God. And the wine press was trodden outside the city, and blood flowed from the wine press, as high as a horse's bridle, for a distance of about two hundred miles.

Chapter 14 concludes with two harvest visions, first of grain and second of grapes. The reaper of the grain harvest is "one like the Son of Man." "Son of Man" links the reaper with Jesus (this phrase is used of Jesus in 1:13). The harvest visions seem to picture judgment (as in Hos 6:11 and Mt 13:30, 39). The meaning here is not totally clear, the reaping is simply described. But since it is Jesus, most likely the idea is to portray salvation, the "judgment" of the followers of the Lamb to be found worthy to join him in paradise (see 2:7; 21:7).

The grape harvest is more complicated, and variously interpreted. Is it a scene of punitive judgment? I'd suggest not. There are good reasons to see the grape harvest as another way that John portrays the style of conquest characteristic of Jesus and his followers. Jesus achieves victory through faithful witness and persevering love even to the point of shed blood and death. Crucially, the "shed blood" comes from Jesus and his followers, not their human enemies.

The reaper in the grape harvest vision is not Jesus but an angel (14:17). That the angel reaps suggests something similar to angels that participate in the plague visions described in chapters 5–10. Likely, the grape harvest, like the plague visions, portrays the present time where followers of the Lamb conquer the evil powers through their persevering love. Such a path may lead to their blood being shed. Evoking the martyrdoms of 6:9, we are told in 14:17 that the second angel "came out from the altar."

The angel reaps the ripe grapes and throws them "into the great wine press of the wrath of God" (14:19). As we learned from the plague visions, the "wrath" may be understood as the outworking of the rebellion of humanity against God. We might also add, from chapter 13, the notion that when humans worship the beast, they empower his conquering. These dynamics call for persevering love from the Lamb's followers, not for retaliation (13:9–10)—a hope for healing rebellious humanity, not punishing it.

We have another reference here that supports the interpretation that the grape harvest is a picture of bloody consequences to the Lamb and his followers as they resist the beast with their persevering love. We are told that "the wine press was trodden outside the city" (14:19). This "outside the city" image was used in Heb 13:12–13 to refer to Jesus's death. Certainly, the model of Jesus's faithful witness that led to his blood being shed reinforces the sense that John uses "blood" here as a symbol for the entire process of "conquering" the dragon "by the blood of the Lamb and by the word of [the comrades'] testimony" (12:11).

The final image in the harvest scene is extraordinarily gruesome. "Blood flowed from the wine press, as high as a horse's bridle, for a distance of about two hundred miles" (14:20). This is a picture of terrible excess. But what does it mean? We are not told directly where the blood comes from. It would be out of character in relation to the rest of Revelation to see this blood as the blood of God's enemies. Every other reference to "blood" in the rest of the book refers to the blood of Jesus or his followers. Nowhere are we told of any other blood being shed. So, most likely in 14:19–20 as well, the "blood" is that of Jesus and his followers.[1]

The excess here should be seen to underscore the importance of the way of life that Jesus embodied and called upon his followers to imitate. I

1. This view of the "blood" in 14:19–20 is not held by most commentators. However, it is not unusual. I first encountered it in Caird, *Commentary*, 192. Among those who have followed Caird are: Johnson, *Discipleship*, 264; Smalley, *Revelation*, 377; Sweet, *Revelation*, 232; and Wright, *Revelation*, 134.

suggest we link the picture here with the vision in chapter 7. The picture there is also of excess, "a great multitude that no one could count . . . [that] have washed their robes and made them white in the blood of the Lamb" (7:9, 14). It would take a lot of blood to wash that many robes! Perhaps the excessive quantity of blood needed for the worship in chapter 7 is what John sees in 14:20.

Finally, we will learn later that in fact the blood of Jesus and his followers turns out to be the precise means that are used to bring Babylon down. Chapter 17 will picture Babylon as a great harlot that "was drunk with the blood of the saints and the blood of the witnesses to Jesus" (17:6). Then, in the next chapter we read how the nations "have drunk of the wine of the wrath of her fornication" (18:3), after which Babylon fall when she drinks "a double draft [from] the cup she mixed" (18:6). The "wrath" that John has in mind with "the great wine press of the wrath of God" alludes to the dynamic during the "three and a half years" of historical existence where the powers resist God in ways that lead to the powers' own demise. When Jesus and his followers give up their lives in loving resistance to the powers, they play a crucial role. God uses their witness to help destroy the destroyers of the earth and to bring ew Jerusalem down as the place of healing.

So, we need to take all the language in Revelation about "conquering" seriously. It is central to the picture John paints of faithful living in a world of domination. Jesus conquers through his faithful witness and his followers share in the conquest with their faithful witness. And this "faithful witness" is bloody. It involves living lives of nonviolent resistance to the empire's hegemony. At points such resistance leads to suffering, even, perhaps, to death. The book promises from the very beginning, though, that such witness is vindicated and that Jesus indeed is "ruler of the kings of earth" (1:5).

HOW TO READ REVELATION

In our all-too-violent world and in our-all-too-violent Christian religion we who seek to follow the Lamb can't afford to squander our amazing resource for peace—the Bible in general and the book of Revelation in particular. Peacemakers, instead of a superficial dismissal of unsettling biblical texts, should (like Jacob of old) wrestle with them until those texts give us blessings. I suggest we take what I like to call a "jiu jitsu" approach to biblical interpretation. Jiu jitsu is a form of martial arts. "Jiu" means "gentle, flexible, or yielding." "Jitsu" means "technique." So, "jiu jitsu" is a gentle technique of self-defense that uses the opponent's force against itself rather than confronting it with one's own force.

Let us allow the difficult, seemingly "pro-violence," texts of the Bible to swing away at us, but step inside the punches and use those very texts as part of our peacemaking repertoire. Such an approach will help us get a blessing when we read Revelation. This jiu jitsu technique will work with a difficult metaphor in chapter 14, the metaphor of "blood." People of good will often are put off by violence in the Bible. Years ago I led a Bible study. We finished with one of the Gospels and somebody suggested we discuss a book from the Old Testament next. One elderly woman protested, "I don't want anything more to do with that bloody book!" I think for her, "blood" signified violence and punishment, the angry and hurtful Old Testament God. She'd had enough of that. I suspect our protester would have said the same thing had someone suggested we study Revelation. Many of the commentaries on Revelation agree that the blood here at the end of chapter 14 indicates God's punishing judgment.[2] The blood that flows "from the winepress as high as a horse's bridle for a distance of about two hundred miles" shows just how widespread God's retribution will be.

I'm impressed with how easy it is for interpreters to assume the worst about chapter 14's grape harvest vision. They seem to forget that this same book also reports the vision of the Lamb's self-giving love in chapter 5 and the vision of the *healing* of the nations in chapters 21 and 22. These interpreters seem to find it obvious that "blood" symbolizes death and punitive judgment. They seem to find it obvious that the God of Revelation of course responds to wrongdoing with massive retaliation and that the universe according to Revelation rests on retributive justice. Some are horrified by this theology that they see in Revelation and reject it.[3] They think Revelation is bad news. Others, such those involved in the Left Behind books and movies, *welcome* this kind of bloody theology—they embrace the idea of God as punisher and see Revelation as a key source.[4]

I once had a mentor who thought this way. We had many discussions about pacifism. He insisted that though Jesus himself in his life was peaceable, both the Old Testament and Revelation give us pictures of a violent God who may well call upon God's people to join in the fight and shed blood. That argument stimulated me to try to understand Revelation for myself—and led to my discovery that Revelation actually is about peace and not violence. We can see that Revelation is *not* about violence if we focus on this most troubling of metaphors—the blood flowing from the wine press in

2. See, for example, several otherwise peaceably oriented studies: Blount, *Revelation*, 281; Koester, *Revelation*, 630; and Krodel, *Revelation*, 276.

3. See Keller, *Apocalypse,* and Kirsch, *History.*

4. See LaHaye and Jenkins, *Left*, the first in a series of novels on the "future" that draw heavily on Revelation.

chapter 14. This is not the first time the image of blood is used in Revelation. Let's look at some of the other places that speak of blood.

The beginning of Revelation tells us about Jesus (1:4–6). He's the faithful witness who followed a path of nonviolent love that resisted the powers and led to his execution. He is described as well as the firstborn of the dead. His life was vindicated when God raised him. Because of his witness and God's vindication of him, he is also described as the true ruler of the kings of the earth. Then we are told that he loves us and frees us from the power of sin by his *blood*, by his ministry as faithful witness. He's a faithful martyr whose life of patient, nonviolent resistance shows the path toward liberation.

The exact same point is made again in chapter 5. Jesus, the executed and resurrected Lamb is the true Lion of Judah (that is, the Messiah) who "stands as if it had been slain" (5:5). He has the power to open the great scroll, the scroll that tells of the ultimate victory of God. Countless creatures then worship Jesus as God, a powerful image of his divinity and of how his life revealed the character of God. "By your blood" you freed a multitude (5:9).

Yet a third time, in chapter 7, the same exact point is made again. Here we have an amazing vision of the 144,000 who are actually a countless multitude who find healing amidst the terrible plagues. They praise God and the Lamb. Who are these multitudes? "These are the ones who come out of the great ordeal; they have washed their robes and made them white in the *blood* of the Lamb" (7:14).

And finally, in chapter 12, "blood" is mentioned one more time. John emphasizes again the faithful witness of the Lamb to the point of crucifixion. And in this witness comes the strength to break free from the powers' death-dealing grip and find wholeness. Those who trust in God's ways "have conquered [the dragon] by the *blood* of the Lamb and by the word of their testimony, for they did not cling to life even in the face of death" (12:11).

So, "blood" signifies Jesus's *life*, and other lives lived in solidarity with his, the willingness to stand against violence and oppression, and for compassion and shalom. Such an approach to life leads to some kind of cross, resistance from the powers-that-be, self-sacrifice or, in Gandhi's term, self-suffering. "Blood," then, is not retributive violence from God. It does not signify death and is not about God punishing those who are found to be outside the narrowly defined boundaries of doctrinal or ritual "truth." In fact, "blood" signifies *life* for the multitudes and the ultimate healing of the nations and even the healing of the kings of the earth. It signifies the battle that was already won in Jesus's faithful living and guarantees that healing is God's final word.

Chapter 14 follows the terrible vision of the beast from chapter 13. The beast embodies the domination system of power politics, nationalism, and "victory" through brute force. The people cry out, "Who can fight against the beast?" We get the answer right away: The Lamb who stands along with the 144,000 (that is the great multitude of chapter 7 who follow the Lamb) is victorious against the beast (14:1). The Lamb wins due to what many translations call "patient endurance" but could just as well be translated "nonviolent resistance," the path of love and compassion followed consistently in face of the beast's terrors.

These who follow the Lamb wherever he goes have no lies in them (14:5), which is a coded way to say that they do not bow down to the beast. They are freed to be "first fruits for God and the Lamb" (14:4). As first fruits, they model nonviolent resistance that plays a sacrificial role. The sacrifice is self-sacrifice (not an appeasing sacrifice to a punitive God). It shows the path to healing and breaks the hold of the powers on people's imaginations. The beast only has power given to him by people's trust. When people believe in the beast's picture of reality, the beast has power. When people don't believe the beast, it is powerless.

In his book *Two Cheers for Anarchism*, political thinker James C. Scott emphasizes just how important throughout history simple refusal of consent to the powers-that-be has been. Stepping out of the elite's coerced consensus gums up the works and makes the mechanisms of domination impossible to sustain.[5] This refusing consent could be seen as a kind of living as "first fruits"—refusing to give the beast the worship he demands because such worship leads to death not to life.

After seeing the Lamb and the 144,000, John sees "another angel flying in midheaven" (14:6). This angel brings the gospel to "every nation and tribe and language," a gospel with three parts—first the proclamation of the healing mercy of God, healing that has already been praised in the book and will find its final fruition in new Jerusalem. But a second element is also required—the fall of Babylon the great. Babylon will be presented as the enemy of God and God's people that demands and receives loyalty and honor and commitment from "all nations." Babylon as spiritual power must be taken down for the human beings enslaved by it to be freed.

The third element of the gospel focuses on those human idolaters. Those who "worship the beast" suffer terrible consequences (14:10–11). I think we need to read this part of the vision not as an ironclad statement of what will happen to specific people so much as a warning. The picture of terrible consequences for those who worship the beast says that it is costly

5. Scott, *Two*.

when we give our trust to the beast. Later, in new Jerusalem, we learn that at least some who worship the beast are healed. But the Bible, Ps 115 for instance, reminds us that we take terrible risks when we do give worship to idols. We can't be sure we'll be able to turn back. "Their idols are silver and gold, the work of human hands. They have mouths, but do not speak; eyes but do not see. Those who make them are like them; so are all who trust in them" (Ps 115:4–8).

John's main concern, though, is not with those outside the churches who trust in the beast. He actually has hope for them once the hold of the beast is broken. He mainly cares about church people who try to go along with the ways of the beast and also maintain a Christian identity. This can't be done, John insists. He warns them of possible self-inflicted torment should they remain loyal to the beast. The message for us here is not encouragement to speculate about what kind of punishments await the heathen. It's rather a challenge to our churches: Are you giving loyalty to the American empire, loyalty that belongs instead to the Lamb?

The chapter concludes with two "harvest" visions. The first is a harvest of grain gathered by "one like the Son of Man." This harvest is Jesus gathering his people for the "wedding supper of the Lamb" that we will see in chapter 19, the celebration that leads to the coming of new Jerusalem. The second harvest is more complicated; how we understand it will depend on what we think the blood metaphor refers to. In light of how Revelation uses "blood" elsewhere—to speak of Jesus's life of persevering love and nonviolent resistance, I think what we have here is another image meant to encourage followers of Jesus to faithful witness. The angel "came out from the altar"—linking back to the image of the martyrs under the altar in chapter 6. The grapes are harvested and thrown into "the great wine press of the wrath of God" that was "trodden outside the city"—a reference to the location of Jesus's crucifixion. Later, we will read of the great harlot (another symbol for Babylon) drunk on the blood of the saints (17:6). And it is this "blood" that will lead to Babylon's downfall (18:6).

What all these images tell us is simple, even if they are messy and complicated. Jesus is our model. He lived his life as a faithful witness, a witness whose commitment to nonviolent resistance led to his death. His life and death, vindicated by resurrection, are what the symbol "blood" refers to. The picture here in Rev 14 means to show that this "blood" of Jesus, joined by the "blood" of his followers, is the very means by which God brings about the world's healing. We see the same dynamic in the two great martyrs of the twentieth century: Mahatma Gandhi and Martin Luther King. Their nonviolent resistance shows the only way our world can move toward healing.

Now, perhaps the most gruesome aspect of this vision is that the blood "flowed . . . as high as a horse's bridle, for a distance of about two hundred miles" (14:20). This is too much blood even to imagine and is a terrible image if we think of it as signifying punitive violence. But it actually signifies something else. Remember back in chapter 7, the 144,000 turns out to be a countless multitude whose robes are made white in the blood of the Lamb. The idea with this bridle-high blood, I think, is that the self-sacrificial love of Jesus and his followers is abundant enough to heal the countless multitudes!

Revelation emphasizes strongly the link between Jesus's self-sacrificial love and the self-sacrificial love of his followers. John's *main* agenda in Revelation is to encourage his readers to follow Jesus's path. This is the path Jesus spoke of in one of his great parables: the path of giving drink to the thirsty, food to the hungry, friendship to the lonely, care for the sick, clothing to the naked, and companionship to the imprisoned—on all occasions, since all people in need are, in a genuine sense, Jesus himself.

So, if we keep Jesus at the center, we will learn how to read Revelation. We will be enabled to see how even the troubling image of "blood" actually reiterates Jesus's main message: Love God and neighbor no matter what. What on the surface seems like a picture of God's punitive judgment in 14:19–20 becomes, upon a more careful reading, another powerful image for the healing work of Jesus and his followers.

FOR FURTHER ENGAGEMENT

1. Summarize and critique the author's discussion of 14:17–20. Strengths and problems? Before you read him, how did you think of these verses? He concludes: "Most likely in 14:19–20, 'the blood' is that of Jesus and his followers. The excess here should be seen to underscore the importance of the way of life that Jesus embodied and called upon his followers to imitate."

2. Once again, the author uses the argument, "we should read the judgment scenes in Rev 14 in light of the book's overall message." How valid is that argument, do you think?

3. Reflect on the call to worship that the angel gives in 14:7. What do you think he had in mind? How might this translate into our present context? Think about the two mentions of worship in this section (14:7 and 14:9). What is being implied by the contrast between worshiping God and worshiping Babylon? Again, think also about our present context.

4. What might it mean to worship the beast (14:9–11) in our world today? What are the cutting edges in the struggle between God and Satan for people's loyalty? Do you find the church (and yours in particular) a help or hindrance in this struggle? How could it help more?

5. Notice that the first direct reference to Babylon in Revelation alludes to its fall. Why might that be important for how Revelation presents Babylon? If our *first* thought of Babylon is of its fall, how might that shape how we think about Babylon's presence in our world today?

6. How adequate of a summary of the gospel do you think Revelation 14:6–12 is with its three elements as summarized by the author: (1) The proclamation of the healing mercy of God; (2) the fall of Babylon; (3) the fate of the human idolaters?

7. The author suggests, "we best understand the troubling imagery of torment linked with the third angel's cry (14:9–11) as mainly rhetorical, not a literal description of what *will* happen." How does that suggestion sit with you? What do you think of the idea of God tormenting forever and ever those who worship the beast?

8. Where do you stand on the symbolism of the term "blood"? In Revelation, is it mainly about Jesus's own life and death as a model of persevering love (or, "nonviolent resistance") or a mixed image that also can allude to God's punitive judgment? Try to unpack the possible meanings of "blood" in 14:17–20.

9. Is it believable to you that suffering and martyrdom could be important means used by God to destroy evil? If so, how does that belief affect how you live?

12

Transforming Babylon

[Revelation 15 and 16]

After the visions of judgment that in actuality focus on Jesus's self-giving love in chapter 14, we turn to chapter 15 for the final series of plagues. Though Revelation gives a sense of progression that moves from the seal plagues in chapter 6 through the trumpet plagues and now to the bowl plagues, we best see the different plague series as three angles on the same picture. They do not actually portray three separate sets of events but rather portray a deeper sense of urgency in relation to the one "event." This single set of "events" is not actually one specific historical moment but a symbolic way of referring to the "three and a half years," that is, the entirety of the time between Jesus's life and the final end. The urgency has to do with the necessity, in John's view, of faithfulness to the way of Jesus as the only way his readers might successfully navigate life in the Roman Empire.

REVELATION 15:1–4

Then I saw another portent in heaven, great and amazing: seven angels with seven plagues, which are the last, for with them the wrath of God is ended. And I saw what appeared to be a sea of glass mixed with fire, and those who had conquered the beast and its image and the number of its name, standing beside the sea of glass with harps of God in their hands. And they sing the song of Moses, the servant of God, and the song of the Lamb: "Great and amazing are your deeds, Lord God the Almighty! Just and true are your ways, King of the nations! Lord, who will not fear and glorify your name? For you alone are holy. All nations will come and worship before you, for your judgments have been revealed."

As the book does earlier when it recounts various plague and trauma visions, here also it gives us a powerful vision of celebration amidst the plagues. One of our big questions in interpreting Revelation is how we understand the relationship between the plagues and the celebrations. I suggest, given the self-identification of the book as a "revelation of Jesus Christ," given the centrality to the entire book of the vision in chapter 5 of the Lamb receiving the scroll, and given the ending vision of new Jerusalem that portrays an amazingly inclusive sense of healing, we should see the celebrations as the fundamental reality and interpret the plagues in light of the celebrations, not vice versa.

We get regular celebratory visions throughout Revelation (4:1–5:14; 7:9–17; 11:15–19; 12:10–12; 14:1–5; 15:2–4; 19:1–10). They offer a constant reminder that the plagues are actually part of God's healing work. The visions do not picture autonomous punishment where God's retributive justice wreaks vengeance on wrongdoing as an independent, self-contained part of God's victory, the punitive judgment side separated from the mercy side. To the contrary, God's relationship to the plagues is part of God's mercy. God used them as part of the healing work to the point that even the worst of God's human enemies, the kings of the earth, find healing and end up in new Jerusalem.

John sees seven angels whose presence brings God's wrath to its fulfillment (15:1). The immediate consequence of the fulfillment of God's wrath is the song of celebration that links with the sight of these angels. The song in 15:2 carries on from the vision in chapter 14 that referred to the "144,000" that follow the Lamb wherever he goes, to the need for the saints to endure, and to the blood that flows from the wine press (which we will see later brings down the great harlot). This victorious song comes from "those who had conquered the beast." All of these figures—the "144,000," the "saints," the bloodshedders, and now the conquerors are all the same people. They gain the victory in the same way Jesus did: persevering love.

The song points to the reasons for everything Revelation tells about. The God of justice, "King of the nations," is the one whom "all nations" will worship. *This* outcome is the fruit of the work of the Lamb and the faithfulness of the Lamb's followers: The nations will be healed and will worship rather than blaspheme God. Thus is borne out the hope of 1:5 (that Jesus is the "ruler of the kings of the earth") and the promise of 21:24 (that the "kings of the earth" will bring their "glory" into new Jerusalem).

The song unites the stories of salvation from the Old Testament ("song of Moses") with those from the New Testament ("song of the Lamb"). These two songs together make up *one* song. This song celebrates God's healing love that generated all of the healing elements of the biblical story from Abraham through Jesus. The biblical salvation events are all variations on the one theme of a merciful God who: (1) respects humanity's freedom, (2) patiently displays love that cannot be defeated, and (3) heals and transforms those who trust and live in light of that love. We must remember this song when we think about the plagues that follow in chapter 16.

The plagues, paradoxically, are portrayed in various places in Revelation as the work both of the dragon and of the One on the throne. Ultimately, they serve healing, even the healing of God's greatest human enemies, "the kings of the earth." They are not to be read as acts of autonomous, end-in-itself, punishment. Nor are they to be read as random acts of destruction that happen outside of God's providential care and the movement of history toward healing.

To say that God's wrath is "ended" with these plagues is not to say that God's anger is completed with the total punishment of all of God's enemies. To the contrary, perhaps we best understand the "end" of God's wrath here as the completion of God's ways of using the dynamics of human freedom, the influence of the powers of evil, and the effect of allowing consequences to work themselves out to lead to the ultimate healing of creation. This process "ends" with the ultimate destruction, not of the worst human enemies of God (the "kings of the earth") but with the destruction of the evil powers that lead human beings astray. And, in fact, what follows in chapters 17–20 will detail how those evil powers will be destroyed.

REVELATION 15:5–8

> After this I looked, and the temple of the tent of witness in heaven was opened, and out of the temple came the seven angels with the seven plagues, robed in pure bright linen, with golden sashes across their chests. Then one of the four living creatures gave the seven angels seven golden bowls full of the wrath of God, who lives forever and ever; and the temple was filled with smoke from the glory of God and from his power, and no one

could enter the temple until the seven plagues of the seven angels were ended.

After the singing of the song of Moses and the Lamb and before the outpouring from the seven bowls that chapters 16 recounts, John sees a picture of the angels that bear the bowls as they emerge from "the temple of the tent of witness in heaven" (15:5). The angels are given the bowls from "one of the four living creatures." To understand the meaning of this picture we need to review some of what we have seen earlier in Revelation. We first met the "four living creatures" back in chapter 4 in John's first vision after he saw the door into heaven opened and was shown the great throne room. Those creatures worship the One on the throne. Here in chapter 15, they seem to be agents of the One on the throne.

In the celebration that follows the Lamb being given the great scroll in chapter 5, the four living creatures sing "a new song" in celebration. They are described as each one "holding a harp and golden bowls full of incense which are the prayers of the saints" (5:9). Then in the first series of plagues that follows the seals of the scroll being opened, "those who had been slaughtered for the word of God" as they cry out from "under the altar" and ask how long before God's justice vindicates their "blood" (6:9–11). Finally, in chapter 8:3–5 we read of an angel with "a golden censer" standing at the altar being given incense to burn along with the "prayers of the saints" that will rise "before God."

So, 15:5–8 seems to make the point that the vindication of the faithful followers of the Lamb is at hand. The faithful lives and the ongoing prayers of the followers of the Lamb are powerful. They are shown to motivate God to complete the work of the "wrath." Note, again, the connection between the healing work of the Lamb emphasized throughout the book but especially in chapter 5 and the outworking of God's "wrath." The four living creatures join in "a new song" as an immediate response when the Lamb receives the scroll due to the Lamb's self-sacrifice. Here in chapter 15, we learn of a song of celebration that repeats the same content of chapter 5's song: "All nations will come and worship before you." The role of the followers of the Lamb in all of this is simply to follow the Lamb's way. When they follow, they imitate his self-sacrificial love, perhaps even to the point of death. The consequence, we will learn, is that God's restorative justice will bring healing to "all nations."

REVELATION 16:1–11

Then I heard a loud voice from the temple telling the seven angels, "Go and pour out on the earth the seven bowls of the wrath of God." So the first angel went and poured his bowl on the earth, and a foul and painful sore came on those who had the mark of the beast and who worshiped its image. The second angel poured his bowl into the sea, and it became like the blood of a corpse, and every living thing in the sea died. The third angel poured his bowl into the rivers and the springs of water, and they became blood. And I heard the angel of the waters say, "You are just, O Holy One, who are and were, for you have judged these things; because they shed the blood of saints and prophets, you have given them blood to drink. It is what they deserve!" And I heard the altar respond, "Yes, O Lord God, the Almighty, your judgments are true and just!" The fourth angel poured his bowl on the sun, and it was allowed to scorch people with fire; they were scorched by the fierce heat, but they cursed the name of God, who had authority over these plagues, and they did not repent and give him glory. The fifth angel poured his bowl on the throne of the beast, and its kingdom was plunged into darkness; people gnawed their tongues in agony and cursed the God of heaven because of their pains and sores, and they did not repent of their deeds.

Revelation 16 describes all seven of the final set of plagues, the "bowl plagues," in which seven angels pour out onto the earth "the wrath of God" (16:1). Unlike the partial destruction that the two early series of seals and trumpets plagues describe (in turn, one-quarter and one-third—perhaps the thunder plagues that were "sealed up" and not reported [10:4] would have told of one-half destruction), here the destruction is total ("*every* living thing in the sea died," 16:3, emphasis added).

With the seventh plague "a loud voice came out of the temple, from the throne, saying 'It is done!'" (16:17). Note that John's reporting of the "revelation of Jesus Christ" is not done. We still have six more chapters in Revelation and several important visions to go. But this is the final plague and the expanding circle of destruction has reached its climax. The dynamics of wrath and destruction have reached their culmination here. As with other scenes of plagues and apparent judgment, also with the plagues in chapter 16 we need to think of them in relation to the outcome of Revelation's revelation of Jesus Christ. We also need to remember the core visions we have already considered, especially chapter 5's vision of the triumph of the Lamb, before we draw conclusions about what this chapter communicates.

The "loud voice from the temple," almost certainly God's voice, tells the angels to "pour out on the earth" bowls of the "wrath of God" (16:1). We should read this description in light of what we have already discerned about God, the plagues, and wrath. We are again going to have described for us the dynamics on earth during the "three and a half years" where the dragon and his minions are wreaking havoc, but not in a way that will actually defeat God. The "loud voice" of God sets the angels loose to pour out their bowls. To say it this way allows some distance between God's actual *direct* involvement on earth and the outworking of God's "wrath." We see God's direct involvement in the witness of Jesus and his followers. God's "wrath" is best seen as more impersonal, an indirect unfolding of cause and effect in a moral universe.

The plagues that follow echo the plagues visited upon Egypt in the story of the exodus. We have been prepared for this by numerous allusions to the exodus earlier in Revelation and, most immediately, with the vision at the beginning of chapter 15. There we read of "those who had conquered the beast" (presumably the countless multitude of Rev 7) who sing "the song of Moses, the servant of God, and the song of the Lamb." They proclaim the greatness and justness of God's deeds that will bring "all nations [to] come and worship before [God, whose] judgments have been revealed" (15:3–4).

The plagues in Exodus had been but a prequel to the blessing of salvation offered the children of Israel. These people of God were a first fruit of the blessing of all the families of the earth. We may infer likewise here that the plagues in chapter 16 that echo the exodus plagues serve God's "just deeds" of blessing all the families of the earth and evoking their worship. The actual plagues that occur when the bowls are emptied are quite similar to the exodus plagues, though each has its own distinctiveness. The first five plagues reflect the dynamic that "God's wrath" is indeed a cause-and-effect series of consequences: Accept the mark of the beast, worship its image, and now get "a foul and painful sore" (16:2). "Shed the blood of saints and prophets" and your "rivers and . . . springs of water . . . become blood" (16:4, 6). "Curse the name of God" and the sun will "scorch people with fire" (16:9).

The effect, though, as we saw earlier in chapter 9, is that these plagues do not lead to repentance (16:11). In what follows here through the end of chapter 18, we will not be given contrasting visions that point to God's actual way of bringing about repentance and healing (the persevering love of the Lamb and his followers). The message in chapters 16 through 18 has to do with the fall of the dragon's kingdom.

However, we know by now that the "purpose" of the plagues is not to be God's method of inspiring repentance. From the picture at the beginning of this plague vision (15:3–4) we do know that God still works to bring healing that will evoke worship from "all nations." This series of visions through the end of chapter 18 pictures the destruction of the destroyers of the earth. These "destroyers" are the spiritual forces of evil. Their destruction will allow the kings of the earth who join with the forces of evil to war against the Lamb ultimately to find healing. That there is no repentance here as the bowls are poured out simply reinforces how powerful the hold the dragon has on human society. The dragon needs to go down before widespread repentance will happen.

The cry of the angel in 16:5–7 reminds John's readers of the means God uses to bring justice. As we saw in chapter 14 and will see more clearly in chapters 17 and 18, the dragon's acts to "shed the blood of saints and prophets" will lead to the dragon, et al., "drinking blood" that is a poison to them. The dragon is not defeated by the Lamb's people shedding blood per se but by their willingness to live as faithful witnesses even to the point of having their own blood shed. This point is reinforced by the response of the altar, echoing 6:9–11: "Yes, O Lord God, the Almighty, your judgments are true and just!" (16:7).

REVELATION 16:12–16

> The sixth angel poured his bowl on the great river Euphrates, and its water was dried up in order to prepare the way for the kings from the east. And I saw three foul spirits like frogs coming from the mouth of the dragon, from the mouth of the beast, and from the mouth of the false prophet. These are demonic spirits, performing signs, who go abroad to the kings of the whole world, to assemble them for battle on the great day of God the Almighty. ("See, I am coming like a thief! Blessed is the one who stays awake and is clothed, not going about naked and exposed to shame.") And they assembled them at the place that in Hebrew is called Harmagedon.

The sixth bowl plague underscores the dragon's efforts to corrupt the kings of the earth. John sees "three foul spirits like frogs coming from the mouth of the dragon, from the mouth of the beast, and from the mouth of the false prophet" (16:13). "These are demonic spirits, . . . who go abroad to the kings of the whole world, to assemble them for battle on the great day of God the Almighty" (16:14). This is a statement both of the actual nature of the ideologies that shape the politics of the kings of the earth ("demonic spirits") and of the main focus of that politics ("assembling for war"). That the spirits come "from the mouths" of the three evil powers signifies the deceptive words they proclaim and underscores that the battle in Revelation is indeed fought with speech.

Read carefully, though, this vision gives a glimmer of hope for the kings of the earth and the nations. Their corrupt politics are fueled by the deceptive message they get from the dragon and his cohorts. The source of militarism, of economic exploitation, and of imperialism is not the inherent character of human political life, nor the sinful nature of the kings of the earth. The dynamics of domination in some sense come from outside. We may hope that as those spiritual forces are "destroyed," their hold on humanity will end and that kings and nations might be set right, healed, and in harmony with God's will for humanity.

It will be crucial as the story reaches its completion that we notice what becomes of this assemblage gathered for battle. We get a hint already. The battle will happen on "the great day of God the Almighty" (16:14). Surely the dragon and the others do not have in mind this kind of "great day" as they join their forces. As it turns out, the great day when it comes will not involve an actual "battle" but only the capture and destruction of the "destroyers of the earth."

The forces that gather to do battle, with all their dynamics of power-over, death-dealing force, and fearfulness, will not set the terms of the actual battle. God does not gather a similar battle force in order to overpower the forces opposed to God with physical force. This should not surprise us. Several times we have been told of God's victory, the way God "conquers" (and how God's people are to conquer), and the weapons that provide the means to conquer. It has been persevering love and the willingness to witness to the way of the Lamb even to the death (see, most clearly, 12:11). We will see in chapter 19 that the actual "great day of God the Almighty" reinforces that message.

In the midst of the picture of the forces of the dragon gathering for "battle," we get an interruption, presumably from the "loud voice" of 16:1, a call to "stay awake and remain clothed" (16:15). We best understand this interruption as a reminder not to let the methods of the dragon determine how God's people respond. Don't be shaped by the dragon's seeming power; don't let the dragon's seeming power determine how you understand power. Do not respond to the sword with the sword. Remember the message throughout of the Lamb's victory through persevering love. That will be all we need. The allusion to "remain clothed" echoes the exhortation to the assembly at Laodicea (3:14–22). The clothing in Laodicea is to be "white robes," the symbol throughout the book for those who follow the Lamb and conquer the way he does.

"Harmagedon" (NRSV) or "Armageddon" (KJV, NIV) is not an actual place. Nor is there ever going to be a "battle of Armageddon." The reference alludes to ancient battles (see Judg 5:19; 2 Kgs 23:29–30). Probably John means here to underscore the self-deception of the dragon and his minions that thinks there actually will be a battle. They will gather at Armageddon simply to be captured and destroyed—not to fight.

REVELATION 16:17–21

> The seventh angel poured his bowl into the air, and a loud voice came out of the temple, from the throne, saying, "It is done!" And there came flashes of lightning, rumblings, peals of thunder, and a violent earthquake, such as had not occurred since people were upon the earth, so violent was that earthquake. The great city was split into three parts, and the cities of the nations fell. God remembered great Babylon and gave her the wine-cup of the fury of his wrath. And every island fled away, and no mountains were to be found; and huge hailstones, each weighing about a hundred pounds, dropped from heaven on people, until they cursed God for the plague of the hail, so fearful was that plague.

The final plague signals the end of the plagues. The final plague will be described in great detail in chapters 17 and 18. The "great city," that is "great Babylon," is not forgotten by God (16:19). As will be stated in the longer story of Babylon's fall to come, God's method of taking down the great city is the "wine-cup of the fury of God's wrath" (16:19). We know this "wine-cup" to be the process of the faithful witness of the Lamb and his followers as they turn the system of domination on its head ("they have conquered . . . by the blood of the Lamb and by the word of their testimony, for they did not cling to life even in the face of death," 12:11).

The various portents here, lightning, thunder, an earthquake "such as had not occurred since people were upon the earth," portents that split the great city into three parts, islands fleeing away, and huge hailstones, all symbolize the significance of the completion of God's work. They are not to be taken literally and are not in the far-off future. In their midst, people are not destroyed but "curse God" (16:21). As history unfolds, the dynamics of love that fight domination lead too many to mistake God's compassion and care for a curse. Again, it will take the destruction of the destroyers of the earth to free people from such deception.

TRANSFORMING BABYLON

We get mixed messages about love. When asked to identify the greatest commandment, Jesus said, it's to love (Matt 22:37). Probably if we were asked what was the most important emphasis for Martin Luther King, we'd say it was love. He called one of his most famous books, *Strength to Love.*[1] And yet it also seems that love is looked down upon. It certainly doesn't seem to come up much when we talk about social policy and social problems, gun violence, economic inequality, terrorism, climate change. When we talk about social issues we tend to use "realistic" language—power, coercion, justifiable violence, finding a seat at the table, self-interest, just desserts. Love may seem sentimental, naïve, emotional, soft. Nice for life on a personal level (perhaps), but not very central as we negotiate social life, not very useful for the work of social justice and social order.

I've read a couple of books that bear this out. Michael Burleigh in his book on World War II, *Moral Combat*[2], and Jean Bethke Elshtein in her book on the American wars in Afghanistan and Iraq, *Just War Against Terror*[3], both write about values and moral standards. However, neither devote any space to love. In the "real world," love seems to be irrelevant. But is it? Have the violent strategies with which the "realists" deal with conflict and wrongdoing actually enhanced human life?

This is a challenging question, given all the terrible things that go on in our world. At the very beginning of World War II, W. H. Auden wrote what became a famous poem called "September 1, 1939"—the day Germany invaded Poland and Britain and France declared war on Germany. Auden realized this was a world-changing moment. He laments: "I and the public know, what all schoolchildren learn, those to whom evil is done, do evil in return." He concludes with the poem's most famous line: "We must love one another or die."

Now, as it turned out, Auden repudiated his poem and especially its final line. He rarely allowed the poem to be reprinted. One time he allowed its reprinting but left that line out. I suppose he thought that it showed him to be too sentimental and weak. After all, what was necessary to stop the Nazis according to the moral consensus after the war was brute force, not love. But

1. King, *Strength.*
2. Burleigh, *Moral.*
3. Elshtain, *Just.*

still, did the Nazi spirit truly lose that war? Was Auden's plea for love refuted? I tend to think not. In fact, were we to summarize the life work of Martin Luther King in just a few words, this phrase, "we must love one another or die" would work pretty well. But we live in a world not all that friendly to love—look at what happened to King, shot to death at the age of thirty-nine.

I think Rev 15 and 16 may be helpful for us as we think about love and the "real world." What we have here is the third of three terribly destructive sets of seven plagues. Each set has gotten worse. First, we read of terrible destruction that brings death to one-quarter of the earth; then, the destruction comes to one-third of the earth. And now, here, in chapter 16, "*every living thing in the sea died.*"

We should not read these visions with precise literalism. Right after we read these visions of death to everyone in Rev 16, the story goes on with people still living in the next chapter. The tales of destruction should be read symbolically. They symbolize the ongoing reality of human life. People die in wars and famine, empires and nation-states wreak havoc, the earth itself is exploited and polluted and poisoned. The brokenness, the alienation, the attempts at domination and control, the conflicts, the corruptions, wars and rumors of war, all stretch back over most of the past two thousand years.

So, John simply reports on human experience in history, not on some future apocalyptic moment or moments. John does not predict a future spiral of three sets of plagues in three moments in time that just get worse and worse. Rather, the movement from one-quarter to complete is rhetorical. It's a way to make a point about how seriously John wants his readers take these problems that plague humanity. He increases the stakes each time in order to grab his readers' attention. These visions *truly* matter.

Let's remember why John writes. He wants his readers, the seven congregations addressed in chapters 2 and 3, to be aware of what kind of world they live in—and what kind of response God wants from them. Many of John's readers are comfortable and relatively secure. They find ways to prosper in their world. But to do so, they must embrace the spirituality of empire and give loyalty to Caesar. John thinks this embrace is tragic. Few of his readers perceive the oppression and destructiveness of the Roman Empire. They themselves do fine; they don't notice the backs upon which the empire is built and rests: the slaves, the oppressed and exploited, the empire's enemies, and souls that the empire destroys for its own gain. Remember the words of the Laodicean congregation: "I am rich, I have prospered, and I need nothing" (3:17).

Even worse, people so oblivious to the actual situation fail to be agents of healing and compassion. They fail to live as heirs of Abraham and Sarah, who were called by God to parent a people who would bless all the families of earth. They fail to live as heirs of Moses, who God called to lead slaves into freedom. They fail to live as heirs of Jesus, the prince of peace. John shares these visions of the terrible reality of actual life in the world in order to challenge his readers to respond to their calling: no to empire, yes to transformative compassion.

Our keys to understanding the bowl plagues come at their beginning and in the third bowl plague. First, we notice the opening picture to these visions. The people of God, those who have conquered the beast, stand by the sea (15:2). Revelation told us earlier *how* they conquer: "By the blood of the Lamb and by the word of their testimony [when] they did not cling to life even in the face of death" (12:11). Remember the key image in chapter 5 of the Lamb, "standing as if slain" worshiped by multitudes from "every tribe and language and people and nation" (5:9). These who stand next to the sea sing the song of Moses and the Lamb. The song praises the justice and truth of God that has these results: "*All nations* will come and worship before you" (15:4, emphasis added). In whatever follows, the purposes of God are joy, healing, solidarity, and celebration.

Of course, what follows with the plagues hardly seems joyful and celebrative. But we should read what follows carefully and not jump too quickly to conclusions. What's going on is the working out of God's "wrath." God's wrath is not the direct finger of God. In fact, the powers of evil (the dragon, beast, and false prophet) are the ones directly responsible for the plagues. But they do not thwart God's purposes in the long run.

God's method is persevering love. We see such a method in the third plague in chapter 16: "The third angel poured his bowl into the rivers and the springs of water, and they became blood. I heard the angel of the waters say, 'You are just, O Holy One; you have judged these things; because they shed the blood of saints and prophets, you have given them blood to drink. It is what they deserve!' And I heard the altar respond, 'Yes, O Lord God, the Almighty, your judgments are true and just!'"

There is something here that may seem surprising, though not if we know how to read Revelation. Notice what happens to the ones who "shed the blood of saints and prophets." What *should* happen to them? You would expect that their own blood would be shed—they should be killed by the sword, it would seem "just" for them to die by the sword. But that is not what happens. Instead, "they are given [the] blood [of the saints and prophets] to drink." What a strange punishment! But let's remember how the metaphor of "blood" works in Revelation. All the people in our day who dismiss Revelation as bloody and violent and vengeful, its "cultured despisers," seem never to have noticed the way "blood" actually is used in the book.

As I have reported above, the only blood that is ever shed in Revelation is the blood the Lamb sheds or the blood his followers shed. Blood is not an image used of punishment. Blood signifies persevering love. Blood is not an image used of God's retaliation. Blood is an image used of the non-retaliation of the Lamb and his followers. Their persevering love actually proves to be the very force that takes down the powers and brings in new Jerusalem. So, in the third bowl plague, saints and prophets are those who witness to life as Jesus did. And, like Jesus, they suffer consequences for doing so. They have their blood shed—the very blood that the powers "drink." And this *defeats* the powers. The prophets and saints conquer by the blood of the Lamb and the word of their testimony, for they do not cling to life even in the face of death.

We will learn more in Rev 17 and 18 about what happens when "they" drink the blood of the saints and prophets. For now, though, the key point is simply to remember that 15:4 tells us that God's purpose is the healing and worship of the nations. Knowing this purpose should govern our reading of everything in Revelation.

In Revelation's portrayal of the domination system, these plagues and most obviously the massive, oppressive corruption in chapter 13, actually have nothing on the American South of the 1950s. In my reading of Taylor Branch's three excellent books on Martin Luther King's life and work[4] I was impressed, as much as anything, with just how oppressive and violent that world was (and continues to be—see Michelle Alexander's book, *The New Jim Crow*[5]), way worse that I had imagined. This is the "real world" at its worse. The American South of the 1950s was a situation of unbearable systemic violence and oppression that crushed the human spirit. The Jim Crow system had to go down. But how could that happen without a terrible bloodbath?

Revelation makes the point that resistance by the sword only furthers the power of domination. Almost always, the powers-that-be benefit from violence. There is a terrible story about the resistance in Czechoslovakia during World War II. Some in the movement wanted to assassinate Reinhard Heydrich, the leader of the Nazi occupation. But those who were in Czechoslovakia actually argued against it. They said it would be counterproductive and only strengthen the oppressors. However, some assassins backed by the British government entered the country and did kill Heydrich. The consequences were disastrous, as Czech citizens had warned. The

---

4. Branch, *Parting*; *Pillar*; and *Canaan's*.

5. Alexander, *New*.

Nazis killed thousands in retaliation.[6] The resistance movement that had been doing a lot of good was smashed. The heightened spiral of violence strengthened the oppressors and crushed the resisters.

In Revelation, in fascinating imagery, the powers of evil (the dragon, the beast, the false prophet) through the use of foul spirits like frogs coming from their mouths to "go abroad to the kings of the whole world, to assemble them for battle" against God (16:14)—the battle of Armageddon. The powers want a war. They spew forth words of war agitation. They know that this will serve their purposes and make it certain that the kings stay on their side and do not defect to God. This is the brilliant insight W. H. Auden had in 1939—even if he could not retain the courage of his convictions: We must love one another or die. The power of hatred and violence can only destroy. The dragon rejoices at any big war, not matter how "just" it is claimed to be, because the winner in all wars is the way of death.

Martin Luther King learned this lesson from Gandhi and from his own experience. The only way the actual enemies (which are the powers of injustice, racism, domination) could truly be overcome was through love. The path of love in face of hatred is costly but is still the only path that will bring healing. King knew that the white racists in the South and the people they hurt were in a crisis that could only be resolved if they came together. This crisis that could only be resolved with a method of conquest that allowed the enemy to win too. And it's an amazing story, or, more accurately an amazing beginning of a story that still needs to be completed. To realize just how entrenched and violent was the regime of segregation is to realize how incredibly courageous and effective King and his colleagues were. They insisted on a path of nonviolent resistance—a path they could follow only in the strength of love.

This path of nonviolent resistance that opens the possibility of victory for both sides is precisely what Revelation will go on to tell about. Chapter 19 tells of when the battle of Armageddon does come—but it is not actually a battle. The only blood that is shed in that vision will be from Jesus. He wins not by shedding his enemies' blood but by making them, in effect, "drink" his. And the consequence, we will see, is that the kings of the earth and the nations they lead win too. They are not destroyed but healed (21:24; 22:2).

Martin Luther King, like Jesus, "won" not by greater firepower but by persevering love that allowed for conversion even while making ongoing violent domination impossible. Of course, King's victory was only partial. Way too many problems remain.

---

6. Beevor, *Second*, 435.

What might Revelation have to say about this victory being only partial? One way to read Revelation is as a promise for full victory in the end. The partial victories are foretastes of the great, complete victory to come. I'm not quite sure what I think of this promise. But I can say with confidence that even if we should interpret Revelation to be a bit ambiguous about where everything will all end up, even if we shouldn't be too confident about a happy ending, still we should see that Revelation tells us urgently about the one and only path that will lead to a happy ending if we are to have one. To find healing from the destructive plagues, if the nations are truly to be healed, will only come by following the path of the Lamb. Martin Luther King got that exactly right. John intensifies his plague visions in Revelation to make this point: It always becomes ever *more* important to follow the Lamb.

FOR FURTHER ENGAGEMENT

1. Reflect on the author's discussion of the relationship between the celebration and plague visions in Revelation. What do you think he has in mind when he writes, "we get regular celebratory visions throughout Revelation [that] help us keep front and center that the plagues are actually part of God's healing work"? Do you agree? Explain.

2. What does it mean that "all nations will come to worship before you" (15:4)?

3. Compare the seals, trumpets, and bowls series of plagues to each other. How are they related in the whole scheme of the book?

4. To what does the conquering of the beast refer (15:2)? Who are the persons who have conquered? Where? When? How? Does this contradict 13:7? What is the basis for the affirmation in 15:2 that God's people have "conquered the beast"? Does their "success" have implications for our struggles versus modern-day "beasts"?

5. What do you make of the connection 15:3 makes between the song of Moses and the song of the Lamb? Is John making a statement of the unity regarding redemption in the Old Testament and in the New? Do you see unity or contradiction between the OT and NT? What can *we* learn from the "song of Moses" (i.e., the Exodus) that's relevant for our struggle with the dragon and beast?

6. Do people "curse" God (cf. 16:9,11) today? Why do they? What is your attitude toward them?

7. What is your emotional reaction to the account of the seven bowl plagues in chapter 16? What role might these plagues play as (like the plagues in Exodus) but a prequel to the blessing of salvation offered all the families of the earth"?

8. The author states that there will never be a "battle of Armageddon." What do you think he means—do you agree? Explain.

9. The author notes that instead of being killed by the sword, the "ones who have shed the blood of saints and prophets" are "given blood to drink" (16:5–7). He suggests that this indicates that "persevering love actually proves to be the very force that takes down the powers." What do you understand his argument to be here? Evaluate it.

13

Seeking the Peace of the City

[Revelation 17]

We read at the end of chapter 16, "God remembered great Babylon and gave her the wine-cup of the fury of God's wrath" (16:19). Now, in chapters 17 and 18, the details of that "remembrance" will be presented. One of the bowl-plague angels comes to John to take him to see the "judgment of the great harlot" (17:1). We should note that it is presumably the same angel who will later come again to John to take him to see "the bride, the wife of the Lamb," that is, new Jerusalem (21:9). The same exact wording is used in both places, indicating that these two visions should be understood in relation to one another. These are the two destinations that John holds out for his readers—trust in the dragon and end up in fallen Babylon or trust in God and end up in new Jerusalem.

REVELATION 17:1–6

Then one of the seven angels who had the seven bowls came and said to me, "Come, I will show you the judgment of the great harlot who is seated on many waters, with whom the kings of the earth have committed fornication, and with the wine of whose fornication the inhabitants of the earth have become drunk." So, he carried me away in the spirit into a wilderness, and I saw a

woman sitting on a scarlet beast that was full of blasphemous
names, and it had seven heads and ten horns. The woman was
clothed in purple and scarlet, and adorned with gold and jewels
and pearls, holding in her hand a golden cup full of abominations and the impurities of her fornication; and on her forehead
was written a name, a mystery: "Babylon the great, mother of
harlots and of earth's abominations." And I saw that the woman
was drunk with the blood of the saints and the blood of the witnesses to Jesus. When I saw her, I was greatly amazed.

We have a central symbol that refers to another symbol. The "great harlot"
refers to "great Babylon." Clearly John does not have in mind an actual prostitute. And by the time of this writing, the ancient city of Babylon no longer
existed. Probably the main source for the metaphors is the Old Testament.
Already in the Old Testament the two images of Babylon and prostitution
were each used to signify the social embodiments of idolatry, rebellion
against God, violence, and injustice.

On the immediate level, John surely means to apply these symbols to
Rome, the "city of seven hills" (17:9) that "rules over the kings of the earth"
(17:18). Rome, who promises peace and insists that it operates with divine
favor, stands as the most profound temptation for John's readers. Those
in the congregations that John most vociferously opposes apparently suggested that followers of Jesus may also function as comfortable actors in
the Roman world—including taking part in the requisite public expressions
of acquiescence to Roman civil religion. The worship moments scattered
throughout Revelation are meant to counter that acquiescence.

As we read this account today, we may recognize that it voices a broader critique than just alluding to the first-century Roman Empire. Babylon,
formerly a great empire but by John's time a distant memory, worked metaphorically to provide insight into the character of the Roman Empire. Likewise, for us, Rome, also formerly a great empire but now a distant memory,
works metaphorically to provide insight into the character of present-day
empires. Most obviously for most readers of this book, the "Babylon" metaphor will evoke the American empire.

Part of what evoked expressions of fealty to Rome, along with its claims
that it served "peace" and "justice," was Rome's great and irresistible power.
The vision of the beast in chapter 13 reflects a sense of that power: "Who can
fight against it?" (13:4). John's agenda has been to counter that feeling about
Rome's greatness. Rome did not serve God but served the powers of evil. To
link Rome with Babylon would signal to John's readers, biblical people that
they were, that the current empire is in continuity with that terrible empire
from the past. Like Babylon, Rome also destroyed the Jerusalem temple.

And, even worse, Rome executed Jesus as a political rebel. In fact, Rome, like Babylon, rebelled against God.

To add to the effect, John adds a new symbol: Babylon/Rome is not an entity of grandeur but in fact a simple harlot. In chapter 17, John means to evoke disgust from his readers, a sense of repulsion. The flash and apparent glamour of Rome are actually superficial impressions that mask deep-seated corruption and rottenness. The use of "harlot" (I prefer this term because being archaic it feels a little less personal) or "whore" or "prostitute" for John's purpose may have been effective as part of his critique of Rome. And we should read the allusion as a social and political metaphor. However, "harlot" certainly is not an innocent metaphor. It tragically reinforces hurtful stereotypes concerning women. I choose to focus on the meaning I understand John to give to the symbol in this context, but I also believe it is a very unfortunate metaphor whose liabilities outweigh its positive value as a useful symbol for us today. We would do well to find other metaphors to convey the message, for example, that today's American empire is built on disgusting violence and injustice even as it claims to be worthy of obedience and loyalty.

It is true that the Old Testament commonly used the metaphor of "harlot," both of those societies who opposed God (e.g., Isa 1:21; 23:16–17; Nah 3:4) and of elements within Israel that sought after gods other than Yahweh (e.g., Hos). We should recognize that Rev 17 intends to convey a political message. It is not that women or sex or even literally prostitution is the problem. The problem is a political system built on the backs of the exploited poor and vulnerable. That system threatens to transform the core values of the community of Jesus's followers with its notion of "conquest" through domination.

The "fornication" that the kings of the earth commit with the great "harlot" probably involves all the various ways human kingdoms violate and exploit. However, the reference to "the wine of [their] fornication" likely links "fornication" most directly to violence against those who stand for genuine justice, especially the Lamb and his followers. We have read already about the "wine" as a symbol for "blood," most especially the blood shed by Jesus and his followers (14:17–20); the link is made explicit at 17:6: "The woman was drunk with the blood of the saints and the blood of the witnesses to Jesus." Later, at 18:24 we read that in Babylon "was found the blood of prophets and of saints, and of all who have been slaughtered on earth."

"The inhabitants of the earth have become drunk . . . with the wine of [their] fornication" as well (17:2). This fact reflects the successful work of the false prophet to gain widespread public support for the dynamics of imperial domination. The notion of being "drunk" points toward deception. Both the kings of the earth and the inhabitants of the earth are being deceived. On the one hand, they are identified here as being profoundly complicit with the works of Babylon. They share in Babylon's status as rebels against God. On the other hand, though, that they are "drunk" and deceived carries with it a hope that they could "turn" (repent) and recognize God as God should they break free from the deception. We will learn that after Babylon goes down and the spiritual forces of evil are destroyed, in fact such a turn happens (21:24).

A link between the harlot and the bride, we will learn, is that both are "adorned with gold and jewels and pearls" (17:3; see 21:18–21). However, the harlot sits "on a scarlet beast" (almost certainly the same as the beast of chapter 13) and holds "a golden cup full of abominations and the impurities of her fornication" (17:4). This cup again alludes to the violent dynamics of empire. This is "Babylon the great, mother of harlots and of earth's abominations, ... drunk with the blood of the saints and the blood of the witnesses to Jesus" (17:5–6).

The problem here is not false religion, per se, but political dynamics of domination and exploitation. At the heart of the political order characterized by such dynamics is ruthlessness toward all who resist (remember the political meaning of the Roman practice of crucifixion—public torture, humiliation, and death in order to maintain social order).

So far in this vision, John reiterates the portrayal of the beast in chapter 13. John emphasizes the beast's overwhelming power but adds an additional dimension of disgust by bringing in the imagery of harlotry. The beast seems overwhelmingly great, but also seems irredeemably evil and not to be sympathized with or acquiesced to. However, between chapter 13 and now, we have seen visions that reemphasize the Lamb's victory over the powers, and we have also traced the denouement of the plague dynamics that express the beast's power—and lead ultimately to the beast's demise. We now turn to the demise.

REVELATION 17:7–14

> But the angel said to me, "Why are you so amazed? I will tell you the mystery of the woman, and of the beast with seven heads and ten horns that carries her. The beast that you saw was, and is not, and is about to ascend from the bottomless pit and go to destruction. And the inhabitants of the earth, whose names have not been written in the book of life from the foundation of the world, will be amazed when they see the beast, because it was

and is not and is to come. This calls for a mind that has wisdom: the seven heads are seven mountains on which the woman is seated; also, they are seven kings, of whom five have fallen, one is living, and the other has not yet come; and when he comes, he must remain only a little while. As for the beast that was and is not, it is an eighth, but it belongs to the seven, and it goes to destruction. And the ten horns that you saw are ten kings who have not yet received a kingdom, but they are to receive authority as kings for one hour, together with the beast. These are united in yielding their power and authority to the beast; they will make war on the Lamb, and the Lamb will conquer them, for he is Lord of lords and King of kings, and those with him are called and chosen and faithful."

The angel who shows John this vision now gets to the point: The beast is about to go to its destruction (17:8). The details of the vision are complicated and hard to decipher. We do learn that "the inhabitants of the earth" will be "amazed" when they see the beast go down (17:8), hinting that their fate is not inevitably to go to destruction with it. We do not get a definitive picture of what happens to "the inhabitants of the earth." Most likely, their fate is linked with the fate of "the kings of the earth" (i.e., ultimate healing once the beast is gone).

Precisely what John means with the account in 17:9–12 of the kings is probably beyond our ability fully to unravel. The general idea is clear, though. The beast unrelentingly opposes the Lamb and gains the support of many kings who unite "in yielding their power and authority to the beast" (17:13). And these kings join the dragon and beast in "making war on the Lamb" (17:13). The "mystery" that John cares about here is not the identity of the beast; surely his readers knew that already. Rather, he means to reiterate once more that the beast and the kings who yielded their authority to the beast serve the dragon, not God. Once more John challenges his readers to discern where their loyalty belongs.

The bottom line is that though the beast gathers all the kings and their authority to wage war on the Lamb, he is doomed. We already know this, so John need not elaborate the nature of the Lamb's victory. He simply states again, "The Lamb will conquer them" (17:14). We should realize by now that the Lamb conquers by persevering love, not military might. Keeping this point in mind will help us interpret the vision of the Lamb's victory in 19:11–21.

We should think back to the beginnings of chapter 17. The harlot has the golden cup full of the "blood of the saints and the blood of the witnesses to Jesus" (17:6). We know from 12:11 that this "blood" is precisely the means Jesus uses to conquer. The harlot's cup had seemed to manifest the beast's dominating power that so impresses "the inhabitants of the earth," those that follow "in amazement" (13:3). But it actually becomes the means by which the *Lamb* conquers—as we will see.

REVELATION 17:15–18

> And he said to me, "The waters that you saw, where the whore is seated, are peoples and multitudes and nations and languages. And the ten horns that you saw, they and the beast will hate the whore; they will make her desolate and naked; they will devour her flesh and burn her up with fire. For God has put it into their hearts to carry out his purpose by agreeing to give their kingdom to the beast, until the words of God will be fulfilled. The woman you saw is the great city that rules over the kings of the earth."

The angel continues to explain to John the meaning of what he sees in the final paragraph of the chapter. Again, the details are difficult to nail down with precision. The first "explanation"—the waters where the harlot sits "are peoples and multitudes and nations and languages" (17:15)—repeats a phrase used throughout the book for both the countless numbers that worship the Lamb (chapter 5) and make up God's people (chapter 7) and the countless numbers that bow down to the beast (chapter 13).

The angel's reference points to what John believes is at stake in Revelation. Which of the countless multitudes that constitutes people from the entire world is most characteristic of the human destiny? As it turns out, the countless multitude who worship the Lamb shows us our end, "end" both as purpose and as ultimate outcome. In chapter 17, John's point may be to indicate that the fall of the beast and harlot will allow the countless multitude to achieve this end.

Then comes a challenging picture. The kings "and the beast will hate the harlot; they will devour her flesh and burn her up with fire" (17:16). So, in some sense the Beast and the Harlot are not identical. This is confusing, because we have learned from the rest of the book (including elsewhere in this very chapter) *is* that they are essentially the same thing; as is Babylon, the "great city." The confusion reminds us to hold such images a bit loosely. John certainly does not simply have Rome in mind as the literal meaning of any of them. Perhaps part of John's thought here is simply that the various structures and ideologies and kingdoms that manifest the spirit of the dragon are actually inherently fragile, unstable, and prone to turning against each other in destructive ways. It certainly rings true to life that the great empires that are dependent upon the blood of the saints for their sustenance tend to act in self-destructive ways.

John adds the profound thought that "God has put it into their hearts to carry our God's purpose" (17:17). Again, as with the plagues, God's purposes are carried out in this "wrathful" dynamic of cause-and-effect consequences where the powers of death ultimately self-destruct and make space for God's healing love to work its transformation.

SEEKING THE PEACE OF THE CITY

I believe that in its idiosyncratic way Revelation gives us perspective on the world we live in. It does so not due to its predictions about the end times but due to its insights into its own times. Those insights tell us about deep structures of human life and the message of the Lamb that spoke then and continues to speak now. An image that comes to mind is of a chair my mother found at a secondhand store when I was a kid. The chair was covered with ugly green paint. She stripped the paint and uncovered the beauty that remained with the original hardwood. Then she put on a finish that enhanced the chair's original beauty, and she had a treasure. Many interpretations of Revelation hide the original beauty of the book. I think we can strip those interpretations away and find in its actual message a great treasure.

I dislike Rev 17's use of "harlot" as a metaphor. Among other things, it seems to disregard the humanity of women who are sex workers. The image is a profoundly negative stereotype. It gives the misleading impression that John's concerns are about illicit sex. However, in terms of what the image intends to communicate, we may see parallels with our current situation. We also have one superpower that corrupts people from around the world to do its bidding and serve its insatiable greed and will to dominate. And we may note the arrogance and lack of self-awareness of this superpower along with its drunkenness on power and its greed that runs rampant.

We may relate as well to the image of the hostility of this one superpower has toward people who resist it. And we are challenged by the idea that the Lamb's way nonetheless conquers the system. This last theme is the one we are most strongly challenged to think about: Does the Lamb and his way of resisting the system truly conquer in our world?

We are also challenged by the rather shocking picture at the end of the chapter. The kings who had earlier allied with the woman turn on her and destroy her. Is this a picture of the self-destructive nature of insatiable greed and lust for power? Do we see in recent history that systems of greed and power politics collapse upon themselves? Is this happening with today's one great superpower? Let me test an idea, though: Even with all the destruction, the picture in Rev 17 actually holds out hope for the city symbolized by the harlot and Babylon. John's vision calls his readers to seek the well-being of *Babylon*. What's my basis for this idea?

At the end of the previous chapter, chapter 16, the seventh of the full-out bowl plagues is visited on the city Babylon. The greatest earthquake the world had ever known splits Babylon into three parts. A loud voice, presumably God's, cries out: "It is done!" (16:17). But then, starting in 17:1, we read of yet more visions. These additional visions offer more detailed elaborations of that final plague. The point, as with all the visions, is not to predict how the world will end. The "revelation of Jesus Christ" is not a vision of the chronological end of time. It, rather, is a vision of the purpose of our existence. The seventh and final plague that completes the vision is about purpose, not future predictions.

The final six chapters of the book elaborate the seventh plague. They make clear the purpose of the plagues—that Babylon would end and that out of Babylon's ashes would arise new Jerusalem. The revelation of Jesus Christ is a revelation of transformation, of healing, of blessing all the families of the earth. We have, I suggest, a revelation not of the literal destruction of Babylon but of the transformation of Babylon itself into new Jerusalem. What matters for us, I believe, is not a promise that for certain this transformation will indeed happen. Rather, it is a statement of the means for this transformation. The visions point not so much to a future outcome as to a present process. They tell us, as does the rest of the book, that we who seek to learn from these visions are called to follow the Lamb resolutely wherever he goes.

One of the seven angels who delivered the great bowl plagues in chapter 16 speaks to John at the beginning of chapter 17. The angel takes John to see the fate of Babylon the Great, the city of the beast that had just received the "wine-cup of the fury of [God's] wrath" (16:20). If we skip ahead to chapter 21, we see that this same exact angel returns for John. This time the angel shows John another city, the city of healing, new Jerusalem. The first city is portrayed as a harlot, the second city portrayed as a bride.

These two cities make a single set of images, a point and a counterpoint. John sets before his readers a stark choice. Accept the empire's way of being in the world, follow the beast wherever he goes, trust in wealth and the sword, and you will be at home in Babylon and meet her fate. Follow the Lamb, trust in generosity and the path of peace, and you will be at home in new Jerusalem. We read that Babylon falls, crushed by the self-destructiveness of its ways of death. Then new Jerusalem comes down, from heaven to earth. But we need to look closely at the dynamics here.

In chapter 17, we get mixed signals. Clearly Babylon has an intimate relationship with the beast. The beast personifies the powers of violence, greed, and exploitation, the insatiable domination of creation and humanity's vulnerable ones. But then, inexplicably, though predictably, the beast turns on Babylon, the beast hates his servant, and the "ten horns" (the beast's kingly minions) devour Babylon. The powers consume and use up their human agents.

Maybe the most terrible manifestations of these dynamics in recent history are the Stalinist terror machine in the Soviet Union and the Maoist terror machine in China. They turned on many of their leaders. Through show trials and purges they massacred many who earlier had themselves killed others on behalf of the system. A much less bloody but parallel dynamic, though, is visible today in most soulless systems of domination—in the corporate world, in the political world, in the military world, in the penal world. The system needs to be fed, and it will devour its own over and over again.

Revelation, however, tells us something quite suggestive. John will see in chapter 20 the three great powers thrown into the lake of fire—the dragon, the beast, and the false prophet. These are the powers of evil behind the human structures that do their bidding. But Babylon is *not* thrown into the lake. What happens to Babylon after the beast is destroyed?

It is not coincidental that the exact same angel who shows John what happens to Babylon then shows him new Jerusalem. After the beast is destroyed, new Jerusalem comes down. And notice, the very kings of the earth who chapter 17 links with Babylon's terrible "abominations and impurities" actually enter into the new Jerusalem. They find healing and bring into it the glory of the nations. The purple and scarlet garments that clothe the harlot in chapter 17 are cleansed to a bright white on the bride. The "gold and jewels and pearls" of chapter 17, grasped greedily in the sweaty hands of Babylon, become part of the commons in chapters 21 and 22. They offer beauty to the entire city, for all who are healed by the leaves of the tree of life.

So, contrary to the standard account of Revelation, we do not have unremitting hostility from John and John's God toward the human city. What happens is not utter destruction of the sinful world of present-day humanity followed by the creation of something completely new and different. Rather, what happens is healing and transformation. That which is beautiful in the human project is welcomed into new Jerusalem. The kings themselves are healed. How does the healing and transformation happen? To answer this question is the point of the entire book of Revelation. And to discern the answer to this question points to the most important message of Revelation has for our century.

Back in the early 1970s, the Watergate scandal shook up the leadership elite of the United States like nothing else ever has. In the investigation of Watergate, the mantra that guided those trying to unwind the tangled web of corruption and deceit was simple but quite profound: "follow the money." "Follow the money" remains a core truism for understanding power and corruption in our world today. However, to understand Revelation and its notion of power, I see something a bit different. "Follow the blood," we could say. Follow the blood. Notice throughout the book how "blood" is used, whose blood is shed, and to what effect. This may seem a bit gruesome. Revelation, perhaps, is not for the squeamish. But we see something profound when we follow the blood, and it is the key to understanding Rev 17.

We read that Babylon is "drunk with the blood of the saints and the blood of the witnesses of Jesus." Jesus is *the* "faithful witness." The saints follow him wherever he goes. They resist Babylon's corruption and injustice, for Babylon's own sake. John has Rome in mind here as the current expression of the spirit of Babylon. Remember what Rome did to Jesus, that crucifixion was Rome's signature way of executing rebels. So, Jesus's blood certainly is also in this cup that makes Babylon so drunk.

The "abominations" and "fornications" are most of all the ways the empire seeks to crush those who resist it. The empire seeks to crush those who do seek genuine shalom and the well-being of vulnerable ones. The city Babylon will try to crush those who seek its true shalom, at least until the city is transformed. And transformation is exactly what John's vision expects to happen. In spite of the best efforts of Babylon to crush the Lamb and his witnesses, the Lamb conquers. Caesar is not the true king but the Lamb, however crazy that may appear to those who understand power in Caesar's terms. The *Lamb* is the true conqueror, the King of kings.

And notice the blood here. We see no hint that the harlot's blood is shed, or that the blood of the kings of the earth or that the blood of the inhabitants of the earth is shed. Only the blood of the saints and of the Lamb is spilled. "Blood" stands for persevering love, consistent resistance, just deeds, staying close to the way of Jesus. So, the blood that makes Babylon drunk alludes to these shalom-enhancing acts. We will see in chapter 18 that this blood takes Babylon down. It does so, though, not by shedding Babylonian blood but by breaking the hold that the beast, the dragon, and the false prophet have on the inhabitants of the earth. The blood the Lamb and his followers shed frees people to embrace the Lamb's ways. Their "conquest" *blesses* the inhabitants of the earth; it doesn't destroy them.

So, what does this all mean for our present Babylon? Much of the imagery in Revelation 17 and 18 seems remarkably foresightful in capturing what the American empire is like. The arrogance, possessiveness, exploitation of the weak, the worldwide commerce that extracts wealth from the hinterlands and puts it in the pockets of the already wealthy, the military bases beyond counting, the assumption that power as dominance is true power. Does Revelation help us to know how to seek the shalom of our city, a different and more authentic peace than that that rests on military might and mass incarceration?

I feel a stronger sense of urgency about this question now that I am a grandparent. I *feel* it when I hear people worrying about what kind of world their grandchildren will be part of. I think often of folksinger Jim Page's song: "Whose world is this?" He asks about what the world will be like that we leave for our children and grandchildren. What kind of teaching can we leave them that will make a difference?[1]

I get some comfort from Revelation when I think about these things. I believe, actually, that the main point of Revelation is to give us a kind of teaching that will help us create a world for our grandchildren. Revelation should not be read as an ironclad promise that everything will turn out okay in the end no matter what humanity does in the meantime. Rather, Revelation tells us of the path we must follow *in order for* things to turn out okay. It's simple: Follow the Lamb wherever he goes. If Babylon is to fall, or, better, if Babylon is to be transformed, it is through faithful witness, willingness to sacrifice one's own blood and resist injustice. This path alone will take care of Babylon.

To give this teaching some heft, Revelation links the Lamb closely with the One on the throne. This confession reminds us that to follow that Lamb is to go with the grain of the universe. To follow the Lamb unites means and ends, pragmatism and principle. This is the only path that will work, and it is also intrinsically life giving. To follow the way of Jesus is to resist, to overcome, and to transform Babylon. Jesus's path to the cross, a path he calls us to join, is the path of persevering love. It commits us to the way of peace even in the face of siren calls to take up the sword. It commits us to trust in God for wholeness, not in the allures of empire. And it promises us that following such a path not only heads us toward wholeness but is wholeness.

1. Jim Page, "Whose World is This?" on the album *Whose World is This?* (Liquid City Records, 2002).

FOR FURTHER ENGAGEMENT

1. The author suggests "the problem here is not false religion, per se, but political dynamics of domination and exploitation. At the heart of the political order characterized by such dynamics is ruthlessness toward all who resist." How would such an analysis apply to us today? Are there such dynamics *inside* of Christianity today? If our congregations were to embody the fruit of the Spirit (see Gal 5:22–26) would they inevitably be "resisting" Babylon? Explain.

2. Note the vivid imagery employed in 17:1–6. What do you think John is trying to convey with this imagery? What dominant suggestions does the vision of the woman give?

3. What does the term "Babylon" refer to? Does it have present-day manifestation?

4. Do you agree that in his condemnatory picture of the harlot, Babylon, John is in reality issuing a strong warning to those in the church who might be allured by her? What might be alluring about the Babylon of John's day? How about the Babylons of our day? How should Christians resist?

5. In terms of your own awareness and life experience, what do you think the most important contrasts between Babylon and the new Jerusalem are?

6. Can you think of examples of how evil turns on itself? Do you think God is behind this phenomenon?

7. Reflect on the use of the metaphor "harlot" in Rev 17. Note the author's concerns. What do you think John means to communicate with this image? Do you find it helpful? Would you use the same metaphor today? Can you think of a good alternative?

8. Also reflect on the term "fornication" as used here. What would you say that "the wine of [her] fornication" (17:2) means? Again, would this be a helpful metaphor for us to use today? Explain.

9. Chapter 17 ends with a confusing image. The kings "and the beast will hate the harlot; they will devour her flesh and burn her up with fire" (17:16). How do you make sense of this?

10. How do you evaluate this idea of the author's: "Even with all the destruction, the picture in Rev 17 actually holds out hope for the city

symbolized by the harlot and Babylon"? What does he mean? How does he support his idea?

11. The author states, to give the teaching "follow the Lamb wherever he goes" some heft, Revelation links the Lamb closely with the One on the throne. How would you explain the significance of that linkage?

12. It seems that Revelation means to contrast the visions of Babylon and new Jerusalem. What lessons can be learned from the way Revelation juxtaposes the characteristics of these two?

14

Confessions of a Birthright Imperialist

[Revelation 18]

Revelation 18 continues the envisioning of God's work of transformation, from Babylon to new Jerusalem. In Rev 17, we read of Babylon's comeuppance. At the end of chapter 16, the seventh of the totalistic plagues had been visited upon the city Babylon. The greatest earthquake the world has ever known splits Babylon into three parts. A loud voice, presumably God's, cried out: "It is done!" (16:17). Yet the visions John reports are far from over.

Chapter 17 focuses on what happens to Babylon—a rather gruesome picture. However, we should not think of this picture as a prediction of what *will* happen in the future. Rather the vision is simply part of Revelation's broader message about humanity's purpose (or "end"). When read in context, then, chapter 17's vision actually joins the bigger movement the book portrays that concludes with new Jerusalem's appearance. In a paradoxical sense, the "destruction" of Babylon might actually be its transformation, or, at least, the transformation of the human city from Babylon to new Jerusalem.

Babylon falls, crushed by the self-destructiveness of its ways. But in the destruction lies the seeds of the city's hope. Babylon is "drunk with the blood of the saints and the blood of the witnesses of Jesus" (17:6). This "blood" links the witnesses with Jesus. This is the "blood" of persevering love that leads to Babylon's downfall, the destruction of the powers of evil (dragon, beast, and false prophet), and the re-creation of Jerusalem as a city of healing. The healing, as we will see, is not only for the faithful witnesses but also for the kings of the earth and the nations. First, though, the destruction of Babylon requires more attention. So, John gives us another vision in chapter 18 of that destruction but from a slightly different angle.

REVELATION 18:1–3

> After this I saw another angel coming down from heaven, having great authority; and the earth was made bright with his splendor. He called out with a mighty voice, "Fallen, fallen is Babylon the great! It has become a dwelling place of demons, a haunt of every foul spirit, a haunt of every foul bird, a haunt of every foul and hateful beast. For all the nations have drunk of the wine of the wrath of her fornication, and the kings of the earth have committed fornication with her, and the merchants of the earth have grown rich from the power of her luxury."

The vision here features a different angel than the angel of chapter 17 who was one of the seven angels who had poured out the plague bowls in chapter 16. The angel in Rev 18 first asserts that indeed "Babylon the great" has met its doom. Instead of being a place of beauty and power, a true city of the gods, Babylon turns out to be disgusting, a home for demons, foul spirits, foul birds, and foul and hateful beasts.

The picture here should not be taken literally, as if the capital city of the great empire has all of a sudden turned into a repulsive place. John would not need to share a vision warning his readers of the true nature of Babylon if common people would find it obviously repulsive. John seeks, rather, to challenge the surface sense of Babylon's greatness. He insists that from the point of view of God, the power of Babylon should be recognized as actually demonic and foul. John once again warns his readers away from their attraction to empire as a way of life.

The problem with Babylon is that it corrupts all those who seek to find their home within her walls. The great ones, the kings of the earth and the merchants of the earth, have placed their trust in her and have been turned from the true God to the idol of empire. The allusions to "drunkenness" and "fornication" are best understood, as we have seen, in terms of injustice, oppression, and violence. The kings and merchants are complicit in the practices of Babylon that exploitatively extract wealth from the vulnerable and oppressed masses. These practices are profoundly life denying.

"Blood" is not explicitly mentioned here. However, the allusion to the nations drinking "of the wine of the wrath of [Babylon's] fornication" (18:3) links with the "woman" being "drunk with the blood of the saints and the blood of the witnesses to Jesus" from 17:6. The nations, the kings, and the merchants join directly with the great harlot Babylon in profound injustices that may make them wealthy for a time. These injustices, though, will turn out to be the seeds of brokenness and self-destruction for the empire and for all who trust in it.

People who drink too much alcohol or who engage in illicit sex are not John's concern here. He has larger concerns. He uses out of control drink and sex as metaphors that speak of social processes that actually are all too controlling and intentional. He has in mind the basic dynamics where the rich and powerful enhance their own wealth and power and bring misery to those they exploit. What are out of control in such social systems, then, are greed and domination. These are the truly insatiable dynamics that attract even those in John's faith communities.

REVELATION 18:4–8

> Then I heard another voice from heaven saying, "Come out of her, my people, so that you do not take part in her sins, and so that you do not share in her plagues; for her sins are heaped high as heaven, and God has remembered her iniquities. Render to her as she herself has rendered and repay her double for her deeds; mix a double draught for her in the cup she mixed. As she glorified herself and lived luxuriously, so give her a like measure of torment and grief. Since in her heart she says, 'I rule as a queen; I am no widow, and I will never see grief,' therefore her plagues will come in a single day—pestilence and mourning and famine—and she will be burned with fire; for mighty is the Lord God who judges her."

The vision in Rev 18 draws heavily on Jeremiah, Ezekiel, and Isaiah. The call to "come out of her, my people" (18:4) references Isa 48:20–22 and Jer 50:8–10; 51:6–10. The message here must not be misread as a call to abandon the faithful witness emphasized throughout the book. John does not call for physical separation but for discernment. He calls for sustained clarity about the appropriate object of worship in readers' lives, and willingness to reject the core values that govern the actions of Babylon, the kings, and the merchants.

"Come out" reiterates what we have seen elsewhere in Revelation. Trust in the ways of the Lamb, not the ways of the beast. Be aware of the differences between these two claims for loyalty. Followers of the Lamb must separate themselves ideologically and religiously from the ideology and religion of empire. The ideology and religion of empire almost invariably include nationalism, militarism, and consumerism that aggrandize the merchants and reinforce the dominating power of the nations. In response, the call to "come out" is a call to resist, to create alternatives, to practice refusal in the midst of Babylon.

The voice from heaven continues when it again emphasizes the true nature of empire as a way of life. Babylon's "sins are heaped high as heaven" (18:5). As we read on, John shows what the character of those "sins" are. The "sins" are the respectable processes of commerce and national security. When the veneer of respectability is torn away and Babylon's true nature is revealed, the "sins" may be boiled down to violence. Their commerce at bottom traffics in "human lives" (18:13), and their national security at bottom results in shedding "the blood of prophets and of saints, and of all who have been slaughtered on earth" (18:24).

The processes of the wrath, the plagues, and the self-destructiveness of greed and exploitation in a moral universe are portrayed graphically in 18:6–8. The moral universe, as it were, takes its vengeance on this great city: "render her as she herself has rendered, repay her double for her deeds;" "as she glorified herself and lived luxuriously . . . give her a like measure of torment and grief"; in face of her arrogance, "her plagues will come in a single day."

We must note that it is "Babylon" (a metaphorical entity, not precisely the same as actual people) that is crushed here—not the kings and merchants themselves. Babylon is "burned with fire" from the Lord God's judgment (18:8). This judgment actually enhances the well-being of kings of the earth themselves who in the end find healing in new Jerusalem (21:24). The notion of city-ness in the social organization of humanity is not destroyed but only this manifestation of it. Cities need not be fueled by greed and arrogance. Babylon goes down in a way that signals the destruction of greed and arrogance, not the destruction of the human denizens of the city. The city as great harlot goes down so that the city as bride might arise and become the true home for humanity, even for the transformed kings. New Jerusalem will welcome the glory of the nations (21:26).

REVELATION 18:9–19

> And the kings of the earth, who committed fornication and lived in luxury with her, will weep and wail over her when they see the smoke of her burning; they will stand far off, in fear of her torment, and say, "Alas, alas, the great city, Babylon, the mighty city! For in one hour your judgment has come." And the merchants of the earth weep and mourn for her, since no one buys their cargo anymore, cargo of gold, silver, jewels and pearls, fine linen, purple, silk and scarlet, all kinds of scented wood, all articles of ivory, all articles of costly wood, bronze, iron, and marble, cinnamon, spice, incense, myrrh, frankincense, wine, olive oil, choice flour and wheat, cattle and sheep, horses and chariots, slaves—and human lives. "The fruit for which your soul longed has gone from you, and all your dainties and your splendor are lost to you, never to be found again!" The merchants of these wares, who gained wealth from her, will stand far off, in fear of her torment, weeping and mourning aloud, "Alas, alas, the great city, clothed in fine linen, in purple and scarlet, adorned with gold, with jewels, and with pearls! For in one hour all this wealth has been laid waste!" And all shipmasters and seafarers, sailors and all whose trade is on the sea, stood far off and cried out as they saw the smoke of her burning, "What city was like the great city?" And they threw dust on their heads, as they wept and mourned, crying out, "Alas, alas, the great city, where all who had ships at sea grew rich by her wealth. For in one hour she has been laid waste."

Revelation 18:9–19 draws on songs of lament from Ezek 27. It poignantly treats the self-destructiveness of Babylon when the chickens come home to roost. We should be clear by now that Babylon's fall is a *good* thing. Babylon's dynamics of domination need to end for humanity to survive, not to mention thrive as God's creatures who live as we are intended to live.

However, the processes of building Babylon have included many elements that have been humane and reflect creativity and beauty. So, the fall of Babylon is indeed to be lamented as well. We even get a whiff of humanity from these characters who joined Babylon's corruption. The shock and grief are genuine, the pain is real, the loss is grievous. The kings cry out, "Alas, alas, the great city" (18:10). And the merchants mourn, "the fruit for which your soul longed has gone from you" (18:14). And then the shipmasters, "What city was like the great city?" (18:18). Even in these laments, though, those who mourn are the wealthy and powerful who gained wealth and power from their commerce with Babylon. They mostly lament the loss of the wealth and the loss of the opportunity to gain more wealth. As the shipmasters lament, "Alas, alas, the great city, where all who had ships at sea grew rich by her wealth!" (18:19).

John's critique runs throughout in subtle ways. The vision has a jarring denouement at the end of the merchants' lament. They mourn the loss of the great buyer of all their cargoes: precious stones, fine wood, spices, food, livestock—and the weapons of war ("horses and chariots"), "slaves—and human lives" (18:13). This fruit of the great city that enriched so many rested on the backs of slaves and human souls. "Repay her double her deeds" indeed!

REVELATION 18:20–24

> Rejoice over her, O heaven, you saints and apostles and prophets! For God has given judgment for you against her. Then a mighty angel took up a stone like a great millstone and threw it into the sea, saying, "With such violence Babylon the great city will be thrown down, and will be found no more; and the sound of harpists and minstrels and of flutists and trumpeters will be heard in you no more; and an artisan of any trade will be found in you no more; and the sound of the millstone will be heard in you no more; and the light of a lamp will shine in you no more; and the voice of bridegroom and bride will be heard in you no more; for your merchants were the magnates of the earth, and all nations were deceived by your sorcery. And in you was found the blood of prophets and of saints, and of all who have been slaughtered on earth."

The vision concludes when John provides more clarity about the moral reality. The fall of Babylon, the lamentations of the great ones notwithstanding, should be celebrated by followers of the Lamb. Babylon's violence and injustice against "human lives" has been enormous. So, "rejoice over her, O heaven, you saints and apostles and prophets" (18:20). One way to interpret the call to celebrate is not as a promise of some future day when this vision will literally be experienced in history, but rather as a statement for the present. People may see Babylon for what it is and withdraw their consent to Babylon's "fornications" with the world's great ones. People may turn from domination toward cooperation. When they do, Babylon will go down. Such an outcome is to be celebrated, even as those who have benefited from Babylon's injustices cry in mourning.

"For God has given judgment for you against her" (18:20) refers back to the cry of the witnesses under the altar in 6:10 for vengeance. We may notice a subtle but important point here, though. The witnesses cried out for vengeance against "the inhabitants of the earth" in chapter 6, but here it is Babylon that is judged. As Babylon goes down, the "inhabitants" (the kings, merchants, and shipmasters) stand to the side and mourn the loss of their meal ticket. But they themselves do not go down. As we will see, the destruction of Babylon (and even more obviously the destruction of the powers that created Babylon—the dragon, beast, and false prophet) allow the kings of the earth to be transformed and healed. And it would not seem farfetched to assume the merchants and shipmasters experience a similar fate. God's justice does not lead to punishment for the "inhabitants" but to their healing.

The vision concludes with quite a poignant recital by another "mighty angel." As this angel throws a great millstone in the sea to symbolize Babylon's fate, it recites what will be lost when Babylon goes down. The litany portrays the human (and humane) side of life in the great city—music, the work of artisans, the light of a lamp, wedding parties—that will no longer be found in Babylon. Though only barely hinted at later, we may assume that these humane elements will actually be quite present in the city as it is transformed into new Jerusalem.

Finally, we are reminded again that Babylon needs to go down. The great ones dominated the earth, and Babylon deceived the nations. Once the "sorcerer" (dragon) is no more, the nations will find healing. To cap the litany that has listed the elements of the life that will no longer be found in Babylon (and powerfully to remind John's readers once more why they need to turn from Babylon), we read of what *was found* in Babylon: "The blood of prophets and of saints, and of all who have been slaughtered on earth," 18:24). This reference to blood reminds us of the blood of the saints and witnesses on which the harlot was drunk (17:6) and the double draught for Babylon "in the cup she mixed" (18:6)—the very dynamics that took Babylon down.

This is what is at stake: Follow the Lamb, respond to enemies with love, center life on compassion and generosity, and be at home in new Jerusalem that even now is at hand. Or follow the beast, respond to enemies with violence, center life on competition and possessiveness, and be at home in doomed Babylon.

CONFESSIONS OF A BIRTHRIGHT IMPERIALIST

Revelation chapter 18 might speak more obviously to the twenty-first century than the chapter that came before it. This chapter focuses on a critique of the great city, called here Babylon. Probably Rome is in mind, but the critique applies to imperial capital cities ever since. John challenges his first readers with how they think about the empire they are part of. As such, I think Rev 18 works as a good challenge for us today to think about how we feel about our empire.

I was born in May 1954 on the ninth anniversary of V-E Day, "victory in Europe," when the Allies defeated the Nazis. My parents were both proud veterans of that "good war," the war to end Nazi tyranny and the tyranny of the Japanese Empire. I wouldn't say that my parents gloried in the war or that they were rabid "patriots." But I grew up with very positive assumptions about America. This was the message: We Americans are a force for good in the world, maybe the greatest force for good ever. We care for the well-being of the world's suffering masses; we are unalterably opposed to tyranny and Communism. We want peace and only reluctantly enter into conflict against the bad guys. And we are winners. Our victories spread goodness: democracy, economic growth, freedom, and the Christian faith. We only go to war when we have no choice, and then we make sure to win. We always win, and it's always for the good of others.

I have vivid memories of childhood playtimes that reinforced the sense of the goodness of our military actions. "Bombs over Tokyo!" we would cry out in joy as we played war. Since then, I have learned what our actual bombs over Tokyo did. They killed upwards of 100,000 defenseless people in just one long night due to intentionally created firestorms. Those firestorms, in the words of the commander of the attack in March 1945, led to people being "scorched and boiled and baked to death."[1] Knowing what those bombs over Tokyo did, I now shudder in horror and shame at our games. I was in school during the Vietnam War years. Again, I only assumed the best. I learned by heart the number one hit of 1966, "The Ballad of the Green Berets." I sang it with my friends during gym class over and over. I actually still know most of the words though I doubt I have heard the song in over fifty years.

This America-the-good message was simply part of the air I breathed as I grew up. I can't imagine that I ever heard a negative critique of my country. So, as I approached draft age, I expected to go fight for my country. I didn't really want to risk my life, but I certainly didn't question whether

---

1. Grayling, *Among*, 171.

I would—or should. As it turned out, the draft ended the year I became eligible for it. When I went to college, though, I began to hear stories. I think especially of the summer of 1974. Instead of going home for the summer, I stayed at college. I got to know a recently returned Vietnam War vet at my job and played on a softball team mostly made up of vets. Their accounts of the horrors they saw and even took part in shook me.

Ironically, the main factor that kept me from being more disillusioned with the American empire was what I continued to hear in my Baptist church. The preacher proclaimed a message of America as God's chosen vessel in this sinful world. That message only slowed my movement to a more negative view of the US for a little while, though. I soon learned a different way to understand the Bible and Jesus; I learned to embrace the crazy idea that Jesus's call to love our enemies might actually apply to how we think about war and empire.

When I met Jesus again for the first time,[2] you could say, I looked at everything related to war and empire and America through new lenses. I learned about some of the things that had happened around the time of my birth that caused me to see my country in a different light. How the CIA overthrew the democratically elected government of Iran and backed the vicious dictatorship of the Shah so our oil companies could get richer. How, with the success of that coup the CIA moved again to overthrow the democratically elected government of Guatemala with a similar result—decades of an even more vicious dictatorship. How, despite the pleas of most of the scientists who had created it, the American government committed itself to building what turned out to be hundreds and hundreds of hydrogen bombs, each one many, many times more powerful than the bombs that devastated Hiroshima and Nagasaki.[3]

Maybe worst of all, I learned how the allegedly noble effort in Vietnam could have been averted back in the year of my birth, 1954, when the Vietnamese defeated the French colonists. Had the US recognized the victors there—in the same way the French, British, and Soviets did—the Vietnam War would never have happened.[4]

Then I started to study the book of Revelation. And I was amazed. Earlier I had been taught that Revelation predicted the bad guys who would be linked with the antichrist (that is, the Russians and the Chinese). Now I looked at Babylon in a new light. First of all, I understood Revelation to be concerned with the first century, not the twentieth century. Babylon was

2. This phrase comes from Borg, *Meeting*.

3. See Carroll, *House*.

4. See Young, *Vietnam*.

indeed a symbol, but not for a future one-world government led by the anti-christ but for the Roman Empire. And as I learned about the Roman Empire as critiqued in Revelation, I began to see discomforting parallels with my own country.

Returning to Rev 18, what does the chapter say is wrong with Babylon/Rome? Well, Babylon may seem all-powerful, full of greatness and of things to inspire awe and respect. Babylon may seem to be a beacon to the world of the good life, the world's one superpower, the renowned bringer of order to the world (the *Pax Romana*—the "peace of Rome"), and the creator of great wealth. But the vision in Revelation states that Babylon is a home for demons, every foul spirit, bird, and hateful beast.

It wasn't obvious to John's readers that Rome was disgusting and foul. Rome's demonic character would not have been an objective statement of clear sociological fact. John offers a moral or theological interpretation. According to John, Rome in actuality, beneath the smoke and mirrors of imperial power and splendor, was corrupt—and corrupting. Rome was not a place of genuine life-enhancing beauty, but the opposite, the haunt of death. Rome did what all imperial centers did and do. It demanded, and by and large received, loyalty. People believed in it, trusted in it, gave it their consent to dominate. Babylon gives wine to the nations that makes them drunk. And it "commits fornication" with the "kings of the earth." And it makes the "merchants of the earth" rich. The problem is not literally alcohol and sex. The problem is that by trusting in Babylon, the nations, the kings, and the merchants join in Babylon's injustice, exploitation, dehumanization, and violence.

Revelation 18 twice details in subtle but powerful ways the dynamics of empire that Babylon follows. First, the chapter portrays the economic dynamics of empire. The merchants of the earth grow wealthy almost beyond measure due to their collaboration with Babylon. They profit from trade of all sorts of things, according to a long list: gold, silver, jewels and pearls, fine linen, purple, silk and scarlet, all kinds of scented wood, all articles of ivory, all articles of costly wood, bronze, iron, and marble, cinnamon, spice, incense, myrrh, frankincense, wine, olive oil, choice flour and wheat, cattle and sheep, horses and chariots.

We would only have to revise this list slightly to apply to today's merchants of the earth who collude with our great empire—fine iPads, costly garments of silk and wool, warplanes, precious metals such as coltan and uranium, Nike and New Balance shoes. Would our list conclude in the same way John's did? At the end of all the cargo comes this, stated as just one more item: "slaves—and human lives" (18:13). Such violence is what is wrong with Babylon. The commerce may benefit many people, but the great wealth it generates for the merchants and Babylon ultimately comes off the backs of the poor, vulnerable, and defenseless—and makes their lives *worse*.

At the end of the chapter we have another list, even more poignant. Babylon will be judged; Babylon will go down. This is the message of chapter 18, following the same message we saw in chapter 17. The merchants mourn the loss of their wealth. And there is more mourning, which is really at the loss of the humane-ness and day-to-day living that characterized this city. The grief is that these humane activities will not be found in Babylon anymore: harpists and minstrels, flutists and trumpeters, artisans and millers, the light of a lamp, and the voices of bride and groom. But this is why they won't be found, because of what *was* found in Babylon: "The blood of prophets and of saints, and of all who have been slaughtered on earth."

Babylon the great, all-powerful, it may seem; beacon of peace and order, it may seem. But it is actually the home of every foul and hateful beast, trafficker in slaves, killer of prophets and saints. Is this America, too? Well, even with the most negative reading, America is not only beastly. My faith community is Mennonites. Mennonites, of all people, have good reasons to appreciate the American traditions of freedom of religion and free speech. Our spiritual forebears came here beginning in the seventeenth century in order to find a safe haven to practice their faith. And we know other ways in which this country has not been and is not beastly. But then, Rome was not only beastly, either.

However, it is precisely the reality that Rome was not only beastly that leads John to make his points so dramatically. He writes to people in his churches who find Rome attractive; too attractive, John believes. John's rhetoric and imagery might be a bit overheated. But it would be a mistake to ignore his point. American Christians too have found our empire too attractive, too benign. We do well to listen to John sympathetically and allow his visions to challenge us. Our nation *has* trafficked in human lives and shed the blood of prophets, saints, and all too many others—it still does.

Since the 1970s, I have continued to learn more about the Vietnam War. A 2013 book by journalist Nick Turse, *Kill Anything That Moves: The Real American War in Vietnam*,[5] chronicles in excruciating detail the systemic war crimes and atrocities our military visited upon the people of Southeast Asia. That particular war is just one example, perhaps the most extensive but hardly alone, of willful slaughter in the name of American national interest. I think reading Revelation can help makes us less gullible in relation to ways the American empire has acted in our names.

5. Turse, *Kill*.

I believe, though, that John's actual agenda is not mainly critique of Rome. I believe that he has a positive agenda, not mainly about criticism and condemnation or about pointing fingers. In fact, he's not mainly about worrying about what empires, including Babylon/Rome, do. John hopes to encourage healing and redemption. What is redemptive in John's vision in Rev 18, and how might this vision help us find redemptive elements in our own setting?

First, we remember that John points ahead to new Jerusalem. Notice that in chapter 18, we have two different kinds of people. The kings, merchants, and shipmasters are the ones complicit with Babylon's exploitive ways, who get riches and power from the global economy. They weep and mourn. "Alas, alas, for this great city that will be no more." The other kind of people *welcome* Babylon's fall. "Rejoice over her, O heaven, you saints, you apostles, you prophets!" (18:20). These are the ones who in the very next vision celebrate the wedding supper of the Lamb and feel at home in new Jerusalem. John means to encourage his readers. When Babylon goes down, it is true there will be no "voice of groom and bride" in Babylon. But in fact, there will be a wedding celebration with countless participants; it just will not be in Babylon. Chapter 19 will tell us of the marriage celebration of the Lamb.

Let's think about this contrast between the two kinds of people. The fact that the kings and merchants and shipmasters mourn Babylon's fall tells us what about their relationship with Babylon? Well, their mourning tells us that they are linked closely enough to grieve, bitterly. But we are told, they all "stood *far off.*" They don't themselves go down with Babylon.

In 18:20, the call to rejoice at Babylon's fall, states, "God has given judgment for you [saints and prophets] against her." God judges because Babylon is where the blood of saints and prophets is found. These images link back to chapter 6 when the witnesses under the altar (surely the same as chapter 18's "saints and prophets") cry out for vengeance. That cry is now answered. However, we realize that the judgment of God is against Babylon, not (as requested in 6:10) against "the inhabitants of the earth" (that is, against the kings and merchants and shipmasters). We were tipped off that this would happen in chapter 16. God is praised for judging those who "shed the blood of saints and prophets" (16:6), that is, "great Babylon" (16:19). So, when Babylon goes down like a large millstone being thrown into the sea (18:21), the human allies of Babylon stand far off and watch.

In the end, God's justice works differently from simple punitive vengeance focused on the inhabitants of the earth. Revelation portrays destruction of the systems of evil. It is the human city as a system, insofar as it is organized for injustice, that goes down. But with what consequence for the human kings of the earth? The consequence for the kings of the earth is that they are healed and welcomed into new Jerusalem.

John wants his readers to know two things, both of which will give us hope and courage, both of which will strengthen us to give our allegiance to new Jerusalem and not to Babylon. The one is this: Be confident that the celebration of new Jerusalem is our fate. It is real. It is the deepest truth of creation. It is the truth of the maker of the universe. And the second is this: Be confident that our own acts of compassion, of resistance, and of solidarity all play a role, a crucial role, in the entry of new Jerusalem.

FOR FURTHER ENGAGEMENT

1. The author sees it as significant that "as Babylon goes down, the 'inhabitants' (the kings, merchants, and shipmasters) stand to the side and mourn." Reflect on the possibility that God's judgment here is focused on the powers and not on the people. What do you think of that idea? What are some of its implications?

2. What is the dominant tone of chapter 18? What contributes to this tone?

3. How is the greatness of Babylon portrayed? How is the sinfulness presented? How is the completeness of Babylon's fall conveyed?

4. What is the point of the social criticism of Babylon (Rome and other empires) in chapter 18? Is it merely condemnatory or meant to motivate John's readers to faithfulness and good deeds?

5. Does it make any sense to you to say that the fate of Babylon is part of God's redemptive work in establishing the new Jerusalem?

6. Do you agree that we should make a distinction between the forces of evil at work in people and the people themselves? If so, how does that affect your attitude toward people in the world? Do you want *your* enemies to be freed from Satan's hold? Does one's view of these things affect one's understanding of how violent Revelation is to humans? How can we say that it is for the sake of the kings and merchants that Babylon is destroyed? Is that true today?

7. The author suggests that "John would not need to share a vision warning his readers of the true nature of Babylon if common people would find Babylon obviously repulsive." Does that point apply to our present-day manifestations of "Babylon"? If so, what aspects of our present Babylon "should be recognized as actually demonic and foul"?

8. What are the bases for the author's statement, "The allusions to 'drunkenness' and 'fornication' are best understood in terms of injustice, oppression, and violence"? Do you agree that as a rule the Bible is more concerned with social sins than personal sins? Explain.

9. How do you relate the call in 18:4, "come out of her, my people" with the emphasis throughout the book on the call for Jesus's followers to give a "faithful witness"? What do you think of the author's explanation to this apparent tension?

10. If the call, "rejoice over her, O heaven, you saints and apostles and prophets" (18:20), is understood to be for the present and if the "her" here could be seen also to refer to present-day "Babylon," then what do you think we should be "rejoicing" over today? Explain.

11. What do you think is significant about how John places at the end of his list of the cargoes the item "slaves—and human lives" (18:13)? Note the author's thoughts.

12. What in our setting is analogous to Babylon—and to new Jerusalem? How do we apply what John seems to teach in Revelation?

15

The War That's Not a War

[Revelation 19]

Though John writes of the completion of the destruction of Babylon both at the end of chapter 16 and chapter 18, the story is not over, not even the destructive elements. However, it is crucial for the story line that Babylon no longer exists as a lure to turn people from God. John turns toward a new celebration at chapter 19's beginning. Here, unlike earlier worship visions, the focus is not on celebrating the Lamb's victory amidst the plagues. The plagues have ended. Now a crucial corner has been turned. Babylon is no more, and new Jerusalem is much closer.

The final "battle" is just ahead, followed in chapter 20 by the dragon meeting its end and the final judgment of humanity. In all of this, John's readers are challenged to remember the Lamb's way as the way of God—and the path to victory for the entire world. The outcome is the healing and genuine justice of new Jerusalem.

REVELATION 19:1–10

> After this I heard what seemed to be the loud voice of a great
> multitude in heaven, saying, "Hallelujah! Salvation and glory
> and power to our God, for his judgments are true and just; he
> has judged the great whore who corrupted the earth with her

fornication, and he has avenged on her the blood of his servants." Once more they said, "Hallelujah! The smoke goes up from her forever and ever." And the twenty-four elders and the four living creatures fell down and worshiped God who is seated on the throne, saying, "Amen. Hallelujah!" And from the throne came a voice saying, "Praise our God, all you his servants, and all who fear him, small and great." Then I heard what seemed to be the voice of a great multitude, like the sound of many waters and like the sound of mighty thunderpeals, crying out, "Hallelujah! For the Lord our God the Almighty reigns. Let us rejoice and exult and give him the glory, for the marriage of the Lamb has come, and his bride has made herself ready; to her it has been granted to be clothed with fine linen, bright and pure"—for the fine linen is the righteous deeds of the saints. And the angel said to me, "Write this: Blessed are those who are invited to the marriage supper of the Lamb." And he said to me, "These are true words of God." Then I fell down at his feet to worship him, but he said to me, "You must not do that! I am a fellow servant with you and your comrades who hold the testimony of Jesus. Worship God! For the testimony of Jesus is the spirit of prophecy."

The worship scene picks up on several images from earlier in the book. The "great multitude" (19:1) points most directly back to chapter 7, though it also evokes the worship scenes from chapters 5, 12, 14, and 15. In chapter 7, in the midst of the seal series of plagues, John sees "a great multitude" beyond counting, "from every nation, from all tribes and peoples and languages" that praises God and the Lamb to whom "salvation belongs" (7:9–10). Both "great multitudes" are dressed in white robes (7:9,14; 19:8).

As with the earlier visions, here we have massive praise, "salvation and glory and power to our God" (19:1). The new dimension is that now we are told that God has "judged the great harlot who corrupted the earth with her fornication." God has brought the judgment due to the harlot for shedding "the blood of God's servants" (19:2). As we know, and which will be confirmed again in the second half of chapter 19, God achieves justice in relation to Babylon because God perseveres in love even in the face of violent bloodletting by the powers. And this justice will result in the destruction of those powers and the healing of the kings of the earth. So, the praise here is not the praise of those who gloat over the punishment of their human enemies. The multitude praises those who welcome God's healing work, work that heals all of creation including *even* their human enemies, and how God ends the reign of violence and centralized power that characterizes the Roman Empire and all other empires before and since.

Though the worship begins with praise for God's justice manifested in the downfall of Babylon, the focus is much more positive. It is as if the taking away of the influence of "the great city" with its "fornications" makes clear just how positive God's agenda is. God seeks healing for the "great multitude" along with the rest of creation. The "salvation" the multitude celebrates here has most of all to do with the Lamb "conquering" the powers of evil and liberating inhabitants of the earth. Salvation is for the multitude, who will live (as we will see) in history on a healed and transformed earth. This multitude will be made into a "bride," worthy to "be clothed with fine linen, bright and pure."

This "fine linen is the just deeds of the saints" (19:8). The way people *live* determines their suitability to be part of this celebration. The idea, though, is not to call for the proverbial "works righteousness" where people prove their worthiness by earning a skeptical God's favor by their accumulation of "good deeds." Rather, the "just deeds" follow from the embrace of God's healing mercy and shape a merciful way of life that, by its nature as life lived in wholeness, simply results in such deeds.

REVELATION 19:11–21

> Then I saw heaven opened, and there was a white horse! Its rider is called Faithful and True, and in righteousness he judges and makes war. His eyes are like a flame of fire, and on his head are many diadems; and he has a name inscribed that no one knows but himself. He is clothed in a robe dipped in blood, and his name is called The Word of God. And the armies of heaven, wearing fine linen, white and pure, were following him on white horses. From his mouth comes a sharp sword with which to strike down the nations, and he will rule them with a rod of iron; he will tread the wine press of the fury of the wrath of God the Almighty. On his robe and on his thigh, he has a name inscribed, "King of kings and Lord of lords." Then I saw an angel standing in the sun, and with a loud voice he called to all the birds that fly in midheaven, "Come, gather for the great supper of God, to eat the flesh of kings, the flesh of captains, the flesh of the mighty, the flesh of horses and their riders—flesh of all, both free and slave, both small and great." Then I saw the beast and the kings of the earth with their armies gathered to make war against the rider on the horse and against his army. And the beast was captured, and with it the false prophet who had performed in its presence the signs by which he deceived those who

had received the mark of the beast and those who worshiped its image. These two were thrown alive into the lake of fire that burns with sulfur. And the rest were killed by the sword of the rider on the horse, the sword that came from his mouth; and all the birds were gorged with their flesh.

The next scene returns us to the drama that has characterized most of the book since the beginning of chapter 6. The breaking of the seals at 6:1 unloosed the first plague series and portrayed the stresses and traumas of humanity's historical existence. There is a method in this madness in Revelation, though, as the plague series and the scenes of judgment lead to the final vision of wholeness for all creation in new Jerusalem.

Back in chapter 4, immediately following the messages "to the seven churches that are in Asia" (1:4; 2:1–3:22), John looked and saw that "in heaven a door stood open" (4:1). Now, in the middle of chapter 19, John again sees "heaven opened" (19:11). This shared image gives us a hint that what follows here in chapter 19 ~~with~~ have affinity with what John saw the previous time heaven was "opened." After the door is opened at 4:1, we saw an extended worship service whose center point is when the slain Lamb "who stands" takes the scroll from the One on the throne (5:7). This turns out to be the key vision of the entire book. The Lamb's persevering love provides the means for the victory that determines the outcome of the human project.

Here in chapter 19, we have what at first glance seems to be something very different. The "war" foreseen at the end of chapter 16 is about to happen. And the key actor is a great warrior on a white horse who rides forth into battle ready to conquer the forces arrayed against him with a sword. However, when we read the description of the vision with Revelation's core vision from chapter 5 in mind, we will see that what John observes when heaven is opened actually is closely linked with what he saw earlier when heaven was opened the first time.

The rider on the white horse is described in the same way as the Jesus of Rev 1–3; this is a picture of Jesus in action. The rider is called "faithful and true" (see 3:14), with eyes "like a flame of fire" (see 2:18), and with "a sharp sword coming" out of his mouth (see 2:12). We must keep in mind that the story we read starting in chapter 4 symbolizes Jesus as a Lamb who "conquers" with persevering love. His most notable act was to resist the powers to the point of shedding his blood. The "blood" of the Lamb is linked in the rest of the book with the faithful deeds of those who follow his way.

So, when we read that the rider "in justice judges and makes war" (19:11), we need to remember the method of "war" that we have seen earlier in Revelation—especially how chapters 7 and 14 use military imagery in relation to the Lamb and his multitude of followers. These, in the words of chapter 12, "conquered [the dragon] by the blood of the Lamb and the word of their testimony" (12:11). As well, when we read that this rider is "clothed in a robe dipped in blood," we realize that this "war" is something very different from our culture's myth of redemptive violence would have us expect. This "war" is not about killing in a physical war. It is about Jesus's self-giving love to the point of shedding his blood in faithful witness against the ways of empire. And he has already done this shedding *prior* to his engagement with the great forces of the dragon at "Armageddon." That is, Jesus *has already conquered* before this alleged "battle."

The rider is joined by "the armies of heaven, wearing fine linen, white and pure, [who] were following him on white horses" (19:13). These "armies," presumably the "great multitude" of earlier in this chapter (19:6) and hence the "great multitude" of chapter 7, from every indication ride into the "battle" also already having conquered. They were given the white robes because of their faithful witness (7:14; 12:10–11; 15:2; 19:7–8)—again, *prior to* this impending "battle." Plus, they carry no weapons of war. Like the rider, they proceed on "white horses" (19:14), the sign of victory.

The only weapon present is the sword the rider carries. That the sword comes out of the mouth of the rider alludes back to the descriptions of Jesus in 1:16 and 2:12. This "sword" is not a literal weapon that soldiers use in military combat, as if Jesus now has become the most violent warrior of all time. Rather, the "sword"—since it comes from his mouth and is not held in his hand—signifies the word of God to which Jesus witnesses. The sword is closely connected with the "name" of the rider: "The Word of God" (19:13).

That the rider is "Faithful and True" and has the sword in his mouth speaks to his faithful witness. Thinking back to Rev 5, we may recognize this witness as nothing other than the Lamb's nonviolent resistance to the powers that was vindicated by God raising him from the dead. The Word that the Lamb proclaims, understood as his entire life of spoken and embodied witness, is precisely the means by which God will "strike down the nations" and "rule them." This is a war of words. The allusion to the "rod of iron" is not implying that Jesus would replace the coercive Roman Empire with a coercive centralized state of his own. Rather, it simply echoes the Old Testament's most famous messianic reference, Ps 2:9. The Lamb that was slain is indeed the "Lion of the tribe of Judah" (5:4) precisely in his nonviolent resistance.

This rider "will tread the wine press of the fury of the wrath of God the Almighty" (19:15). This image links to the grape harvest of 14:17–20. It also links with the fall of Babylon in chapters 17 and 18 when the great harlot drinks the cup full of the wine of the blood of the saints and prophets. That drink expresses God's wrath that uses the cause-and-effect dynamics of Babylon's violence to bring Babylon down (17:6; 18:6). The actual dynamic of "judgment" here is the faithful witness of the rider and the "armies of heaven." Their witness involves suffering and undermines the authority of Babylon and lead to its demise. The rider is identified further in 19:16: "King of kings and Lord of lords." This title alludes back to the beginning of the book. This is a "revelation of Jesus Christ" (1:1), who through his "faithful witness" is affirmed as "the ruler of the kings of the earth" (1:5).

The imagery in 19:11–15 portrays the rider as already victorious and the "armies of heaven" not as actual fighters but as the already victorious multitude. Then, when we get to what we would expect to be a battle scene with the gathered forces of the dragon, there is no battle. "The beast and the kings of the earth with their armies [are] gathered to make war against the rider on the horse and against his army" (19:19). However, what happens, shockingly, is that the beast and the false prophet, powerful as they had seemed back in chapter 13, are simply captured without a fight. And they are thrown "into the lake of fire" (19:20).

We are not told why the beast and false prophet were so easily taken down. Revelation, as a whole, shows us that the power of these figures was mostly a façade, based on their ability to deceive (as noted here also, 19:20). With their deception unmasked, there is no power. By what means is the deception unmasked? The faithful witness of the Lamb and his multitude of followers. The very experience of seeming defeat at the hands of the evil powers proves to reveal the true character of those powers, undermining their ability to deceive.

The fate of the human actors in this vision is a bit unclear. On the one hand, they are not thrown into the lake of fire with the beast and dragon. There is a separation between the spiritual forces of evil and the humans who were deceived by them into opposing God. This would seem to allow for the possibility of a different kind of fate for the "kings of the earth" (19:19). On the other hand, we are told they were "killed" and "the birds were gorged with their flesh" (19:21). However, we should note that they were "killed" by "the sword that came from [the rider's] mouth" (19:21). Since we know this sword is not literally a killing weapon but instead is the word of God, perhaps there is a hint here that the "killing" is metaphorical, a purifying process more than some kind of eternal punishment or separation from God.

The ultimate outcome, we will discover when we read of new Jerusalem, is that "the kings of the earth" actually find their way into God's paradise. They do not get thrown into the lake of fire. Perhaps the "killing" by the sword and the "devouring" by the birds actually turn out to be elements of the *transformation* of the kings of the earth from those who trusted in the dragon to those who could be at home in a city where nothing unclean was to be found (21:27).

THE WAR THAT'S NOT A WAR

Over and over again in Revelation we are told that the beast, the dragon, the city Babylon, these powers that symbolize the domination system, are defeated. They go down, and "it is all over." Yet the powers keep coming back, they keep showing up. You may remember the old folk song, "The Cat Came Back." It has also been turned into a children's book. Mr. Johnson wants to get rid of this pesky old yellow cat. "He gave it to a little man who was going far away, but the cat came back the very next day." And it goes on, a little boy takes the cat on a boat trip. The boat capsizes; lives were lost. But still the cat came back. In one version, even after the hydrogen bomb falls, the cat comes back. "They thought he was gone, but the cat came back, he just wouldn't stay away."

This is kind of like the dragon and its minions in Revelation. They go down in chapters 11 and 12. They go down in chapter 17. And then in chapter 18. And at the beginning of chapter 19, the great harlot has been judged and smoke goes up from her forever and ever. And yet, in chapter 19 the powers of evil are back at it, gathered for the battle of Armageddon. That the powers keep coming back is a literary technique. It pushes the narrative ahead. We come to the end but know there is still more of the book to come. Then we circle back, and it happens again. This drama holds readers' interest. But I also think there is a theological message here too. The return of the doomed powers is a way to say that history, the three and a half years we live in, is not simply linear. Certainly, the outcome that matters isn't only in the future.

That the powers keep coming back and that the Lamb's followers keep celebrating tell us that what matters is what we do now. The story in Revelation is not about the future. It's about the present—the present of John the writer but also the present of all the readers throughout history. The powers are always present, but so too is the celebration, if we but choose to join it.

My phrase, "the war that's not a war" is actually a good title for Revelation as a whole. Why so? Well, Revelation tells us about an ongoing conflict, a conflict that is deadly and that requires, in the words of Harry Potter's teacher Alastor "Mad-Eye" Moody, "constant vigilance." Revelation frames the conflict in terms of living in a life-enhancing way in the midst of the death-dealing ways of the Roman Empire. There is a war, yet Revelation makes it clear that this war is not to be fought with conventional weapons. It's not to be a typical war with winners and losers, death and destruction. The "conquering" that needs to happen comes about through love, not through force. So, it's a war that's not really a war.

Revelation 19 directly gives this kind of picture. Back in chapter 16, at the conclusion of the series of visions where the bowls of God's wrath are poured out, we read that the beast and false prophet will gather "the kings of the whole world, to assemble them for battle on the great day of God the Almighty . . . at the place . . . called Armageddon" (16:14,16). However, then come two chapters' worth of visions of the destruction of the city Babylon, the great harlot—the home for the kings of the earth, the social manifestation of the influence of the beast. There is no battle here, just what amounts to this great city committing a kind of suicide as its death-dealing dynamics bring self-destruction. Then there is a celebration; the city is gone. The marriage of the Lamb and the Lamb's followers is at hand.

Yet the story has not forgotten the expected battle. We return to the "battlefield" at 19:11. The great warrior figure rides forth on a mighty white horse accompanied by "the armies of heaven." So, it's Armageddon time. But read carefully here. As happens earlier in the book, with chapter 19 many interpreters seem to forget the operating dynamic of the book as a whole. They seem to forget that the Lamb who gave his life to love and nonviolent resistance to the powers has been vindicated by God and expresses the ultimate power of the universe.

We must keep the vision of the victorious Lamb (chapter 5) in mind. If we do, we shouldn't have much trouble seeing that in fact what happens with the coming of the rider on the white horse is a creative way of portraying a war that is not a war. There is no battle. The powers have been fooled. Still, it is not accidental that the rider is portrayed with battle-like imagery. In fact, he is said to "make war." He rides a great white horse. He wields a powerful sword. Think Aragorn in *The Return of the King*, bearing the reforged "sword that was broken" into battle.[1] The rider is joined by massive armies of heaven.

As I said, Revelation insists we are in a terrible conflict. Life during the three and a half years is life that requires "life-and-death ethics." "Life-and-death ethics" comes from philosopher Philip Hallie's book *Lest Innocent Blood Be Shed* about the people of Le Chambon, the French village that saved the lives of over 5,000 Jewish refugees during World War II. By "life-and-death ethics," Hallie means a fundamental commitment that all

1. Tolkien, *Return*.

human life is precious beyond measure. Because life is precious, we avoid harming others. Even more, we act to prevent harm.[2] The story Hallie tells certainly takes place in an emergency situation. I think Revelation means to tell its readers that this entire three and a half years is an emergency situation. Life-and-death ethics always apply because harm-doing always lurks around us. The follower of the Lamb recognizes the presence of the "war" that the Lamb wages against harm-doers.

Let's look more closely at the imagery in chapter 19. We will see that in waging war the Lamb actually does not wage violent war. First of all, there is only one mention of "blood" in this entire scene. And it is completely consistent with the way "blood" is portrayed in the entire book. Shockingly, if we are expecting a battle, it is one without any combatant's blood being shed. The blood here belongs to the rider himself, and it is shed before he rides forth.

The rider "is clothed in a robe dipped in blood" (19:13). Clearly the rider is Jesus the Lamb that was slain from chapter 5. This blood on his garment is the blood that chapter tells us about. None of the armies of heaven that join with the rider carry weapons. They wear "fine linen, white and pure" (19:14). Back in chapter 7 we meet the multitudes who are given white robes washed and made white in the Lamb's blood. According to chapter 12, they "conquer the [dragon] by the blood of the Lamb and by the word of their testimony." Their method of waging "war" is self-giving love. They fight without fighting in a war that is not a war.

Then, what happens when the "battle" is joined? No bloodshed. No battle. The powers of evil, the beast and false prophet, are simply captured. A war that's not a war. The issue is not the intrinsic power of the powers. The beast and false prophet actually are powerless when people don't believe in them. Sadly, though, people do still believe in the message of the powers. People keep believing in, say, the necessity of violence to stop evil or in the need to defer to people in power. People still believe in the need to find scapegoats to blame our problems on or in "my country right or wrong."

Such beliefs are why Revelation emphasizes that the weapon that conquers the powers is the word of testimony that Jesus gives. The way to salvation is this: Love your neighbor (Luke). Forgive seventy times seven (Matthew). Understand that the Sabbath is for humankind not humankind for the Sabbath (Mark). Let the one without sin cast the first stone (John). Know that the rulers of the nations lord it over others and that it must not be so among you (Mark). Recognize that the greatest among you shall be the servant of all (Luke). Understand that blessed are the peacemakers

---

2. Hallie, *Lest*, 269–87.

(Matthew). And so on. The approach taken by the "armies of heaven" (which is made up of you and me, all who seek to follow the way of the Lamb) that leads to conquest is simply to return to the core message of Jesus. When there are questions or doubts, go back to the path of love. Then the beast can't touch you.

The imagery at the end of Rev 19 challenges us. First the beast and false prophet are simply captured and thrown into the lake of fire. I understand this to be an image of their destruction. We must keep in mind what John means by "beast" and "false prophet" in Revelation, though. These are symbols and personifications. They are not human persons. They symbolize prejudice and the structures of injustice: Human culture insofar as it dehumanizes, belief systems that exclude as fully human those outside the circle of "truth," the dynamics of racism and patriarchy and homophobia that socialize us to fear, to other, and to scapegoat.

The image of the beast and false prophet being thrown into the lake of fire is not about revenge against human beings. Rather, this image is about destroying the destroyers of the earth (11:18) for the sake of all life. However, the images here do get a bit complicated. If we expect to find revenge and punishment of human beings in Revelation, we might find some here. This is so because, after the beast and false prophet go into the lake of fire, we do read of something happening to their human allies. "The rest [meaning the kings of the earth and their armies] were killed by the sword of the rider on the horse, the sword that came from his mouth; and all the birds were gorged with their flesh" (19:21). Sounds pretty harsh. However, we need to look at this carefully and keep in mind what we already know about this rider and what we learn about the kings of the earth as we read on.

The rider clearly is Jesus, whose blood brought victory through persevering love. The blood of Jesus's opponents is never shed in all of Revelation. And the sword that "kills" here is the "sword that came from his mouth," meaning his words—not words of condemnation but words of welcome and healing. That these are words of healing is confirmed by what comes later in Revelation. The kings of the earth, these very minions of the beast who go to Armageddon and expect to fight against Jesus, end up in new Jerusalem and eat the healing fruit from the tree of life. What we have at the end of Rev 19 is a gruesome picture of *healing*, not punishment. We sense that life transforming mercy turns the world of the kings of the earth upside down. We have a fascinating precedent in the New Testament.

The apostle Paul, in his pre-Christian days as a zealous fighter for truth (as he understood it) literally had wielded the sword of punishment. He shed the blood of Jesus's followers. He totally sold out to the politics of purity and fought in many little Armageddons against followers of the Lamb.

But then he met Jesus on the Damascus Road and had his world turned upside down. The violence of love.

When Paul met Jesus, he was blinded and rendered speechless. It took him months, maybe years, to piece things back together. His healing required a sort of being killed, a sort of being devoured by the birds of heaven. And then he himself became a bearer of the gospel of mercy and did as much as he could to tear down the very walls that had led him to violence. To think about the images in chapter 19 in light of Paul makes it pretty believable that they actually are consistent with the message of the Lamb in Rev 5.

The terms "apocalypse" and "eschatology" are relevant today. You don't have to believe in the rapture to think we live in times of crises. There is a fascinating book by Eugene, Oregon anarchist John Zerzan, *Elements of Refusal*.[3] Zerzan offers a radical and in many ways persuasive critique of modern civilization. His articulation of the Babylon-going-down motif in relation to twenty-first-century America is perceptive. His is indeed an "apocalyptic" vision. We are doing ourselves in. That which seems solid may well soon melt into air. Perceptive as Zerzan's critique may be, though, it is not "*biblical* apocalyptic" nor "*biblical* eschatology." It has only some things in common with Revelation. These are important things, but not the whole picture. Along with its critique of civilization (just as radical and thorough-going as Zerzan's anarchist critique), Revelation adds another dimension that I find missing in *Elements of Refusal*.

Throughout Revelation, more important than the critique, we hear of worship happening, praises being sung, human solidarity, even celebration in face of civilization's destructiveness. Zerzan has nothing comparable in his vision. He portrays destruction without much healing. In contrast, Revelation's apocalyptic sensibility actually is hopeful and joyful. We do well to notice that Revelation's worship is not mainly about going to church.

Worship in Revelation is about celebrating life here and now. Revelation does not point to the future saying hold on in your present of life as nasty, brutish, and short and in the by-and-by all will be well. No. Revelation says sing, celebrate, and live joyfully *right now*. The way of the Lamb is the way of life. You may suffer grievously as you seek to embody it, but you will also know joy, you will know life.

Our future does look pretty grim right now—global warming, expanding drone warfare, unrelenting corporate domination, cold-heartedness toward vulnerable people, austerity, dead oceans. I do feel a sense of urgency to try to create a better future. Revelation can remind me that only peace is

3. Zerzan, *Elements*.

the way to peace. For there to be a usable future, the paths of transformation must be built and sustained. However, we also need to remember always to see value in celebration, in hugging, and in laughing. The best preparation for the future is to learn to love in the present. Human beings are pretty resilient when we find ways to live in love.

FOR FURTHER ENGAGEMENT

1. Summarize the argument that the author makes to support his statement, "This 'war' is not about killing in a physical war. It is about Jesus's self-giving love to the point of allowing his blood to be shed in faithful witness against the ways of empire." Evaluate that argument.

2. What does the symbolism of "the marriage supper of the Lamb" convey?

3. What is the significance of the bride "making herself ready" for the marriage supper of the Lamb? What is the role of the "righteous deeds of the saints" (19:8)? What *are* these "righteous deeds"? Reflect on the author's comments regarding the "just deeds of the saints" (19:8): "The 'just deeds' follow from the embrace of God's healing mercy and shape a merciful way of life that simply by its nature as life lived in wholeness results in such deeds."

4. Note the description of Jesus in 19:11–16. What is the significance of the various symbols associated with him? How does this description compare with others in the book? What is the mission of the rider on the white horse? Do you see the picture in 19:11–16 as consistent with the Jesus of the Gospels? Should it be?

5. What do you make of the apparent absence of a real battle where one is expected (19:19–20)? Assuming that this is a way to emphasize the all-sufficiency of Jesus's cross and resurrection for defeating the forces of evil, do you think this has any relevance for present-day struggles with evil?

6. Revelation 19 begins with "the loud voice of the great multitude" singing praise because God "has avenged on [the great harlot] the blood of her servants" (19:2). This seems likely to be a reference to the cry for vengeance from the martyrs of 6:9–11. Given what we have read in Rev 17 and 18, who (or what) has the vengeance been visited upon? Is this seemingly violent and punitive vengeance consistent with the character of God as revealed in Jesus? Explain.

7. Instead of having an actual battle, the beast and false prophet are simply captured and thrown into the lake of fire (19:20). Why do you suppose in the end there is no battle, and these powers are so easily overcome?

8. How do you interpret this statement in Rev 19:21: "The rest were killed by the sword of the rider on the horse, the sword that came from his mouth, and all the birds were gorged with their flesh"?

9. What do you think the role of the saints is in the "battle" of 19:11–21? How would you summarize the role of the saints in the entire process of the "Lamb's war" in Revelation?

16

The Judgment That's
Not a Judgment

[Revelation 20]

Revelation 20 comes in the middle of the final set of visions that complete the book of Revelation. The first part of chapter 19 shows the great celebration of the Lamb's marriage following the fall of Babylon the Great (chapter 18). Then comes the battle that's not really a battle where the rider on the white horse (Jesus, crucified and resurrected) captures two of his main enemies, the beast and the false prophet, and dispatches them (without an actual battle) to the lake of fire. The book concludes in chapters 21 and 22 with a vision of new Jerusalem, the city of peace and healing that has been in the background from the beginning of Revelation. Tears are wiped away never to return, and ceaseless celebration and praise of the Lamb and the One on the throne ensues.

In between, in chapter 20, comes a series of cryptic visions that complete the judgment and destruction of the powers of evil (finally, the dragon, the power behind Babylon, the beast, and the false prophet). The visions portray the judgment of all of humanity and the final destruction of Death and Hades. These visions (like the rest of Revelation) should not be read strictly in terms of chronology. One interpretive approach that especially makes the visions in chapter 20 confusing is to assume that this chapter presents events that will happen in the future after everything else shown earlier in the book. A better approach sees this chapter as a kind of recapitulation of some of the main themes from earlier in the book. Rev 20 is also best understood as a picture of *present* reality. And it offers a theology of judgment that is quite different from what is usually assumed to characterize Revelation.

REVELATION 20:1–3

> Then I saw an angel coming down from heaven, holding in his hand the key to the bottomless pit and a great chain. He seized the dragon, that ancient serpent, who is the Devil and Satan, and bound him for a thousand years, and threw him into the pit, and locked and sealed it over him, so that he would deceive the nations no more, until the thousand years were ended. After that he must be let out for a little while.

Chapter 19 concludes with a gruesome picture of the rider "killing" the armies of the beast and then the birds "gorging" themselves on the armies' flesh. This vision is followed in 20:1 by one of John's standard uses of "then I saw" that emphasizes both that there is a change of scene coming up and that there is continuity between what was just seen and what is coming next. But the "next" should not be understood in terms of historical chronology, rather simply as the order in which John sees these various aspects of his present reality.

One of God's angels enters the scene and takes the dragon (identified as "the Devil and Satan"), binds it, and throws it into the pit that is locked and sealed. This imprisonment lasts for "a thousand years." We know that the dragon (Babylon's animating spirit) is the power behind the beast and false prophet. And we know that when the "battle" of the beast and his armies against the Lamb actually happens, there is no battle. The spiritual enemies of the Lamb are simply captured and thrown into the lake of fire. So, it's not surprising that the power behind the beast also is simply captured. We may see the capture of the dragon as the reason why the beast could be so easily defeated. Their power actually cannot stand in face of the Lamb.

That is, along with everything else that is mentioned beginning with 6:1, the fate of the dragon must be seen in light of the victory already won, described in Rev 5, by the faithful Lamb. The dragon's lack of power echoes the picture in the Gospel of Mark of the "strong man" who is bound, easily, by the power of Jesus (Mark 3:22–27). Jesus's power over demons points ahead to his power over the dragon. The "thousand years" clearly is a symbolic number, though its precise meaning is unclear. Reading it in light of the rest of Revelation, probably the best interpretation is to see it as another symbol for the time we live in, historical time (three and a half years, forty-two months, and 1,260 days). This time is marked by sin, suffering, and brokenness—as well as by faithfulness, healing, and celebration. We could say the three and a half years is "plague time" and the thousand years is "worship time"—and that they are simultaneous.

The purpose of the dragon's binding is that "he would deceive the nations no more until the thousand years were ended" (20:3). This statement does not make sense if we take it literally. Precisely what characterizes the thousand years is that the dragon is indeed deceiving the nations—that's why it is a time of sin, suffering, and brokenness.

Maybe the point, though, is not that this reference to the one thousand years states precisely what will happen so much as giving the *purpose* of the binding. The dragon is bound *in order that* it not deceive. The trouble, though, is that the dragon doesn't actually stay bound, even during the thousand years. When that time is up, we are told, "He must be let out for a little while." The dragon being "let out" might symbolize the sad reality that "the nations" have continued to give the dragon power even while he is rendered powerless ("bound") by Jesus's revelation. But being loosed "for a little while" is a reminder that the dragon is not an inherent part of creation, it can be resisted and even rendered powerless when people don't worship it.

REVELATION 20:4–6

> Then I saw thrones, and those seated on them were given authority to judge. I also saw the souls of those who had been beheaded for their testimony to Jesus and for the word of God. They had not worshiped the beast or its image and had not received its mark on their foreheads or their hands. They came to life and reigned with Christ a thousand years. (The rest of the dead did not come to life until the thousand years were ended.) This is the first resurrection. Blessed and holy are those who share in the first resurrection. Over these the second death has no power, but they will be priests of God and of Christ, and they will reign with him a thousand years.

The next paragraph contains more cryptic imagery. We will better understand these verses if we read them in light of the rest of Revelation. Here, too, we have a brief restatement of what has already been shown in previous chapters. Special emphasis is placed here in chapter 20 on the fate of the dragon. This paragraph focuses on those who have resisted the dragon and the beast and how crucial their witness has been and will be.

These who "had not worshiped the beast" are the same as the "countless multitude who were given white robes" in chapter 7, the "two witnesses" of chapter 11, and the "144,000" of chapter 14. It is a mistake to take the imagery too literally or to assume that in some direct sense John has in mind two classes of saved people, the martyrs and everyone else. Rather, the point more simply is to highlight how important the witness to the way of Jesus is in resisting the dragon—for everyone. "Those who had been beheaded" is an image meant to inspire all kinds of resistance (certainly including the possibility of literal death). Such resistance will echo the "testimony to Jesus and . . . the word of God" that leads to a refusal to "worship the beast or its image." John expects such resistance from of all followers of the Lamb, not just a special class of martyrs.

John challenges all his readers to be part of the multitude that "reigns with Christ" during this "thousand years"—that is, during historical time. His point here is analogous to what we meant by the earlier references to worship amidst the times of struggle (see chapters 7 and 14, for example). We "reign with Christ" when we witness to his way powerfully and effectively amidst the struggle. Followers of the Lamb "reign" when they remain faithful amidst suffering and in the face of the hostility of the powers. In doing so, they are "priests" who mediate to the nations (including the "kings of the earth") the message of the Lamb's victory through persevering love.

The reference in 20:4 to "thrones" inhabited by those who "were given authority to judge" is a bit unclear. The dragon, who is the power behind the emperors and kings of the earth whose "judgment" resulted in the "beheading" of those who witnessed to Jesus, is actually the one being judged here. What happens here is a reversal; the judgment that matters is a reversal of how "authority" works among the nations. It remains to be seen what the consequences of the judgment will be. In this paragraph, though, it is clear that those who the dragon's minions judged to be worthy of execution (the witnesses to the Lamb's way) are vindicated in God's authentic judgment.

REVELATION 20:7–10

When the thousand years are ended, Satan will be released from his prison and will come out to deceive the nations at the four corners of the earth, Gog and Magog, in order to gather them for battle; they are as numerous as the sands of the sea. They marched up over the breadth of the earth and surrounded the camp of the saints and the beloved city. And fire came down from heaven and consumed them. And the devil who had deceived them was thrown into the lake of fire and sulfur, where the beast and the false prophet were, and they will be tormented day and night forever and ever.

This paragraph repeats the account of 19:11–21 in almost every detail except that here the role of the dragon ("Satan" [20:7] and "the devil" [20:10]) is emphasized. The "battle" (that turns out not to be a battle) in chapter 19 comes at the end of the story of the beast attempting to destroy the Lamb and the Lamb's people. In chapter 20, the "battle" comes after the 1,000 years has ended. In chapter 19, "the kings of the earth with their armies" gather for battle (this force had first been mentioned in 16:14). In chapter 20, Satan gathers nations "from the four corners of the earth . . . for battle."

The key parallel between 19:11–21 and 20:7–10 is that we don't actually have a battle. In chapter 19, the beast and his false prophet are simply captured and thrown into the lake of fire (19:20). Here, "the devil" (i.e., the dragon) is simply captured and thrown into the lake of fire (20:10). That is, "the devil who deceived them," the devil who deceived the nations and their kings to trust in his way and to oppose the way of the Lamb.

We have reason, because of the close parallels, to perceive in chapter 20 the same dynamic of victory over the powers that chapter 19 presents: The Lamb's shed blood prior to the "battle" provides the only needed basis for victory. Going back to chapters 4 and 5, the faithfulness of the Lamb to the path of persevering love is in fact the most powerful force in the universe. That faithfulness provides the bases for fulfilling the purpose of human history. In the end, the final expression of the "Lamb's war" is that the dragon himself is captured and sent to the lake of fire to join the beast and the false prophet "forever and ever."

The capture and destruction of the dragon is crucial for what follows as Revelation comes to a close. The power that the dragon wields is *deception*, that's all. When the conflict actually comes to a head, the dragon (like the beast and the false prophet) is simply captured, seemingly without a struggle and sent to its end. For John, this powerful metaphor points to the source of the power that matters in our world. The power of truth, the power of the Lamb, trumps the seemingly all-powerful dragon whose only actual power is the power to deceive.

Hence, the motif that defines the book as a whole: The *revelation* of Jesus Christ. How is the dragon to be defeated? Through following the Lamb wherever he goes. Which is to say, the dragon is defeated when people *see* that love is truthful and that domination and nationalism and materialism and fear and violence are not truthful. It's a simple thing; simply learn to see what is for what it is.

Details about the "dragon" are not given in Revelation. Is this symbol meant to convey a sense of an actual personal being? Or does it have more to do with a personification of cultural dynamics that corrupt human beings by causing people to trust in empires and ideologies and institutions of injustice and brokenness for their ultimate reality? Is the "dragon" another way of talking about dynamics that foster idolatry? When the dragon is thrown in the lake of fire, does God punish an actual personal being or is this rather a symbolic way of portraying the death of ideologies and values and spiritualities that foster alienation and death? Maybe what follows the end of the dragon can help us discern how to answer these questions.

REVELATION 20:11–15

> Then I saw a great white throne and the one who sat on it; the earth and the heaven fled from his presence, and no place was found for them. And I saw the dead, great and small, standing before the throne, and books were opened. Also, another book was opened, the book of life. And the dead were judged according to their works, as recorded in the books. And the sea gave up the dead that were in it, Death and Hades gave up the dead that were in them, and all were judged according to what they had done. Then Death and Hades were thrown into the lake of fire. This is the second death, the lake of fire; and anyone whose name was not found written in the book of life was thrown into the lake of fire.

The next "then I saw" (20:11) reminds us that what follows presupposes what we have just seen. The "judgment" of 20:11–15 happens with the dragon out of the picture; the great deceiver's web of deceit has been broken. The "One on the throne" is great, "the earth and heaven fled from his presence" (20:11). We must remember, though, that the One on the throne is closely identified with the Lamb. The fleeing away of earth and heaven is not to be understood as terror from a violent and retributive judge.

The One on the throne works throughout Revelation in harmony with the persevering love of the Lamb. The love of the Lamb opens the great scroll of chapter 5 and that leads to new Jerusalem. The "fleeing" here is not related to judgment as punitive justice. Rather, most probably, the fleeing has to do with what is actually the healing of earth and heaven that involves the disappearance of the brokenness and alienation that had been fostered by the dragon.

The use of two books as the bases for judgment is an ingenious, if complicated, touch. Notice that the first book, the one that contains a record of human beings' "works," is not named. It is of secondary importance, in service to the second book. The second book *is* named: "the book of life." The naming of only the second book reiterates what we have read earlier. The default stance of God is to welcome everyone who wants to be there into God's presence. All people are in the book of life unless they act in such a way as to lead to the "blotting out" of their name (3:5). The first book, then, is not a list of good works that must be sufficient in order for one to overcome their default exclusion from paradise. Rather, it more likely tells of the active acts of hostility toward peace and justice that would lead to having one's name "blotted out."

Let's remember that the main dynamic behind such acts of hostility was the dragon's deception. We surely best understand that this final judgment reflects God's awareness of the true status of human hearts once the deceiver's deceptions have been taken away. The picture here suggests a distinction between human agency freely expressed and the powerful influence of the fallen powers that try to separate us from God's love. When the deceiver, the fueling energy behind the systems of domination, is taken away, people are freed to see God and the Lamb for who they truly are.

We also need to think of the notion of "judgment" here in light of the overall trajectory Revelation. "Judgment" links with "justice." We could say that the purpose of God's judgment is to bring true justice to bear on the human condition. How do we understand God's justice? Our starting point should be that God's justice has to do with God making things right. That is, God's justice is about God bringing healing, reconciliation, and the restoration of relationships.

All that being said, the picture in 20:11–15 does leave open the possibility that even with the deceiver out of the picture, some human beings may still truly be blotted out the book of life and doomed to join the dragon and his minions in the lake of fire. I understand this possibility to mainly be a metaphorical way of emphasizing human freedom. We *can* choose against God. But *will* we? We need to look at Rev 21 before responding to that question. But let's remember that the human beings throughout Revelation who surely are most likely to have their names blotted out are the "kings of the earth."

THE JUDGMENT THAT'S NOT A JUDGMENT

One of the things many see when they look at Revelation is judgment. But what kind of judgment? Maybe what we see when we see scenes of judgment is itself kind of a Rorschach test. What we make of judgment reveals a lot about our psychological makeup—or at least our theological makeup.

Back in the late 1990s. I went with some students to hear the theologian Miroslav Volf speak. Volf wrote a well-received book called *Exclusion and Embrace*.[1] It drew in poignant ways on his experience as a Croatian with the terrible violence in the Balkans conflicts he had lived through. He powerfully emphasized the need for forgiveness, compassion, and reconciliation in the face of brokenness. However, there was a key element of Volf's argument, about judgment, with which some of us felt uneasy. He suggested that a major reason why Christians might advocate and practice this radical "embrace," even of enemies, is because of our trust that in the end God will *judge* evildoers. This judgment will be punitive. We don't have to do violence against offenders because we count on God's violence in the end.

I can picture the room where we met. The audience was in a U-shaped set of chairs with the speaker at the open end of the U. I was directly to one side of him and one of my like-minded students was on the opposite side. During the discussion we started firing questions from both sides, and Professor Volf was kind of whipping his head, first clear in one direction and then, right away, clear to the other direction. Back and forth. It was a friendly if intense debate, and we didn't resolve it.

Certainly, though, Volf's is a common way to read Revelation's sense of judgment. For those with such views, sin and wrongdoing shape human history. We can't successfully fight against all of it. It may even seem that evil people are going to win. But we have the promise of Revelation. God will have the final say. For such interpreters, "Vengeance will be mine, saith the Lord," means that God will ultimately punish those human beings who have so egregiously violated the commandments. When I argue against that kind of theology, I go against the grain of most other interpreters of Revelation. Some see Revelation preaching punitive judgment toward human beings and they rejoice. Others see Revelation preaching punitive judgment toward human beings and they are repulsed.

Revelation 20 is one of the main "judgment" texts in Revelation. I think one of the problems when we think about judgment in a passage like this is that we tend to assume that "judgment" has to do with "punishment." The time of judgment is when people get punished. But what if judgment

---

1. Volf, *Exclusion*.

actually has to do with something else? Maybe judgment has to do, not with punishment so much as with making things right. Maybe God is "judge" not as the Great Punisher but as the Great Healer.

The book of Revelation ends with a surprise. The kings of the earth surely were terrified of God after God sent their bosses (the beast and the false prophet) into the lake of fire. They thought they would be next, expecting God to rule with the same kind of brute, retributive force the beast and dragon used. But it doesn't turn out that way. There are two types of judgment going on in Rev 20—the judgment of the dragon and the judgment of human beings. It seems important to see them as separate. The dragon's judgment results in its destruction. But what happens to the people? Their fate actually turns out to be something quite different than punitive destruction, even the fate of those who had trusted in the dragon.

Let's focus on the dragon first. To understand the dragon, we must first understand John's agenda. His concern is that people get sucked into beliefs and practices that usurp God. For example, people trust in their nation as the lynchpin of their identity and hence are seduced into violence and exploitation—for John the Roman Empire, for us the American empire. With this trust, people see the world through the eyes of those in power. The false prophet in Revelation is the master of propaganda; in the US, over and over, it has been the corporate media and pundits that push the US toward war in Iraq or Syria or Libya or Russia or . . .

Self-destructive trust in power and wealth abounded in ancient Rome, trust that John perceives even among those in the churches. And we certainly see a similar problem today. I think, as a random example from news reports, of a frightening article about how jellyfish are taking over the oceans of the world.[2] For millions of years they have been held in check, essentially by the health of oceanic ecosystems. But the modern world's mad trust in economic growth at all costs has created unhealth in the oceans and turned them into the gathering point of the poisons and ecological degradation of modern civilization. The continued idolatry of economic growth and the inability of societies to resist corporate obsession with profits make it hard to imagine the tide being turned (so to speak).

Why is it that we can't turn the tide? What is it that pulls cultures into spirals of death? A crucial factor is that we have belief systems and worldviews that act on us, that shape us, that *pull* us into the spiral. Such "currents" toward dehumanization concern John in Revelation. He uses the metaphor of "the beast" to characterize a culture that shapes people toward domination as it utilizes cultural myths such as the belief in the redemptive

2. Giggs, "Imagining."

power of violence. And John goes deeper. Behind the culture of domination is another force. Behind the beast is the dragon.

The "dragon" is a fascinating and appropriate image. What are dragons? They are mythological creatures. They are not exactly real. But they can seem real. They exist, we could say, in our collective and individual subconscious. The "dragon" is an image for the deep-seated sense that the universe is dangerous, malevolent, hostile, a hierarchy of power. The dragon, in Revelation, is the force that cultivates fearfulness, a fearfulness that tempts us to trust in idols for our security, even idols that ultimately devour us. The dragon represents the beliefs, traditions, and structures that act on us from the time we are born. Such dynamics feed our culture's racism, sexism, nationalism, and exploitation of creation.

There is something real about idolatrous powers. However, they have little or no power over those who are not deceived by them. Hence, the visions in Rev 19 and 20 imagine the powers of evil actually to be easily "bound" and "conquered" by those who aren't afraid, those such as the Lamb and his followers who trust in the God of love. Chapter 20 actually repeats the vision of chapter 19, though with a focus on the dragon instead of the beast as the *deepest* source of alienation and idolatry. The story is the same. The powers of evil and their human minions (led by the kings of the earth) gather to battle against the Lamb.

As we discussed above, there is *no* battle. The weapon that wins is the Lamb's self-giving love of chapter 5. So, the judgment against the dragon is not God using violence to conquer. It is God revealing the love that breaks the deception. The weapon that works is persevering love, all the way down. To try to crush the dragon (or anything else) with brute force only empowers the dragon. When people see and trust in the way of the Lamb, they break the hold of the dragon and send it into the lake of fire. This is the first kind of judgment: God's condemnation of the idolatry of death for the sake of liberating humanity. When the militarism-racism-nationalism-economic exploitation are disbelieved they lose their power and are "destroyed."

What about the second kind of judgment? What happens to people in this story of judgment? Let's notice that the "great white throne" judgment comes after the dragon's destruction. And to what effect? The scene that depicts the judgment of humanity focuses on two kinds of books. The first books, those that contain a record of human beings' "works," do not have names. They serve the second kind of book that is named: "The book of life." The book of *life* is about God's generosity and abundance. We have been told already in Revelation that the default stance of God is to welcome everyone who wants to be in God's presence. John assumes everyone is in the book of life. So, when some are warned about identifying too closely with the dragon, they are told that their names—already in this book—*may* be "blotted out" (3:5). This warning is a threat, not a certainty.

We should not understand the first book, a book that focuses on human deeds, to suggest that God keeps close track of our good deeds and if we do enough, we might earn our salvation that otherwise would not be offered. Rather, the "works" here are more likely the evil deeds that reflect hearts in harmony with the dragon. They are works of hostility toward peace, compassion, and restorative justice. They are the ways of life that blind people to God's love and in that way lead toward the blotting out of names from the book of life. It is dangerous to trust in idols because you may become just like them—lifeless.

Still, though, let's remember the strong message of Revelation that people live lives of hostility to love because they are deceived by the dragon and his minions. We surely best understand this picture of final judgment to reflect God's awareness of the true status of human hearts once the deceiver's deceptions have been taken away. We may hope that when the deceiver is taken away, when the deceptions end, when the powers that try to separate us from God's love are truly conquered, people might find the freedom to see God and the Lamb for who they truly are.

The destruction of the dragon is part of the process of the judgment of human beings that provides for healing even for those people most deceived by the dragon. So, contrary to Miroslav Volf's view, the story is about mercy *all the way down*. Those who maim and murder and oppress need healing too. Our task is to follow the Lamb wherever he goes—to help that healing happen because all of life is precious.

The true message of Revelation is not that healing will certainly come—though we should hope for ultimate healing. But the true message is about the means, the method, about *how* healing comes. The *only* way that healing will come is through consistent, persevering love. All of life is precious. As followers of the Lamb, our task is to embody that love.

To draw from the letter to the Ephesians, our struggle is not with flesh and blood, but with the powers and principalities (Eph 6:12). We are not to hate and seek to kill human kings and their human servants—though we certainly must resist their actions and their lies. Rather, we are to resist the dragon, the ideologies, and the structures of violence for the sake even of the kings themselves. The means for such a struggle remain the way of the Lamb.

FOR FURTHER ENGAGEMENT

1. What do you think is going on in what seems to be a scene of final judgment (20:11–15)? Do you expect this to happen? If so, what do you think your fate will be? Based on what? If not, what do you think this scene means for us? How do you understand a person's fate to be determined? What allows a person to have one's name in the book of life? Do you know anyone that you think has been or will be thrown in the lake of fire? Explain.

2. What is your understanding of the millennium? What other biblical parallels to the 1,000 years of chapter 20 are there? Do you agree with the 1,000 years is a symbol for the time between Christ's first and second comings? If not, how do you understand it? How important do you think this issue is? Why?

3. What do you make of the binding of Satan (20:2)? Is it conceivable that Satan is bound now, given the rampant evil in our world?

4. Only at 20:11 is God's throne described as "white." Is the color symbolism important? What is the meaning of 20:11b? What does the great white throne add to the consummation of the judgment of God?

5. Is the idea of the great white throne judgment a comfort or a threat to you? Why? How is your attitude toward this related to your view of God and God's predisposition toward you?

6. How do you make sense of the vision concerning the dragon in 20:1–10? Do agree that this is a recap of material already presented in Revelation, just from a different perspective? What is similar between these verses and the vision concerning the beast and false prophet in chapter 19?

7. The author suggests that the dynamics around the defeat of the dragon in chapter 20:7–10 are the same as those in 19:11–21 around the defeat of the beast. Do you agree or disagree? Explain.

8. Reflect on the image of the dragon joining the beast in the lake of fire and being "tormented day and night forever and ever" (20:10). Is this a comforting vision? Or troubling? Is this scene compatible with believing that God is a God of love who conquers through self-sacrifice?

9. How would you explain the dragon (or Satan, 20:7, or the devil, 20:10)? Is this a personal being? A personification of the spiritual and social dynamics of evil? A mere metaphor?

10. Respond to this comment by the author: "We tend to assume that 'judgment' has to do with 'punishment.' The time of judgment is when people get punished. But what if judgment actually has to do with something else? Maybe judgment has to do, not with punishment so much as with making things right. Maybe God is 'judge' not as the Great Punisher but as the Great Healer."

17

What is Paradise For?

[Revelation 21–22]

The book of Revelation reaches its conclusion following the destruction of the beast, the false prophet, the dragon, Death, and Hades in chapters 19 and 20. The vision of the completion of God's healing work in 21 and 22 leaves us with the fundamental contrast of the book: The spiritual forces of evil are gone, they are not part of the fulfilled city; new Jerusalem, and the spiritual forces of good are ever-present.

Even in the end, though, things are left ambiguous about the human element of the final scene. Revelation as a whole makes clear what kind of person will be at home in new Jerusalem—one who follows the Lamb's path of persevering love. And we are told numerous times what kind of person will not be at home there—one who trusts in the dragon and follows the ways of domination. What is ambiguous is what happens to human beings after the dragon is gone. Shockingly, the very kings of the earth who throughout the book symbolize humanity at its most hostile to the Lamb are present in new Jerusalem. The nations, allied with the dragon as they were, find healing in new Jerusalem. So, we don't know precisely *who* will be there. Some Christians mentioned in chapters 2 and 3 might not; kings of the earth will be. It is not about religious affiliation. It is about the ultimate response to God's call.

REVELATION 21:1–8

> Then I saw a new heaven and a new earth; for the first heaven
> and the first earth had passed away, and the sea was no more.
> And I saw the holy city, the new Jerusalem, coming down out of
> heaven from God, prepared as a bride adorned for her husband.
> And I heard a loud voice from the throne saying, "See, the home
> of God is among mortals. He will dwell with them; they will be
> his peoples, and God himself will be with them; he will wipe ev-
> ery tear from their eyes. Death will be no more; mourning and
> crying and pain will be no more, for the first things have passed
> away." And the one who was seated on the throne said, "See, I
> am making all things new." Also, he said, "Write this, for these
> words are trustworthy and true." Then he said to me, "It is done!
> I am the Alpha and the Omega, the beginning and the end. To
> the thirsty I will give water as a gift from the spring of the water
> of life. Those who conquer will inherit these things, and I will be
> their God and they will be my children. But as for the cowardly,
> the faithless, the polluted, the murderers, the fornicators, the
> sorcerers, the idolaters, and all liars, their place will be in the
> lake that burns with fire and sulfur, which is the second death."

With the vision of "a new heaven and a new earth" and the statement that
"the first heaven and the first earth had passed away" (21:1), John reports
the social and spiritual healing of the world we live in. We read a few verses
later that God is "making all things new" (21:5), not making all new things.
The process of the plagues turns out to be not the total destruction of the
physical world but the destruction of the destroyers of the physical world
(i.e., the dragon et al., the spiritual dynamic of domination).

Throughout the book we have been told about various moments of
worship in the midst of the time of tribulation that characterizes the "three
and a half years" of human historical existence. These worship moments
point ahead to Rev 21's vision of life lived in the presence of God and the
Lamb, a kind of constant worship. So, when the destroyers of the earth are
destroyed, the earth is renewed ("made new") and humanity is renewed
("made new") with it. The holy city, new Jerusalem, "comes down out of
heaven from God, prepared as a bride" (21:2). This reference alludes back to
the bride in chapter 19, which is the same as the multitude beyond counting in chapter 7. That is, the renewed earth provides a home for a healed
humanity in numbers beyond counting.

The connection between healed humanity and God is direct, immediate, and life-giving. That "the first things have passed away" (21:4) refers

not to the physical world but to the dynamics of domination, dynamics that characterized human life during the "three and a half years." The new world is, we could say, the old world with the powers of domination excluded—a place where tears of sorrow, idolatry, and death dealing are no more.

The One on the throne utters words of healing and assurance to describe the coming down of new Jerusalem, words that are "trustworthy and true" (21:5). For John, this is one more statement of the contrast between the ways of the true God and the ways of the dragon. John challenges his readers on the level of fundamental disposition. Whose words do you believe are "trustworthy and true"? Whose words actually empower healing and transformation? Too often, in John's view, the words of the empire and its agents have been seen as trustworthy, even by those within the congregations of chapters 2 and 3. But it all comes down to this: Do you trust that new Jerusalem is our true end as human beings, or is it Babylon? Which is more realistic in addressing human needs and aspirations?

This passage ends with a reminder of the contrast Revelation centers on. There is the path of a "conquest" that involves telling the truth, to courageously resist the powers, trust in the visions of worship that emphasize that God and the Lamb are worthy of praise and seek to live as children of God. And there is the path of trusting in the dragon, a path that ultimately proves to be the path of cowardice, faithlessness, violence, and dishonesty. John has made this contrast clear throughout the book, because in the end one must choose sides: Either death or life.

REVELATION 21:9–21

Then one of the seven angels who had the seven bowls full of the seven last plagues came and said to me, "Come, I will show you the bride, the wife of the Lamb." And in the spirit he carried me away to a great, high mountain and showed me the holy city Jerusalem coming down out of heaven from God. It has the glory of God and a radiance like a very rare jewel, like jasper, clear as crystal. It has a great, high wall with twelve gates, and at the gates twelve angels, and on the gates are inscribed the names of the twelve tribes of the Israelites; on the east three gates, on the north three gates, on the south three gates, and on the west three gates. And the wall of the city has twelve foundations, and on them are the twelve names of the twelve apostles of the Lamb. The angel who talked to me had a measuring rod of gold to measure the city and its gates and walls. The city lies foursquare, its length the same as its width; and he measured the city with his rod, fifteen hundred miles; its length and width and height are equal. He also measured its wall, one hundred forty-four cubits by human measurement, which the angel was using. The wall is built of jasper, while the city is pure gold, clear as glass. The foundations of the wall of the city are adorned with every jewel; the first was jasper, the second sapphire, the third agate, the fourth emerald, the fifth onyx, the sixth carnelian, the seventh chrysolite, the eighth beryl, the ninth topaz, the tenth chrysoprase, the eleventh jacinth, the twelfth amethyst. And the twelve gates are twelve pearls, each of the gates is a single pearl, and the street of the city is pure gold, transparent as glass.

The same angel who showed John the fall of Babylon (17:1) now returns to show John the opposite of Babylon, new Jerusalem. Given the close parallels in how these two cities are introduced, as well as scattered parallels and contrasts between them in the details, we are meant to see that in some sense new Jerusalem is what Babylon should have been. The problem is not that human beings live in cities. The outcome of the human project here is an urban outcome. The problem is when cities become organized for injustice. Since we are not told that Babylon is destroyed in the same way that the dragon, beast, and false prophet are destroyed, it may not be totally farfetched to imagine that Babylon itself actually is transformed into new Jerusalem. Regardless of how we think about the precise relationship between the two, clearly there is some continuity between them. The outcome of God's work of healing as presented in Revelation is the healing of the nations, of the kings of the earth, and of the entire social and political dynamics of human life, not to mention of the human relationship with the rest of creation.

This renewed city is portrayed in terms of glittering jewels (21:9), a description not meant to be taken literally but as a statement about how blessed and beautiful this city will be. It is "the bride of the Lamb." That is, the city is made up of the multitude that has been created from the followers of the Lamb. This is in contrast with the gaudy harlot of chapter 17. Even more, though, it is a positive affirmation of the status and impressive character of those who have "conquered" through their faithful witness, again underscoring the importance of that witness.

The city is a community of people, most directly a community of the multitude of those mentioned in chapter 7. To emphasize this point, John notes that the city has twelve gates inscribed with the names of the twelve tribes of Israel and twelve foundations inscribed with the names of the twelve apostles. The twelve tribes actually were named back in chapter 7 as another way of designating the countless multitude (7:5–9). Now John continues with the same imagery but with a more explicit statement of continuity between the tribes and the apostles. He points back to the description at 15:2–3 of "those who had conquered the beast" and sing the "song of Moses, the servant of God, and the Lamb" (note that "song" is singular; it's sung by the *one* people of God).

The description of the city in 21:15–21 expands on its beauty, couched in terms of precious jewels along with a peculiar reference to "pure gold, transparent as glass" (21:21). John also makes a point of telling how the angel that has brought him to this city carefully "measured the city with his rod" (21:16). The city turns out to be a perfect cube. It measures 1,500 miles in each direction, a description surely meant to convey the city's enormous size. Even more, John's readers would surely recognize the allusion to the holy of holies in the temple, that was also a cube (1 Kgs 6:20; see also the description of the temple in Ezek 40–48). We will learn in a moment that indeed the holy of holies, in the Old Testament temple accessible only to a very few elite priests as the carefully segregated presence of God in the world, has been turned on its head.

REVELATION 21:22–27

> I saw no temple in the city, for its temple is the Lord God the Almighty and the Lamb. And the city has no need of sun or moon to shine on it, for the glory of God is its light, and its lamp is the Lamb. The nations will walk by its light, and the kings of the earth will bring their glory into it. Its gates will never be shut by day—and there will be no night there. People will bring into it the glory and the honor of the nations. But nothing unclean will enter it, nor anyone who practices abomination or falsehood, but only those who are written in the Lamb's book of life.

John's next statement is self-contradictory if read literally; he doesn't see something that he actually sees: "I saw no temple in the city, for its temple is the Lord God the Almighty and the Lamb" (21:22). What John means is that he did not see a temple as a building but instead the true temple is revealed as God and the Lamb themselves. This is an enormously suggestive statement on several levels. Most if not all of the major cities in the Roman Empire (including the seven cities mentioned in chapters 2 and 3) had temples devoted to various deities. By John's time, they all served the civil religion of the Roman Empire and the deification of the emperor. So, one point John makes with his temple reference is that new Jerusalem is utterly different from the empire's cities. There is no emperor worship here. To the contrary, this vision is another example of John's insistence that Caesar and God are direct rivals that require a clear choice by his readers. "The temple *is* the Lord God the Almighty and the Lamb," which means, among other things, that new Jerusalem's temple exists *instead of* the various temples scattered throughout the empire.

The lack of a temple building does not repudiate Israel's past. The temple was only ever meant to be a symbol of God's presence. Now, the reality behind the temple is present without limit. There is no need to symbolize God's presence on earth physically with a temple building. The reality behind the symbol is present in new Jerusalem. God is present; God is the temple, and no other representation of that presence is needed. At the same time, the lack of a temple building also could be seen as a critique of the what the temple became in Israel. The temple evolved into a politically shaped means of limiting access to God in ways that enhanced human authority in the community. There is no justification for such a political dynamic now. God clearly repudiates human hierarchies—even within Israel when Israel imitates empire's ways of domination.

To reinforce the anti-hierarchical message, we are told that the temple is God the Almighty *and* the Lamb. The Lamb indeed is being exalted here, but even more importantly for John's message God is being defined in relation to the Lamb. The power of God is Lamb-power. God's way of conquering is Lamb-like. To say that the temple is God and the Lamb is to say that the kind of power and authority associated with the temple is the power and authority of servanthood that lifts up the lowly, not domination and elite power-over.

The text reiterates the close linkage of the One and the Lamb with the statement about needing no sun or moon, but only the glory of God as the city's light and the Lamb as its lamp. The reference to sun and moon might also allude to the ways the gods of the empire were linked with those two celestial entities. That this is a place of healing and welcome, the desired outcome of the human project, is underscored by the somewhat surprising presence of the kings of the earth and the glory of the nations who walk by God and the Lamb's light (21:24). These "kings" and these "nations" surely are the same "kings" and "nations" mentioned throughout the book. They had been opposed to God. John used those terms here intending to evoke his earlier usage and make the point that God has healed God's human enemies.

We may hearken back to the opening of the book, where 1:5 describes Jesus as "the ruler of the kings of the earth." We may read the entire book as the story of how Jesus established his kingship in relation to the nations and kings. Jesus's conquest through persevering love brings down the empires and establishes his rule in relation to the kings of the earth. Both the repeated calls to John's readers themselves to conquer in the same way and this image of the ultimate healing of the nations and kings mean to challenge and encourage John's readers. They give the message: "Your work is crucial."

It is actually not surprising that new Jerusalem would contain the healed citizenry. To "follow the Lamb wherever he goes" is to cultivate the Lamb's justice, a desire to restore wholeness, not a desire to punish. Those who conform to the image of the Lamb will share his love and his desire for healing. We get a hint of this dynamic when we follow the process of the answer to the cries of the "martyrs" in 6:9–11. They cry out for vengeance. They then receive white robes (a powerful symbol of sharing the Lamb's path) and are told to wait. As they wait, they (we may imagine) come to understand better the meaning of "vengeance" (or, taking justice) in light of the Lamb. So finally, those human beings who, being deceived by the dragon to shed the blood of the saints and prophets, themselves find healing.

Not only do we read of the kings and nations being in new Jerusalem; we also note how it is that they can be there. The city's "gates will never be shut by day and there will be no night there" (21:25). The city, as a light to the nations, draws all who want to be inside its ever-open gates. We see here a fulfillment of the Bible's core promise going back to the call of Abraham and Sarah that their descendants would bless all the families of the earth (Gen 12:3). "People will bring into it the glory and honor of the nations" (Rev 21:26). The story Revelation tells, and the story the Bible as a whole tells, is that God acts to bring healing to all of creation in harmony with God's creative intent from the very beginning.

In the light of the expansiveness of this vision of the kings of the earth and the nations finding healing, it is crucial to note the caveat that follows immediately: "Nothing unclean will enter it" (21:27). God's work to empower the Lamb's faithful witness and to destroy the destroyers of the earth brings healing and wholeness. God's holiness is not an attribute of God that makes it impossible for God to be in the presence of uncleanness. If we recognize Jesus as the clearest manifestation of God in the world, we know that staying separate from unclean human beings can't be what God's holiness is like. God's holiness empowers human beings to be made clean. Just as Jesus ministered among sinners in order to help them find wholeness, so new Jerusalem welcomes everyone in order to help them find wholeness.

The stipulation that nothing unclean will be found in new Jerusalem follows on the heels of the emphasis on the kings' presence. This juxtaposition indicates that the main point here is not that the city remains discriminatory and exclusive. Rather, one key purpose of the city is to be a place where even the worst of God's human enemies are transformed. It's a tremendous message of hope and should serve as a great motivation for Lamb-followers to be agents of transformation.

To say "only those who are written in the Lamb's book of life" will be present, hearkening back to Rev 20:11–15, is not a statement of exclusivity but of identity. God's call is a wide-open call, one that countless multitudes embrace. It appears from earlier in Revelation that everyone starts out in the book of life, and only those who explicitly turn against God run the risk of having their names erased from that book (3:5). We should recognize the possibility that erasure may be permanent for some, but the presence of at least some of the kings of the earth in new Jerusalem indicates that the erasure threat is only that, a threat. God's intent is that as many names as possible will indeed remain in the book of life. That it is the *Lamb's* book of life should be enough to make that intention clear.

REVELATION 22:1–7

> Then the angel showed me the river of the water of life, bright as crystal, flowing from the throne of God and of the Lamb through the middle of the street of the city. On either side of the river is the tree of life with its twelve kinds of fruit, producing its fruit each month; and the leaves of the tree are for the healing of the nations. Nothing accursed will be found there anymore. But the throne of God and of the Lamb will be in it, and his servants will worship him; they will see his face, and his name will be on their foreheads. And there will be no more night; they need no light of lamp or sun, for the Lord God will be their light, and they will reign forever and ever. And he said to me, "These words are trustworthy and true, for the Lord, the God of the spirits of the prophets, has sent his angel to show his servants what must soon take place." "See, I am coming soon! Blessed is the one who keeps the words of the prophecy of this book."

The final "then the angel showed me" allows John to see what we may understand to be the ultimate contents of the scroll that the Lamb gained the ability to open through his faithful witness. John sees a vision that evokes the very beginning of the human project in the garden of Eden in Gen 2. Now at the culmination, this garden is in the middle of a city. The centerpiece of the vision is the "river of the water of life" that flows from the "throne of God and the Lamb." This river is flanked on each side by "the tree of life" with its fruit and leaves that are "for the healing of the nations" (22:1–3). It is difficult to imagine a clearer statement of the message of the book of Revelation, and this vision serves as a powerful conclusion to the Christian Bible: Life-giving power comes directly from God's throne in order to heal the nations.

The vision of the tree of life gives a final point of emphasis to counter notions that the God of the Bible is a punitive God or that sinful human beings have removed themselves from the reach of God's healing love. "The nations" in Revelation, and actually throughout the Bible, are usually human beings organized in opposition to God and God's people. In Revelation, the city of Babylon links closely with the nations. To have this final allusion to the healing of the nations makes the point that indeed God loves God's enemies (Rom 5) and shows that the final word will be a healing, not a punitive word.

This final vision also underscores that the Lamb reveals to us God's very character. The throne here is not a throne with two distinct seats, as it were. We are not dealing here with two distinct characters with different wills, God and the Lamb. There is no hint here that Jesus represents God's loving mercy, and "God the Father" represents God's holiness and punitive wrath. The close identification between the Lamb and the One on the throne emphasizes that they are one; the Lamb reveals the one will of God. If we want to know what God is like we look to the faithful witness of the Lamb, who Revelation asserts, rules "the kings of the earth" (1:5). The rule of the Lamb, though, is a rule of healing, not a rule of domination. As such a ruler, as "king," as "Christ," the Lamb reveals the nature of God's rule over all creation.

Right after the picture of the nations being healed, John reiterates the point from the prior chapter that, though the "nations" are present in the city, "nothing accursed will be found there anymore" (22:3). Earlier, he wrote, "nothing unclean will enter [new Jerusalem]" (21:27). This assertion does not stand in tension with the expressions of healing mercy. It is not that John now wants to emphasize those who are excluded. Rather, that "nothing accursed" will be present emphasizes that the nations truly are healed. This is a word of assurance. New Jerusalem as a place of wholeness is an invitation and a promise—if you want, you will be healed.

A radical theological reorientation lies behind the promise that the Lamb's "servants" (meaning the countless multitude of chapter 7) will "see God's face" (22:4). This underscores the identification of God with the Lamb. God is present to God's people as a face who can be seen. This contrasts with earlier notions of God as unseen (Exod 33:20 and Deut 4:12). God, in the end, is not the unknowable and inscrutable Other. God is known in the Lamb, the author of healing and persevering love.

Not only will the servants see God's face, they will also be given light that empowers them to "reign forever and ever" (22:5). The work of God that Revelation recounts has as its goal social transformation. The nature of the "city" that provides humanity's home is transformed—from Babylon's domination and definition of "reign" as power-over to new Jerusalem's servanthood as embodied by the Lamb where "reign" now means power-with. That these visions relate to "what must soon take place" and that God is "coming soon!" (22:6–7) does not mean that Revelation is predicting a near end to human history (which, of course, did not happen). Rather, the point is that this message is urgent and is for today. John and his readers can (and must) embody new Jerusalem "soon" (that is, immediately).

REVELATION 22:8–21

I, John, am the one who heard and saw these things. And when I heard and saw them, I fell down to worship at the feet of the angel who showed them to me; but he said to me, "You must not do that! I am a fellow servant with you and your comrades the prophets, and with those who keep the words of this book. Worship God!" And he said to me, "Do not seal up the words of the prophecy of this book, for the time is near. Let the evildoer still do evil, and the filthy still be filthy, and the righteous still do right, and the holy still be holy." "See, I am coming soon; my reward is with me, to repay according to everyone's work. I am the Alpha and the Omega, the first and the last, the beginning and the end." Blessed are those who wash their robes, so that they will have the right to the tree of life and may enter the city by the gates. Outside are the dogs and sorcerers and fornicators and murderers and idolaters, and everyone who loves and practices falsehood. "It is I, Jesus, who sent my angel to you with this testimony for the churches. I am the root and the descendant of David, the bright morning star." The Spirit and the bride say, "Come." And let everyone who hears say, "Come." And let everyone who is thirsty come. Let anyone who wishes take the water of life as a gift. I warn everyone who hears the words of the prophecy of this book: if anyone adds to them, God will add to that person the plagues described in this book; if anyone takes away from the words of the book of this prophecy, God will take away that person's share in the tree of life and in the holy city, which are described in this book. The one who testifies to these

things says, "Surely I am coming soon." Amen. Come, Lord Jesus! The grace of the Lord Jesus be with all the saints. Amen.

The book concludes with a variety of exhortations that underscore the importance and immediacy of John's message. The angel tells John, "Do not
seal up the words of the prophecy of this book, for the time is near" (22:10).
We need the message of this book now; it is not for some distant future time
(contrary to the way present-day future prophecy interpretation understands Revelation). As a book of ethical exhortation, Revelation spoke first
of all to the late first century when it was written. With such a focus, then,
it speaks to future generations through the perennial value of the message
about the late first century.

The emphasis on "the time is near" is to say that this message is for
now. The time to learn from and embody the message is in the present. John
has made it clear throughout Revelation that its message is for the long haul.
He has no sense that the "three and a half years" will be a brief time; the call
he makes is not hang in there for this brief time before history ends. To the
contrary, he calls for *persevering* love. What is at hand is the "end" in the
sense of purpose and meaningfulness of life lived in the Lamb's way—not
"the end" in the sense of the ending of time and history.

The closing section of Revelation contains numerous elements of the
letter style of communication, as does the opening section. One effect of this
beginning and end is to underscore that the message the book contains is
first of all intended for actual people in actual congregations in John's present, a letter of exhortation. Also, the structure underscores the importance
of reading Revelation as a whole. It has a beginning and then a middle that
move toward the conclusion.

WHAT IS PARADISE FOR?

We tend to read the Bible expecting a happy ending. Even though a lot of
people don't like the book of Revelation all that well, it does end happily,
with a vision of paradise. The book contains several allusions that go clear
back to Genesis, and I think we are meant to read Revelation as in some
sense the conclusion to the entire Bible. I like the vision in Rev 21 and 22.
It makes me feel good. But I am attracted to these chapters for somewhat
different reasons than I used to be. I checked back on the first book I wrote,
published in 1987. It was about Revelation. This is something I wrote back
then:

> The affirmation of Revelation 21 and 22 is that this fulfillment, this conclusion of history, will be worth all the pain and struggle which humankind has experienced throughout the ages. The completion of God's work is the New Jerusalem—the establishment of the holy city—within which God's people will reign forever and ever.[1]

I'm not sure I would write the same thing now. That is, actually, I won't write the same thing, at least not exactly. Back then, I read Revelation to predict the future. It was not in the details like the rapture, antichrist, millennium, and all that, but in a more general sense that I read it to assure its readers that indeed everything will end up okay. But I don't read it that way now. I think Revelation is all about the now of its author and the now of its readers, not about what will *certainly* happen in the future.

When I read the vision of new Jerusalem, I see three key points that I want to write about that have to do with now as the truest picture of reality. (1) The vision affirms that the brokenness of the plagues that dominates much of the book of Revelation is not the truest picture of reality. The vision envisions healing. (2) The vision of resolution is not predictive so much as exhortative. It does not say: This is what will be. It says, more, this is the direction you should live toward. (3) The vision re-emphasizes that Revelation's main concern is method, not prediction. It's not that God has this set-in-concrete plan for the future where the dragon and beast are defeated, and the kings and nations healed. It's that God shows us *how* to go about the work of defeating the dragon and healing the nations.

So, first, the plagues, chaos, and conflict of the earlier visions are not the truest picture of reality. The plague visions show human history in the present time. The present time, looked at from a certain angle, is a time of sorrow, of pain, of domination, of oppression. It's a time when the dragon and the beast exercise a lot of power. I'm reminded of how a speaker I had a formal debate with once portrayed things. His parents were Holocaust survivors who settled in Israel. This speaker loves peace, but he believes ultimately that life requires violence. The bad guys are still at work, he said, and we have to be able to fight better than them to survive.

Revelation 21 and 22, though, envisions an alternative way to see human history. It's a history where the plagues and turmoil can end, even now. It's a history of healing. There are people who remain humane, who, in Revelation's terms, "conquer." They conquer the brokenness and cycle of retaliation with love, and they reject the ideology of necessary violence. Follow the Lamb's way of peace instead. They do this even when they suffer as

---

1. Grimsrud, *Triumph*, 164.

a consequence. Rev 21 promises vindication. The conquerors will be made whole.

Something else, though, is that those human actors who had tried to conquer Lamb-following conquerors with their violence will also find healing. When the spiritual forces of domination (the great dragon, and its minions, the beast and the false prophet) are themselves destroyed, those humans who had trusted in the dragon's distorted picture of reality are set free. They are still created in the image of God and may find their way to wholeness.

The nations are healed as well. The kings of the earth catch up the biblical tradition of human leaders who oppose God. Pharaoh in the exodus story, the leaders of the Assyrian empire that crushed the kingdom of Israel, King Nebuchadnezzar of Babylon who destroyed Judah's temple, the Roman Empire's puppet king Herod the Great who massacred newborn sons, and the various Caesars who oversaw the killing of Jesus and of Peter and of Paul are only some examples. Throughout the Bible, the kings of the earth indeed do side with the beast in gathering their forces to crush God and God's people. But in Rev 21 and 22, the beast is gone, and the kings find healing. So too do the nations themselves, the human collectives organized so often to exploit, to buy and to sell even human souls, and to shed the blood of prophets.

I don't think the vision of healing that resolves the plagues is a prediction. It is more a vision of what can be that tells us that the kings and the nations are not inherently broken. The Lamb's witness can indeed find a response in the world. We should never become fatalistic and give up hope. Witness is always possible and always can bring transformation.

I still have memories of the 1980s and 1990s when the Iron Curtain was torn down, when apartheid ended, when the Pinochet dictatorship was ended—each, against every expectation, without bloody warfare.[2] Few thought those systems of domination could go down peaceably. Those transformations didn't usher in new Jerusalem; many, many problems still remain. But what happened shows us that our world is not a closed system. Change is possible.

The second point: The vision of resolution in Revelation is not predictive so much as exhortative. It's not telling us about the future so much as challenging us about how to live in the present. It pictures the nature of reality even now, worship amidst chaos. And we are called to live in light of the world seen in the worship visions, a world of solidarity and healing.

2. See the accounts in Ackerman and Duvall, *Force*.

An interpretive key here is the close parallel between two city visions. First, in chapter 17 is the vision of Babylon, the city of the world of plagues. John is told by an angel, "Come and I will show you . . ." And he sees chaos and violence. Then in chapter 21, he is told by this same angel, "Come and I will show you . . ." And he sees healing and worship. The judgment of Babylon in chapters 17 and 18 is now seen, in chapters 21 and 22, as the healing of the nations and their kings. The judgment leads to the destruction of the powers behind the kings, the dragon and beast and false prophet. And, as we see in the new Jerusalem vision, the judgment leads to the healing of the kings themselves and their nations. Let me suggest that we may actually be seeing here two visions of the same city at the same time—the time of John's present and, in a genuine sense, our present too.

The two visions of the contrasting cities show two ways to interpret the present. There are plagues and there is worship. There is violence toward prophets and the vulnerable and there is healing. There is warfare and there is reconciliation. Remember, John wants to challenge people in the churches to follow the Lamb wherever he goes. The book of Revelation gets its name from its first verse: "the *revelation* of Jesus Christ." This word, "revelation," in Greek is apocalypse. But its original meaning is simply "unveiling," not catastrophe or punitive judgment.

"The unveiling of Jesus Christ" has two senses. One sense is unveiling who Jesus is and who God is. Paradoxically, Jesus and God are seen most definitively in the resurrected Lamb. The second sense is unveiling what the Lamb wants of humanity—persevering love. John wants his readers to see that they have a choice: the way of the Lamb or the beast. He tries to "unveil" the reality of both ways, conquer through force or conquer through love. The city that is most real is the city of love. The vision does not predict the distant future but exhorts us (as John's readers throughout all time) to live in new Jerusalem now.

The third point is that this vision is about method. *How* is the dragon defeated? *How* is the beast resisted? *How* are the kings of the earth converted? *How* are the nations healed? Revelation makes it clear that God's agenda is transformation, in history, from brokenness to blessing. And there is only one way for this transformation to happen: The message that is revealed in Jesus. Follow the Lamb wherever he goes. Return hatred with love. Welcome vulnerable people. Counter the tyranny of the great ones with care and compassion. Refuse to let the domination system shape your values. Resist empire. Even to the point of suffering.

Revelation's final vision, of new Jerusalem, gives us some powerful images. These images inspire us to live in paradise *now*—not to wait, not to hope for something in the future while we endure the present. As well, these images confront Christians in comfortable circumstances who remain complacent in the confidence that God will work things out in the future. The images call Revelation's readers to active and costly present-day resistance.

Here's one nice image: The door to the city is always open. The invitation to return, to turn back to God's true city, to find healing, this vision is *permanent*. It's for everyone. Another image: Even the kings of the earth, the most unlikely people may find healing. If no one is beyond the pale, Jesus's call to neighbor love extends to everyone. One last image I want to mention looms very large in the context of the Bible as a whole. "I saw no temple in the city, for its temple is the Lord God the Almighty and the Lamb" (21:22). God is present everywhere. God is not contained in some restricted institution, not protected by some spiritually elite guardians, not accessible only through authorized rituals. God is present everywhere, to everyone, at all times. And, God is present in the form of the Lamb—gentle, persevering love. This is paradise; this is now.

Let me end this chapter with a story about paradise in the midst of the plagues and chaos of present history. Rebecca Solnit, in her book *A Paradise Built in Hell*, tells about an eight-year-old girl, in 1906, who lived through the great San Francisco earthquake, one of the worst natural disasters in American history. Many died; much of the city was destroyed. But, amazingly, in the midst of the chaos, people came together. The caring, compassion, sharing, and solidarity were remarkable. This is believable to me. I remember the one-hundred-year flood that devastated my hometown in Oregon in 1964. People joined together in amazing ways to help each other. For this young girl in San Francisco, the earthquake, likewise, was a time of joy amidst the carnage because genuine love and caring, the impulse to help and share, were enormously powerful.[3]

This experience of a kind of paradise remained a living memory for the girl, whose name was Dorothy Day. Twenty-some years later, motivated in part by a desire to embody that same kind of solidarity, Dorothy Day founded the amazing movement that she called the Catholic Worker. The Worker located itself in the midst of the endemic carnage and chaos of Depression-era inner city North America. It has and continues to bring a little bit of paradise into the present. The witness of the Catholic Worker shows indeed that following the Lamb wherever he goes is possible. Such following leads to witness against war and violence and it leads to witness for the healing reality of radical hospitality.

3. Solnit, *Paradise*.

FOR FURTHER ENGAGEMENT

1. What do you think about these comments by the author: "It is ambiguous what happens to human beings after the dragon is gone. Shockingly, the very kings of the earth who throughout the book symbolize humanity at its most hostile to the Lamb are present in new Jerusalem. The nations—allied with the dragon as they were—find healing in new Jerusalem. So we don't know precisely who will be there." What is at stake with how we think about this?

2. What is the meaning or significance of the word "new" in 21:1? Does the remainder of the passage throw any light on its meaning?

3. Note how the city in chapter 21 is portrayed. What is the meaning of: "coming down out of heaven" (21:2,10)? "as a bride," "the bride" (21:2,9)? the measurements of the city (21:15–16)? the absence of the temple (21:22)? the gates, the wall, and the names of each (21:12–14)? the gates are never closed (21:25)? "the river . . . flowing from the throne" (22:1)? the tree of life (22:2)?

4. What do you associate with new Jerusalem? Do you see it as totally future? or in some sense present? Or is it pie-in-the-sky by-and-by, a means of avoiding the present-day reality?

5. Does the promise that there will be no more mourning and crying help one to embrace mourning and crying in the present?

6. Do you agree that new Jerusalem "coming down" (21:2) indicates a transforming of things and not a destruction and recreation? How much continuity is there between human history and new Jerusalem? Do you see evidence in your own experience (and what you know of history) that God is in the process of transforming the fallen world into the new Jerusalem? If so, what evidence do you have? Is there evidence that evil is not ultimate and all-powerful?

7. What significance, if any, do you see in the outcome here where human beings end up with an "urban outcome"? What do you see to be the relationship between Babylon and new Jerusalem?

8. When John writes, "I saw no temple in the city" (21:22), what seems to be in mind? Why would there be no physical temple here?

9. At the end of Revelation, we read of a vision where both God and the Lamb sit together on one throne (22:3). Reflect on Christology. How would you describe the relationship between the Lamb and God?

How does Revelation think of this relationship? Do you agree with this view?

10. How do you respond to the author's assertion: "The vision of resolution in Revelation is not predictive so much as exhortative. It's not telling us about the future so much as challenging us about how to live in the present"? How important to you is the expectation that Revelation's vision of new Jerusalem will in some fairly direct way certainly come true? How do you understand "Behold, I am coming soon" (22:7,10)?

Conclusion

Why We (Should) Read Revelation

One of the burdens of *To Follow the Lamb* has been to make the case that Revelation should not be seen as a marginal or peripheral part of the Christian Bible. Revelation makes its own distinct and essential contribution to the story of Jesus that the New Testament tells. I believe that the key to understanding Revelation is to understand that it is a book about conflict that promises victory and that, most importantly, presents the *means* that make victory possible.

The arena for the fight is not the future nor is it a literal battlefield that features weapons of war that kill, maim, and destroy God's good creation. The arena is the present of the readers of Revelation across the years of its existence. And the battlefield is the world of words, the world of deception and truth telling. The means to achieve victory are steadfastness in embodying the message of Jesus, a message of love, compassion, and resistance to all that negates love and compassion. That Revelation presents the life of faith as a "war of words" is actually pretty clear when we take time to note the various allusions to words and speech throughout the book.

The future-prophetic approach[1] to Revelation fails to recognize the symbolic character of the book's imagery. Partly this is due to a failure properly to understand the message of Jesus from the Gospels as being a message of peace for *this* world. These interpretations of Revelation then add another failure to that failure, which is to fail to recognize that the character of the Lamb in Revelation reveals that this imaginative book itself brings a message of peace. I am convinced that we read Revelation appropriately when we read it to be in full harmony with the life and teaching of Jesus presented in the Gospels. When Rev 1:1 tells us that what follows is a "Revelation of

---

1. Probably the best-known concise statement of this approach is Lindsey, *Late*.

Jesus Christ," it makes a point that is indeed to be taken *literally*: The purpose of the account of this "revelation" is to help us better to follow the way of the Jesus of the Gospels.

Of course, Revelation does contain some harsh imagery (such as the flowing blood of 14:20, the devastating fall of the "great harlot" in chapter 17, the destructive sword of 19:11–21, and numerous others). However, the book makes it clear that its governing image is that of the Lamb, who wins the victory the book celebrates with his self-giving love (see especially 5:5–14 and 12:10–11). If we read the book in light of this governing image, then we will come to a peaceable understanding of the "war" that is portrayed in the book—and of the means to fight that war that the book advocates.

The book does use the image of the "Lamb's war" (17:14). When we note all the other violent imagery, it is understandable that peaceable people would find it difficult to embrace the war image. I respect those who sense that we need to reject the use of war imagery of Jesus because that imagery is irredeemable in our modern world. At the same time, this is the imagery we have, and I tend to think that by embracing the imagery in Revelation and orienting it in light of how the book actually uses that imagery we may find important resources for actively resisting the domination system in the midst of which we live.

A "WAR OF WORDS"

I like the idea that what Revelation is concerned about is what we could call a "war of words." If we read carefully, we will see that over and over the book presents the conflict in terms of what comes out of the mouths of various characters (both those on God's side and those who oppose God). We also will note the importance of the book's critique of the deception of the anti-God powers—and the importance of the truthfulness of those aligned with God. This "war of words" becomes even more apparent when we think a bit about the historical setting for the writing of the book. Most scholars place the book near the end of the first century, though a few place it earlier. For my point here, either time works. The point would be that the book was written to challenge the tendency among early Christians to allow themselves to become too comfortable with the Roman Empire, too easily to accept the vision of reality presented by Rome.

So, those in John's intended audience when he wrote Revelation were indeed engaged in a kind of war of words, a battle of stories about reality. John seeks to challenge his readers to recognize what is at stake in their disposition toward Rome. He wants them to recognize that indeed they are in the midst of a battle over their loyalties and ways of understanding the world they live in and their place in it. I think it is safe to say that John's agenda has remained a relevant agenda for people of faith ever since, down to the present. Whose words provide our sense of the world we live in: the prophetic, countercultural, peace-centered words of the Lamb or the words of the various human kingdoms, empires, or corporations that center on wealth, power, national security, and domination? Once we are sensitized to the possibility that Revelation indeed recounts a war of words, we can't help but begin to notice how many images throughout the book confirm that possibility. I will mention the key ones here.

John begins the book by naming it "the revelation of Jesus Christ"— who is then identified as "the faithful witness" (1:5) who is risen and currently rules. The "faithful witness" label is used several times in the book of Jesus, the Lamb, and also of Jesus's followers. I understand this term to refer all at once to Jesus's faithful life, to his teaching, and to his execution. This label establishes Jesus's teaching ministry as a key element of his identity as the emissary of the One on the throne.

Present-day readers of Revelation do not always pay enough attention to the emphasis the book makes on discipleship, on actively following Jesus's way. Revelation offers, as much as anything, an ethical exhortation to its readers to embody that way. We see this emphasis right away when John writes that those who read, hear, and keep the words of Revelation's prophetic exhortation will be blessed (1:3).

Later in chapter 1, John reiterates the sense that Jesus the prophet proclaims authoritative words of truth when he reports that as he receives this vision of Jesus Christ, he sees Jesus ("one like the Son of Man") with a sharp, two-edged sword coming from his mouth (1:16). This image of Jesus's sword is a crucial element of the conflict that Revelation portrays—and Jesus's (and his followers') means of engaging the conflict.

The "sword from the mouth" should be linked closely with the "faithful witness." It is the prophetic proclamation of Jesus (both his actual words and the witness of his life) that confronts the enemies of God (and those who give their loyalties to those enemies). These images, in the context of Revelation's vision of Jesus as the Lamb whose victory was won through his persevering love that leads to death and resurrection (5:5–6; 12:10–11), combine *both* the nonviolence of speech and works of love *and* the reality of confrontation. Jesus challenges those who depart from shalom, so the "sword" does connote judgment. But the judgment comes in words, not in coercive violence.

The call to join Jesus and confront and resist the forces of injustice and oppression defined the messages to the seven congregations (chapters 2 and

3) that establish the agenda for the book as a whole. The core exhortation that John shares with each one calls them to listen to what the Spirit says to the churches (2:7, 11, 17, 29; 3:6, 13, 22). Listen to the words of the Spirit of Jesus. They speak to the shape of faithfulness amidst the Roman Empire in the late first century CE.

The message to the congregation in Pergamum (2:12–16) brings into sharpest focus John's agenda. John presents Jesus to this congregation as the one with the sharp, two-edged sword, an allusion back to the picture of Jesus in 1:16 with the sword coming out of his mouth. This image reminds those in Pergamum of Jesus's prophetic life and speech that led to his execution by the representatives of the Roman Empire.

This reminder gains potency in face of problems that John sees in the congregation. "I have this against you—some hold to the teachings of Balaam and the Nicolaitans" (2:16). This cryptic reference most likely alludes to those teaching the congregation that collaboration with the empire is fine for Christians. Jesus disagrees, in part because this same empire responded to his resistance with execution. Revelation as a whole may be read to challenge those in the congregations who were too comfortable within the empire and, as a consequence, too complicit with the empire's injustices and too dismissive toward Jesus's call to transformative justice.

If John's readers ignore this message's call to repentance (i.e., turn away from giving loyalty to Rome and return to the gospel way of life that Jesus modeled), the Jesus of the messages promises to "make war against them with the sword of my mouth" (2:16). I believe that this "making war" is a war of words, confrontation, prophetic critique. The conflict John has in mind here is a sharp, meaningful debate between two sets of loyalties and two ways of life.

We get the picture in the seven messages that the battle that matters is a battle of ideologies, of ways of being in the world, of ways of understanding what deserves our loyalties. John's Jesus wages war against those in the congregations who teach that the empire is an agent of their God and guarantees their peace and security. This is a war of perceptions, of the truths of Torah and the gospel over against the deceptions and falsehoods of the empire (which are, John insists with his imagery, the deceptions and falsehoods of Satan himself).

THE STRUGGLE BETWEEN THE TWO WAYS

Several references later in the book underscore that what's going on is a battle of words. In chapter 9, the forces of the dragon practice violence and oppression in the form of deadly cavalry horses with "fire and smoke and sulfur coming out of their mouths; . . . the power of the horses is in their mouths and their tails" (9:17–19). I interpret the image here to refer to the words of deception and agitation that come out of the mouths of the leaders of the empire and its satellites in the areas where the seven congregations of chapters 2 and 3 are located.

Then, in chapter 11 we get a picture of the other side in this struggle. God calls "two witnesses" (a parallel image with the seven congregations in chapters 2 and 3 and the 144,000 that turns out to be a countless multitude in chapter 7—all are the communities of God's people) to exercise authority and stand against the powers. These two witnesses are powerful as "fire pours from their mouths and consumes their foes" (11:5). The key image here is that the weapon "pours from their mouths." This image surely alludes to their words of prophecy, clarity, critique, and encouragement that underscore the truthfulness of the message of Jesus, the "faithful witness" who assures the success of these two witnesses.

The imagery of conflict continues in chapter 12, where the dragon is now explicitly identified as the true power behind the human leaders of the empire. The comrades of Jesus are victorious in the conflict. They "conquer the dragon by the blood of the Lamb and the word of their testimony" (12:11). Jesus's life, teaching, execution, and resurrection show how to be impervious to the deceptions of the powers—that is, how to conquer. And the word of testimony from those who seek to follow him is their part in the conquering process.

However, the dragon never gives up. The struggle for truthfulness continues. The dragon pours water like a river from his mouth, hoping to "sweep away" the Lamb's people (12:15–17). The words of deception and idolatry will continue to pour forth from all later iterations of empire. In chapter 13, we learn of a powerful representative of the dragon, the beast (another image for empire), whose "mouth utters haughty and blasphemous words as it exercises great authority" (13:5–6). Yet another beast, called the false prophet, joins in and adds to the deceptive dynamics where empire takes the place of God as the source of "truthfulness" and recipient of loyalty (13:11–18).

Again, though, John reminds his readers of the Lamb's victory. The countless multitude of chapter 7 is re-envisioned in 14:1–5 as "the 144,000" (note 7:4–9) who follow the Lamb wherever he goes, join him in celebrating his victory on "Mt. Zion," and—crucially, given the "war of words"—are shown to have no lies found in their mouths (unlike the many lies of the beast and his representatives).

One more time, John shows the continuing efforts of the dragon to win the war of words. Three foul spirits like frogs come from the mouths of the dragon, beast, and false prophet and perform signs and draw together the kings of the earth for battle with God (16:13–14). These words are deceptive and persuade the "kings" of the falsehood that there actually can be a physical battle between the dragon and the Lamb—though this will never happen.

The drama reaches its end in chapter 19 when the "battle" that was promised in chapter 16 with the gathering at Armageddon is described—and turns out not to be a battle at all. The rider on the white horse (Jesus) simply captures the three powers of evil (dragon, beast, and false prophet), throws the latter two into the lake of fire (19:20), and sets the dragon up for its destruction when it joins them (20:10). A careful reading of the description of this rider reveals crucial theological affirmations and a confirmation that the war in Revelation is a war of words. The rider "is clothed in a robe" that is "dipped in blood" *prior* to the encounter with the powers (19:13). The "blood" here surely is the same as the "blood" of 12:11 that conquered the dragon. This is the "blood" that is the basis for the Lamb taking the scroll from the One on the throne and being worshiped as victorious by all of creation (5:9–14). There is no actual battle in chapter 19 because the conquest has already happened through the faithful witness of Jesus as described in the Gospels.

Further, the only weapon mentioned in chapter 19 is one we are already familiar with: "from his mouth comes a sharp sword" (19:15). This sharp sword surely stands for the "faithful witness" of Jesus, his prophetic proclamation of words and practices that "conquered" the dragon, in part by exposing the dragon's lies and deceptions about the meaning and purpose of life for what they are. The sharp sword is Jesus's effective weapon that wins the war of words that Revelation reveals.

The final use of the sword image is a bit difficult to understand. After the beast and false prophet are thrown into the lake of fire (19:20), we are told, "the rest were killed by the sword of the rider, the sword that came from his mouth" (19:21). Let's assume that the reiteration of the "came from his mouth" is meant to make it clear that the reference is to Jesus's words. In what sense would these words "kill" the "kings of the earth with their armies," i.e., "the rest"? It is doubtful that there is anything literal about this killing since we will read in chapters 21–22 of "the kings of the earth," healed and bringing the nations' glory into new Jerusalem.

One possible explanation is that this "killing" is a bit of rhetorical hyperbole that makes the point that those who identify with the dragon truly are completely defeated by the Lamb. Left unstated is the reality that such a defeat for human beings might well result in their healing, once their loyalty to the dragon is broken. As we see in the end, the defeat and destruction of the powers of evil frees their human loyalists (i.e., the "kings of the earth") from their idolatries and leads to their healing.

So, Revelation, indeed, is not telling us about a literal war of coercive firepower vs. coercive firepower. Nor is it predicting some great end times battle royal without a predetermined outcome. Rather, Revelation describes a struggle over worldviews, over loyalties, over understandings of truth. The struggle happens in the realm of ideas, of speech, of ideologies. John presents as most truthful the message of Jesus that centers on God's love for creation, on Jesus's faithful witness to that love, and on the embodiment of that message by those human beings from all tribes and peoples and languages and nations who identify with the Lamb.

Revelation's portrayal of a war of words between the forces loyal to the Lamb and the forces loyal to the dragon remains relevant for all times and places. To conclude *To Follow the Lamb*, I will reflect on the relevance of this portrayal for two themes of perennial interest, the occurrence of major catastrophes and the dynamics of imperialistic warism.[2]

THE WORDS OF REVELATION SPEAK TO CATASTROPHES

As long as the book of Revelation has existed, interpreters have applied it to large-scale catastrophes that either were present or easily imagined to be. Quite often, the applications have presented Revelation as predicting such catastrophes and their presence as signs of the end. And each time, history continued as the catastrophe passed. I think the mistake was in thinking that Revelation was predictive. It was not a mistake to think that Revelation was relevant. As I write these words, we are still in the midst of the catastrophe that is the COVID-19 pandemic. Thinking about this pandemic provides a good opportunity for thinking about how Revelation remains relevant as a resource for morally faithful living.

I begin with an assumption that we should read Revelation in the same way that we read other books in the New Testament. We understand it to be written by a person of the first century addressing readers in the first century about issues that mattered in the first century. It is indeed prophetic

---

2. By "warism" I mean a society's widespread and largely uncritical devotion of extraordinary resources to the preparation for war, generally based on a faith in the efficacy of war to provide security. As far as I know, my wife Kathleen Temple coined this term.

writing, in the same sense that Paul's writings were prophetic writing. These writings follow the Old Testament prophets in speaking on behalf of God to people of their own time, offering challenges and exhortations that their readers live faithfully in light of the message of Torah and (in Paul's context) the message of Jesus.

So, I do not read Revelation to offer predictions about the long-distant future. It is "non-predictive prophecy." As a "revelation of Jesus Christ," it is basing its critique and exhortation on the message of Jesus. Too often, interpreters of Revelation have (and still do) miss the ways that the book is oriented around Jesus. They miss, that is, the relevance of the book's first verse that identifies itself as the revelation of Jesus Christ.

As it turns out, reading Revelation as non-predictive prophecy oriented around the message of Jesus makes it *more* relevant and helpful for Christians living in a time of worldwide pandemic than reading it as future predictive prophecy. Revelation provides insights and encouragements that are true and relevant for all times. Perhaps, though, given the importance of the plague visions in Revelation, it has particular application to us in a moment of an especially intense experience of plagues with the COVID pandemic.

The center point of Revelation, and the center point for all Christian theology, will be found in chapter 5: The vision of the slain and risen Lamb taking the great scroll from the right hand of the One on the throne. This vision, that includes worship of the Lamb by all creation, emphasizes that the peaceable life of Jesus that elicited a violent and deadly response from the Roman Empire and was vindicated by God in raising Jesus from the dead shows us what God is like and how the victory of God has been, is, and will be achieved. This vision underscores the truth that Jesus embodied love of God and neighbor as the meaning of the law.

Revelation's great contribution is that the understanding it presents of Jesus's way as a counter to the way of the Roman Empire remains enormously insightful for later Christians, including those of us living in the twenty-first century in a time of pandemic. However, the insights are not due to some magical kind of awareness about the future that John might have been given. Rather, they are due to the parallels between John's times and ours. Let me mention several examples of how Revelation's teaching might speak to us amidst our catastrophes.

On the one hand, Revelation is not a book of predictive prophecy with a planned-in-advance calendar for the "end times" where events such as our pandemic are markers on the schedule for the consummation of human history. On the other hand, it is indeed meaningful to think of Revelation as giving us a portrayal of the "end times." It's just that the "end times" according to Revelation began with Jesus. Revelation presents the "end times" as the current history within which we live, and the urgency is not due to chronology. The urgency is an always present call for active discernment and resistance.

The drama Revelation recounts indeed should be understood as getting its intensity from the struggle between the forces of God and the forces opposed to God (symbolized as the forces of the dragon). This is a struggle that occurs during the "great tribulation" that marks the "end times." However, the key point here is that this is Revelation's way of asserting that *all* times and places are the arena for the call to follow the Lamb wherever he goes. All times are part of the great tribulation and the end times. We do not live in a predetermined series of different eras (or dispensations) that one after another lead to a final time of catastrophic battles and the ushering in of a new age. Rather, we are simply living during human history where the struggle to follow the Lamb always remains central and urgent. Revelation is encouraging us for our present, just as it encouraged John's original readers for their present.

We may appropriately think of the COVID-19 pandemic as a kind of plague of the same type as those envisioned in Revelation. The link, though, is not as if our current plague fulfills an ancient prediction. Rather, the link is that these plagues in Revelation are characteristic of all of human history. Revelation's relevance is how it calls the followers of the Lamb to faithful witness during *all* plagues.

Revelation contains a powerful critique of the realities of the Roman Empire. It is the great example of early Christian resistance to the mindset of empire. A big factor in Rome's domination, as portrayed in Revelation, is the work of the False Prophet, the "minister of propaganda." Revelation encourages a strong sense of suspicion toward the powers-that-be. John especially seems to care about how the empire's ways of presenting reality attracted many in the congregations to whom he wrote.

We certainly see a lot of need for suspicion in our current context. Powerful economic and other social forces exploited the chaos of the coronavirus for their own interests. The rich only got richer. They may have presented their efforts as being for the sake of the well-being of the general population, but a sense of suspicion as encouraged by Revelation can help counter the momentum toward exploitation. We live in the time of the "great ordeal" (or "great tribulation," another way Revelation refers to the "end times," or the three and a half years) as have all human beings since Revelation was written.

Crucially, Revelation also insists that we are in the time of worship (see for example, Rev 5, 7, 15, and 19). "Worship" in Revelation seems not so much about people attending Sunday morning services as about a general sensibility of gratitude toward God and commitment to understand reality in the terms presented by the Lamb. "Worship" in Revelation also underscores the importance of solidarity among those committed to the Lamb's way. Only with such solidarity may the empire's propaganda and hostility be successfully resisted.

The dragon plays a crucial role in Revelation's visions. The presence of the dragon makes it apparent that the plagues are not the direct hand of God at work in the world. There are evil forces, in some sense independent of God and malevolent toward humanity and all other life. Throughout the past 2,000 years, wars and rumors of wars, the destruction of nature, famine, and widespread disease have reared their ugly heads. Revelation helps us understand these events as the expression of the deep-seated brokenness of our fallen and too often malevolent structures, ideologies, and institutions. These "powers" seem at times to have an independent will that shapes human life for injustice (e.g., nationalism, white supremacy, patriarchy, economic exploitation). This brokenness can be personified as the work of the dragon (or, as Revelation states, Satan). All too often, powerful people contribute to the brokenness and figure out how to exploit the brokenness to increase their wealth and power.[3]

Thus, the COVID pandemic was not strictly random. Revelation's portrayal of the dragon can help us see the dragon at work in that crisis: the breakdown of ecological balance, vulnerability of the poor, social stratification, mindless commitment to warism, out of control global capitalism. Yet, Revelation also portrays the dragon as ultimately powerless against the Lamb. The ways of peace and persevering love will not be conquered by the dragon.

The victory of the Lamb over the dragon in Revelation may inspire and guide our response to the pandemic. We should always seek to act in ways that echo the Lamb's generosity, welcome of and care for the vulnerable, and critique of the powerful. We should also celebrate and encourage all the ways that people do act to enhance life and healing during these times of stress and trauma and fearfulness. Ultimately, Revelation contains a central message: "Fear not!" The agenda with the plague visions includes a portrayal of life in the world as intensely frightening. This is not a world where an all-powerful, controlling, interventionist God protects God's people. It is not a world where the existence of brokenness constitutes a scandal where we should doubt God's existence because bad things happen to good people.

---

3. For an extraordinarily perceptive analysis of this type of exploitation in the contemporary world see Klein, *Shock*.

The world Revelation portrays is a world with brokenness but not a world without meaning or love. In fact, it is the opposite.

The God of Revelation is actually the kind of God you would expect if you trust in a God of love in the world in which we live. It is a God who intervenes with healing love, not with coercive domination. It is a God who coexists with the dragon and the dragon's malevolence, breaking the dragon's hold with unyielding and suffering love. Revelation tries to help its readers find meaning amidst the plagues, meaning grounded in work to heal and to resist evil and to further the effects of love.

Revelation's call to "fear not!" rests on its presentation of the Lamb's victory as powerful and stable. Remarkably, the only means in the entire book that works to gain the victory is the suffering love of the Lamb and his comrades. This is the point that chapter 5 makes and that it is reiterated numerous other times in the book. The victory, though, leads to enormous consequences. The praise from all creation in chapter 5. The uncounted multitude of chapter 7 that have "washed their robes white" (a sign of their being made whole). The defeat of the dragon in chapter 12. The defeat of the beast and the false prophet in chapter 19. And the healing of the nations (and, it appears, the kings of the earth) in chapters 21 and 22.

The Lamb's victory by means of suffering love involves liberation from the deceptions of the dragon, and deception is actually the only power the dragon has. The basic message of Revelation is fearlessly to trust in God and in the way of the Lamb. That is the needed response to the oppression of the Roman Empire in the first century, to all the plagues since, to the American empire today, and to our pandemic.

THE WORDS OF REVELATION SPEAK TO THE GREAT EMPIRES AND THEIR WARISM

One of our big problems within the American empire (like so many other empires) is the destructive influence of embedded biases, fears, and idolatries that we grow up absorbing—our institutions, ideologies, structures, and the like shape us toward violence, hostility, and stereotyping and othering people. Racism, sexism, heterosexism, nationalism, warism, consumerism, classism. The list goes on.

Revelation actually gives us insights into these dynamics and clues about how to resist and overcome them. One of the key sets of metaphors in the book involves figures such as the dragon, the beast, and the false prophet. These figures lure and deceive people into giving loyalty to the Roman Empire and its central value system, parallel to how those in the

United States now are shaped by the American empire. Revelation shows that these powers ("the destroyers of the earth") are our central enemies, not the particular people who are corrupted by the powers. One point, then, is the need to differentiate the spiritual forces of evil from the actual human beings we confront. The problems, for us, then, are best seen as, say, racism more than racists. That is, the social dynamics that enslave and divide and push to violence are what must be overcome.

If we read Revelation as a resource for helping us to seek peace amidst our struggle against the forces of violence and warism, especially amidst our sense of powerlessness versus those forces, we should focus on Revelation's critique of the powers and its vision of how to "conquer" those powers. I don't understand Revelation as a promise of a certain happy outcome to the human project. I don't think an ancient text can credibly make such a promise. The actual message of Revelation is to illumine *the path* toward the harmony, joy, and wholeness captured in the book's final vision of new Jerusalem. That is, Revelation is about process and method more than about outcome. As Gandhi taught about social ethics, the truth that matters is the truth of means (the means of *satyagraha* or peace) not the truth of ends.[4] We could say, what matters is not a new Jerusalem achieved by whatever means might be necessary but rather the truthful means, which are the only possible ways actually to achieve new Jerusalem.

A message of means taking priority over ends is actually a hopeful message. Revelation teaches us that we may find intrinsic meaning in the means of embodying the way of peace and restorative justice, the way of the Lamb. Such a path is the only way ultimately to achieve new Jerusalem, but it is also in and of itself valuable and meaningful. That sense of the intrinsic meaning of this path is what I understand the various visions of worship scattered throughout the book to mean. We may crucially note that the worship takes place *in the midst* of the struggles and traumas of life in the present historical moment. Life is meaningful in a rich and profound way right now. To borrow Jesus's image: The kingdom of God is present among us. This is our basis for hope.

We see portrayed in Revelation the relative powerlessness of the dragon and other powers of evil. They do seem powerful, but such an appearance is simply part of their deceptiveness. When it comes down to it, the dragon, beast, and false prophet are simply captured and thrown into the lake of fire. These destroyers of the earth are destroyed. Crucial for an accurate interpretation of Revelation, we must recognize the actual means

---

4. For an analysis of Gandhi's political philosophy that illumines this point, see Bondurant, *Conquest*.

used in this destruction. We get a concise statement at 12:11: The followers of the Lamb conquer the dragon by "the blood of the Lamb and the word of their testimony." The means of victory are the pattern of Jesus, a life of self-giving love lived in resistance to the domination system of the dragon, a life ultimately vindicated by the One on the throne.

Revelation, thus, provides a straightforward strategy for constructive, healing, hopeful living that remains relevant for life in our twenty-first-century caldron of anxiety and turmoil. The obvious key to understanding and applying Revelation is given in the book's very first words: "A revelation of Jesus Christ." These words call us to look back to the gospel story and to recognize that that story provides what we need to shape our vision of reality. When we do that, the various unsettling visions and images in Revelation come together as a restating of the basic message Jesus left us with: "Love God with all your heart and your neighbor as yourself."

The Jesus of Revelation, most often symbolized as a lamb, is the same Jesus we meet in the Gospels. Thus, Revelation reinforces and expands the message of the Gospels: Love God and neighbor, seek healing and not retaliation, and refuse to imitate the tyrannical ways of the world's leaders. Interpreters of Revelation tend to lose sight of how the book is anchored in Jesus and thus fail to note all the ways throughout the book that Jesus and his way are evoked. In the end, the healing ministry of Jesus extends to the nations and the kings of the earth.

The key moment in Revelation comes in chapter 5 when we first encounter the Lamb, who is portrayed as the victor, the (only) one who is worthy to take the scroll from the hand of the One on the throne. Because of the Lamb's faithful witness, all creatures in the earth worship him alongside the One (5:8–14). Crucially, this victory is based on the past faithfulness of Jesus, the story told in the Gospels. Revelation does not picture history as heading toward some future drama with the outcome in doubt until some final cataclysm. The victory *has been achieved*, the Lamb *has conquered*, the dragon *has been defeated*.

Jesus's followers are called to conquer like he did. The practical agenda of Revelation as a whole has at its core the call for Jesus's followers to share with him the healing ministry that will transform the world. Once the reader of Revelation is alerted to this motif, we see it throughout the book. A few key examples include the direct exhortation in chapters 2 and 3 to the readers to "conquer." These chapters give us the seven messages from Jesus "to the seven churches that are in Asia" (1:4). These churches are at work in seven different cities. The seven messages identify important strengths and important problems in the congregations, and each message concludes with the call to "conquer." That is, resist the spirit of the Roman Empire and witness faithfully to the way of Jesus.

In chapter 7 we read of a countless multitude of those "robed in white" who "have washed their robes and made them white in the blood of the Lamb" (7:14). This image captures the call to follow Jesus in the path of love and resistance that caused the empire to shed his blood in a vicious execution and that led to God's vindication of Jesus and affirmation of his path as the model for faithful, healing human practice.

Chapters 11 and 12 recount the drama of faithful living during the time of struggle and conflict in face of the dragon's efforts to deceive and overturn the rule of God. Faithfulness is pictured in chapter 11 in terms of the two witnesses who in some sense represent the churches, the communities of Jesus's people. After reading in chapters 6 through 9 of the intransigence of those who resist God, finally in chapter 11 we learn of a large group that does repent and give glory to God (11:13). They do so in response to the faithful witness, even to death, of the two witnesses. Then in chapter 12, we read again of successful witness, the defeating of the dragon by Jesus's comrades due to the "blood of the Lamb and the word of their testimony" (12:11).

In chapter 14, immediately following an intimidating vision of the beast and the false prophet who seemingly run roughshod over human societies and receive the worship of the deceived multitudes ("who can fight against [the beast]?" 13:4), we are relocated to Mt. Zion to observe the Lamb and his faithful followers (14:1–5; numbered here 144,000, a symbolic number we learned in chapter 7 that signifies the countless multitude of those whose white robes were washed in the Lamb's blood). This faithful multitude does stand strong and defiant in face of the beasts, singing songs of victory.

When we get to the final "battle" (that is not actually a battle) of chapter 19, Jesus rides forth victoriously before any battle is fought (19:11–13) and is joined by weaponless "armies" who are also already wearing victorious white linen (19:14) due to their faithful conquering. In the end, new Jerusalem is shown to be not so much a physical structure, but a human community made up of the twelve tribes of Israel and the twelve apostles of the Lamb (21:12–14). The creation of new Jerusalem, thus, is seen in Revelation as a *co-creation*. It is the work of the One on the throne, the Lamb, and the Lamb's faithful people.

The Lamb and his followers in Revelation win their victory with the weapons of the Spirit—nonretaliatory resistance to the domination system, love of neighbor, truthful speech. This victory has actually in many ways been achieved prior to the beginning of Revelation in the story told in the Gospels. At the same time, Revelation does emphasize an ongoing conflict. The powers (dragon, beast, false prophet) continue to resist God and to deceive and dominate. So, it's not inaccurate to recognize a battle motif in Revelation. We must notice, though, the true parameters of this conflict.

The enemies of God are the "destroyers of the earth," and these powers must be "destroyed" (11:18). However, we must note that the successful carrying out of this destructive work leads not to the destruction of God's human enemies (e.g., "the kings of the earth"). The powers are destroyed, and this leads to the *healing* of those human enemies. The means of destroying the destroyers may be seen as the model means for all engaging all subsequent interhuman conflicts: The effort to break the deceptive hold of the powers' ideologies and propagandas and false loyalties in order to free human beings to worship the true God. This deception is broken, going back to the Gospels, through Jesus's faithful living, love of neighbor, and truthful speech. When the powers execute Jesus, they reveal themselves to be agents of the dragon, not of God. Their credibility is broken, and their deception can be ended.

Thus, Jesus wars against the powers using the weapons of love, courage, solidarity with the vulnerable, clear talk, and suffering love (all captured in the metaphor of "blood"). Jesus' "blood" and the "blood" of his followers defeat the powers, destroying their credibility and their hold on deceived humanity. Violence, in this story, is not violence visited upon God's enemies by God, but it is violence accepted by God, the Lamb, and the Lamb's people as the consequence of their faithful witness. This violence witnesses to liberation and healing. Revelation concludes with a vision of new Jerusalem, a place of healing (Rev 21–22). God heals the nations and the kings of the earth, those who earlier in the book rebelled against God. They join the faithful multitude of chapter 7 in establishing the city that practices the politics of the Lamb.

The peaceable message that Revelation proclaims, I suggest, is not a message that everything will turn out okay in the end. It is not a message of an interventionist God who is in control of history. It is a message of the sovereignty of *love*. It is a message of the call to have love shape our values and ideals and convictions and loyalties in all areas of life. It is a realistic message embedded in the pain and alienation of life in history, in this world. The plagues reflect the difficult realities we face in our present world. They are the context for Revelation's call to "conquer" with love, a call that remains valid for those of us today who are sensitive to the same Spirit that fueled John's creative imagination.

FOR FURTHER ENGAGEMENT

1. Reflect on the author's assertion that the conflict Revelation presents is set in the present of its readers (throughout time) and not in the future. Also, that the arena for the conflict is the realm of words, deception, and truthtelling and not a literal battlefield. What are attractive and problematic with those proposals? What are the ramifications for us today?

2. The author writes: "We read appropriately when we read [Revelation] to be in full harmony with the life and teaching of Jesus presented in the Gospels." Does his presentation of this idea persuade you? What are some reasons why this is an important issue?

3. What do you make of the "war of the Lamb" image as a way to characterize the message of Revelation?

4. The author argues that the sword that comes from the rider's mouth in Rev 19 is a central image in Revelation to indicate the *means* for defeating the dragon. What are some of the ramifications of this view for interpreting Revelation as a whole?

5. The author makes a distinction between saying that Revelation is "relevant" and saying that it is "predictive." He affirms the former while denying the latter. What are some of the ways this distinction affects his interpretation? How do you evaluate his perspective on this issue? What seem like the strongest evidence in favor and in opposition?

6. The author suggests that Revelation speaks to our present not due to its foreseeing events of the future but due to parallels there might be between Revelation's time and our time. What might some key parallels be? Should present-day readers share Revelation's intensity about the importance of its message? Why or why not?

7. Revelation seems to give us mixed messages about the power of the dragon and the beast. At times they seem overwhelmingly powerful, and yet they are easily dispatched in the end. How would you resolve this apparent conundrum?

8. How best might Revelation help us in our struggle with systemic evil? Reflect on the author's point that what matters most about Revelation is not that it promises certain ultimate healing but that it provides a vision of *how* to move toward healing? What is the significance for this question of the assertion in Revelation that the Lamb's comrades conquer the dragon through the Lamb's blood and their faithful witness (12:11)?

A guide for further reading

The books I mention here are ones that I have read over the years as I have studied the book of Revelation. I am including only books that I have found helpful. The books marked with an asterisk are books that to some degree at least advocate what I call a "peaceable reading" of Revelation. Only some of these designated books are explicitly pacifist, but as a rule they are books that interpret Revelation as portraying a merciful (as opposed to punitively retributive) God and that interpret Revelation as a positive resource for contemporary peacemaking work. Full publishing information may be found in the bibliography.

POPULAR-LEVEL COMMENTARIES

This section contains books written for a popular audience that provide interpretations of the entire book. One of the strengths of such works is that they tend to provide a sense of the sweep of the book as a whole that is often missed in more detailed commentaries. On the other hand, they by necessity only touch on a few of the main themes in Revelation.

*Carter, *What*, *Farmer, *Revelation*, and *Rossing, "Revelation," are all excellent and leave the reader wishing these authors might provide more detailed commentaries in the future. All give strong support to a peaceable reading of Revelation—as does *Grimsrud, *Triumph*. *Boesak, *Comfort*, and *Schüssler Fiorenza, *Revelation*, offer readings informed by liberation concerns. Wright, *Revelation*, is also frustratingly brief but solid.

MID-LEVEL COMMENTARIES

These commentaries cover the entire book. They tend to range from two hundred to four hundred pages and are aimed at preachers and students. They tend to focus on paragraphs from Revelation more than close readings of individual verses. Some are more scholarly and technical than others.

The commentary that exerted a major influence in spelling out a peaceable reading of Revelation was *Caird, *Commentary*, in 1966. Some of the later commentaries that seem the most clearly influenced by Caird's peaceable reading include *Boring, *Revelation*; *Harrington, *Revelation*; *Rowland, "Revelation;" *Sweet, *Revelation*; and *Yeatts, *Revelation*. The Yeatts commentary, along with *Eller, *Most Revealing*, present an overtly peace church approach.

Beasley-Murray, *Book of Revelation*, *Blount, *Revelation*, and Wilcock, *I Saw*, are commentaries that I have found especially helpful in my work. Beasley-Murray packs a great deal of helpful analysis into a fairly compact book. Blount helpfully emphasizes the centrality in Revelation of the call to what he calls "nonviolent resistance" (often translated as "patient endurance"). Wilcock helped me to see the importance of centering on Revelation as a whole and reading it in the context of the rest of the Bible, over the more typical scholarly approach of focusing more on particular words and on extra-biblical sources. Mangina, *Revelation*, and *Ressaguie, *Revelation*, also helpfully emphasize reading Revelation as a whole.

TECHNICAL COMMENTARIES

As a rule, I have not used the books in this section much as they tend to focus on detailed word studies, on surveying scholarship on Revelation, and on extensive accounts of sources from outside the book of Revelation. Whatever the value might be of such emphases, they were not particularly helpful for my approach to Revelation. The one important exception is the commentary by Craig Koester in the Anchor Bible series. While Koester's book does indeed contain much of the detailed work typical in the books listed here, he also provides in-depth analyses of Revelation's theology— mostly fitting in the peaceable Revelation perspective.

Beale, *Revelation*, while quite detailed, is actually an abridged version of an even more detailed and more technical commentary. Osborne, *Revelation*, and Smalley, *Revelation*, both do write some about theological issues amidst their technical studies.

STUDIES

This section contains studies that vary widely, from highly technical to introductory level. I will point to several of the most useful books. *Friesen, *Imperial Cults,* and *Johns, *Lamb Christology,* are quite technical but well-written and examine carefully key aspects to Revelation in ways that support a peaceable reading. *Bauckham, *Climax,* is a helpful collection of scholarly essays on various themes in Revelation. *Howard-Brook and Gwyther, *Unveiling,* combines a solid and detailed introduction to Revelation with an analysis of how Revelation serves as a helpful resource for social justice work today. The collected essays in *Barr, *Reading;* *Grimsrud and Hardin, *Compassionate;* and *Hays and Alkier, *Revelation,* vary in both content and quality, but all three books contain some excellent analyses in support of a peaceable reading.

Several of the books offer a more popular level introduction to Revelation and its theology, all supportive of a peaceable reading: *Bauckham, *Theology,* *Gorman, *Reading,* and *Kraybill, *Apocalypse.* *Blount, *Can I,* *Bredin, *Jesus,* *Ellul, *Apocalypse,* and *Maier, *Apocalypse,* helpfully analyze Revelation as a resource for present-day ethics. *Rossing, *Rapture,* combines a sharp, perceptive critique of the approach to Revelation taken in the Left Behind books with a strongly peace-oriented alternative approach.

*Aukerman, *Reckoning,* and *Stringfellow, *Ethic* and *Conscience,* are examples of peace activists finding helpful resources in Revelation. Finally, two older and now little-known books are worth looking at as pioneering efforts to counter the punitive and retributive interpretation of God's wrath in Revelation: *Hanson, *Wrath,* and *King, *God's.* Keller, *Apocalypse,* is an important example of a stream of interpretation that combines perceptive and liberative feminist theology with an unfortunately hostile misreading of Revelation.

Streett, *Here,* is noteworthy in that Streett overtly presents a counter perspective to the peaceable Revelation approach. Wainwright, *Mysterious,* is a useful survey of the history of the interpretation of Revelation.

Bibliography

Ackerman, Peter, and Jack Duvall. *A Force More Powerful: A Century of Nonviolent Conflict.* New York: Palgrave Macmillan, 2000.

Alexander, Michelle. *The New Jim Crow: Mass Incarceration in the Age of Colorblindness.* New York: New, 2012.

Aukerman, Dale. *Reckoning with Apocalypse: Terminal Politics and Christian Hope.* New York: Crossroad, 1993.

Aune, David E. *Revelation.* 3 vols. Dallas: Word, 1997.

Barr, David L., ed. *Reading the Book of Revelation: A Resource for Students.* Atlanta: Society of Biblical Literature, 2003.

Bauckham, Richard. *The Climax of Prophecy: Studies in the Book of Revelation.* Edinburgh: T. & T. Clark, 1993.

—————. *Theology of the Book of Revelation.* New York: Cambridge University Press, 1993.

Beale, G. K. *Revelation: A Shorter Commentary.* Grand Rapids: Eerdmans, 2015.

Beasley-Murray, George B. *The Book of Revelation.* Grand Rapids: Eerdmans, 1974.

Beevor, Antony. *The Second World War.* New York: Little, Brown, 2012.

Berrigan, Daniel. *The Nightmare of God: The Book of Revelation.* Marion, SD: Rose Hill, 1983.

Berry, Wendell. *Standing by Words: Essays.* Berkeley: Counterpoint, 1983.

Blount, Brian. *Can I Get a Witness? Reading Revelation Through African American Culture.* Louisville: Westminster John Knox, 2005.

—————. *Revelation: A Commentary.* Louisville, KY: Westminster John Knox, 2009.

Boesak, Allan. *Comfort and Protest: The Apocalypse from a South African Perspective.* Philadelphia: Westminster, 1987.

Bondurant, Joan V. *Conquest of Violence: The Gandhian Philosophy of Conflict.* Princeton: Princeton University Press, 1988.

Borg, Marcus. *Meeting Jesus Again for the First Time: The Historical Jesus and the Heart of Contemporary Faith.* New York: HarperCollins, 1994.

Boring, M. Eugene. *Revelation.* Nashville: Abingdon, 1989.

Boyarin, Daniel. *Border Lines: The Partition of Judaeo-Christianity.* Philadelphia: University of Pennsylvania Press, 2004.

Boyd, Gregory A. *Crucifixion of the Warrior God: Interpreting the Old Testament's Violent Portraits of God in Light of the Cross.* Minneapolis: Fortress, 2017.

Boyer, Paul S. *When Time Shall Be No More: Prophecy Belief in Modern American Culture.* Cambridge, MA: Harvard University Press, 1992.

Branch, Taylor. *At Canaan's Edge: American in the King Years, 1965–1968.* New York: Simon & Schuster, 2006.

———. *Parting the Waters: America in the King Years, 1954–1963.* New York: Simon & Schuster, 1988.

———. *Pillar of Fire: America in the King Years, 1963–1965.* New York: Simon & Schuster, 1998.

Bredin, Mark. *Jesus, Revolutionary of Peace: A Nonviolent Christology in the Book of Revelation.* Waynesboro, GA: Paternoster, 2003.

Burleigh, Michael. *Moral Combat: A History of World War II.* London, UK: Harper, 2010.

Caird, George B. *A Commentary on the Revelation of St. John the Divine.* New York: Harper & Row, 1966.

Carroll, James. *House of War: The Pentagon and the Disastrous Rise of American Power.* Boston: Houghton Mifflin, 2006.

Carter, Warren. *What Does Revelation Reveal? Unlocking the Mystery.* Nashville: Abingdon, 2011.

Crossan, John Dominic. *God and Empire: Jesus Against Rome, Then and Now.* San Francisco: HarperSanFrancisco, 2007.

Ehrenreich, Barbara. *Dancing in the Streets: A History of Collective Joy.* New York: Metropolitan, 2007.

Eller, Vernard. *The Most Revealing Book of the Bible: Making Sense Out of Revelation* Grand Rapids: Eerdmans, 1974.

Ellul, Jacques. *Apocalypse: The Book of Revelation.* New York: Seabury, 1977.

Elshtain, Jean Bethke. *Just War Against Terror.* New York: Basic, 2003.

Engler, Mark, and Paul Engler. *This is an Uprising: How Nonviolent Revolt is Shaping the Twenty-First Century.* New York: Nation, 2016.

Farmer, Ronald. *Revelation.* Nashville: Chalice, 2005.

Farrer, Austin. *Rebirth of Images: The Making of John's Apocalypse.* London: Dacre, 1949.

Friesen, Steven. *Imperial Cults and the Apocalypse of John: Reading Revelation in the Ruins.* New York: Oxford University Press, 2001.

Galbraith, John Kenneth. *Economics, Peace, and Laughter.* Boston: Houghton Mifflin, 1971.

Giggs, Rebecca. "Imagining the Jellyfish Apocalypse." *The Atlantic Monthly,* January, 2018. https://www.theatlantic.com/magazine/archive/2018/01/listening-to-jelly fish/546542/.

Gorman, Michael. *Reading Revelation Responsibly: Uncivil Worship and Witness: Following the Lamb into the New Creation.* Eugene, OR: Cascade, 2011.

Grayling, A. C. *Among the Dead Cities: The History and Moral Legacy of the World War II Bombings of Civilians in Germany and Japan.* New York: Walker, 2006.

Grimsrud, Ted. *The Good War That Wasn't—And Why It Matters: The Moral Legacy of World War II.* Eugene, OR: Cascade, 2014.

———. *Triumph of the Lamb: A Self-Study Guide to the Book of Revelation.* Scottdale, PA: Herald, 1987.

Grimsrud, Ted, and Michael Hardin, eds. *Compassionate Eschatology: The Future as Friend.* Eugene, OR: Cascade, 2011.

Hallie, Philip P. *Lest Innocent Blood Be Shed: The Story of the Village of Le Chambon and How Goodness Happened There.* 2nd ed. New York: Harper Perennial, 1994.

Hanson, Anthony Tyrell. *The Wrath of the Lamb.* London, SPCK, 1957.

Harrington, Wilfrid J. *Revelation.* Collegeville, MN: Liturgical, 1993.

Havel, Václav. "The Power of the Powerless." In *Open Letters: Selected Writings, 1965–1990*, 125–214. New York: Knopf, 1991.

Hays, Richard B., and Stefan Alkier, eds. *Revelation and the Politics of Apocalyptic Interpretation*. Waco, TX: Baylor University Press, 2012.

Howard-Brook, Wes, and Anthony Gwyther. *Unveiling Empire: Reading Revelation Then and Now*. Maryknoll, NY: Orbis, 1999.

Johnson, Darrell W. *Discipleship on the Edge: An Expository Journey Through the Book of Revelation*. Vancouver, BC: Regent College, 2004.

Johns, Loren L. *The Lamb Christology of the Apocalypse of John: An Investigation into Its Origins and Rhetorical Force*. Eugene, OR: Pickwick, 2014.

Keller, Catherine. *Apocalypse Now and Then: A Feminist Guide to the End of the World*. Boston: Beacon, 1996.

King, Martin Luther, Jr. *Strength to Love*. Minneapolis: Fortress, 2010.

King, Rachel H. *God's Boycott of Sin: A Consideration of Hell and Pacifism*. Nyack, NY: Fellowship, 1946.

Kirsch, Jonathan. *A History of the End of the World: How the Most Controversial Book in the Bible Changed the Course of Western Civilization*. San Francisco: HarperSanFrancisco, 2006.

Klein, Naomi. *The Shock Doctrine: The Rise of Disaster Capitalism*. New York: Metropolitan, 2007.

Koester, Craig R. *Revelation: A New Translation with Introduction and Commentary*. New Haven, CT: Yale University Press, 2014.

Kraybill, Donald B. *The Upside-Down Kingdom*. 3rd ed. Scottdale, PA: Herald, 2003.

Kraybill, J. Nelson. *Apocalypse and Allegiance: Worship, Politics, and Devotion in the Book of Revelation*. Grand Rapids: Brazos, 2010.

Krodel, Gerhard A. *Revelation*. Minneapolis: Augsburg, 1989.

LaHaye, Tim, and Jerry Jenkins, *Left Behind: A Novel of the Earth's Last Days*. Carol Stream, IL: Tyndale, 1995.

Lawrence, D. H. *Apocalypse*. New York: Penguin, 1974.

Lindsey, Hal. *The Late Great Planet Earth*. Grand Rapids: Zondervan, 1970.

Maier, Harry O. *Apocalypse Recalled: The Book of Revelation after Christendom*. Minneapolis: Fortress, 2002.

Mangina, Joseph L. *Revelation*. Grand Rapids: Brazos, 2010.

Marshall, Christopher D. *Beyond Retribution: A New Testament Vision for Justice, Crime, and Punishment*. Grand Rapids: Eerdmans, 2001.

———. *The Little Book of Biblical Justice: A Fresh Approach to the Bible's Teachings on Justice*. Intercourse, PA: Good, 2005.

Osborne, Grant R. *Revelation*. Grand Rapids: Baker Academic, 2002.

Penton, M. James. *Apocalypse Delayed: The Story of Jehovah's Witnesses*. 3rd ed. Toronto: University of Toronto Press, 2015.

Pippin, Tina. *Death and Desire: The Rhetoric of Gender in the Apocalypse of John*. Louisville: Westminster/John Knox, 1992.

Resseguie, James L. *The Revelation of John: A Narrative Commentary*. Grand Rapids: Baker Academic, 2009.

Rossing, Barbara R. *The Rapture Exposed: The Message of Hope in the Book of Revelation*. Boulder, CO: Westview, 2004.

———. "Revelation." In *The New Testament: Fortress Commentary on the Bible*, edited by Margaret Aymer et al., 715–71. Minneapolis: Fortress, 2014.

Rowland, Christopher C. "The Book of Revelation: Introduction, Commentary, and Reflections." In *The New Interpreter's Bible*, edited by Leander E. Keck et al., 12:501–736. Nashville: Abingdon, 1998.

Rowling, J. K. *Harry Potter and the Deathly Hallows.* New York: Levine, 2007.

Schell, Jonathan. *The Unconquerable World: Power, Nonviolence, and the Will of the People.* New York: Metropolitan, 2003.

Schüssler Fiorenza, Elisabeth. *Revelation: Vision of a Just World.* Minneapolis: Fortress, 1991.

Scott, James C. *Seeing Like a State: How Certain Schemes to Improve the Human Condition Have Failed.* New Haven, CT: Yale University Press, 1998.

———. *Two Cheers for Anarchism: Six Easy Pieces on Autonomy, Dignity, and Meaningful World and Play.* Princeton: Princeton University Press, 2012.

Sider, Ronald J. *Nonviolent Action: What Christian Ethics Demands But Most Christians Have Never Really Tried.* Grand Rapids: Brazos, 2015.

Smalley, Stephen S. *The Revelation to John: A Commentary on the Greek Text of the Apocalypse.* Downers Grove, IL: IVP Academic, 2005.

Smith, Norma. *Jeanette Rankin, America's Conscience.* Helena, MT: Montana Historical Society, 2002.

Solnit, Rebecca. *A Paradise Built in Hell: The Extraordinary Communities That Arise in Disaster.* New York: Viking, 2009.

Streett, Matthew J. *Here Comes the Judge: Violent Pacifism in the Book of Revelation.* New York: T. & T. Clark, 2012.

Stringfellow, William. *Conscience and Obedience: The Politics of Romans 13 and Revelation 13 in Light of the Second Coming.* Waco, TX: Word, 1977.

———. *An Ethic for Christians and Other Aliens in a Strange Land.* Waco, TX: Word, 1973.

Sweet, J. P. M. *Revelation.* Philadelphia: Westminster, 1979.

Tolkien, J. R. R. *The Return of the King: Being the Third Part of the Lord of the Rings.* Boston: Houghton Mifflin, 1956.

Turse, Nick. *Kill Anything That Moves: The Real American War in Vietnam.* New York: Metropolitan, 2013.

Volf, Miroslav. *Exclusion and Embrace: A Theological Exploration of Identity, Otherness, and Exclusion.* Nashville: Abingdon, 1996.

Wainwright, Arthur W. *Mysterious Apocalypse: Interpreting the Book of Revelation.* Nashville: Abingdon, 1993.

West, Cornel, ed. *The Radical King.* Boston: Beacon, 2015.

Wilcock, Michael. *I Saw Heaven Opened: The Message of Revelation.* Downers Grove, IL: InterVarsity, 1975.

Wink, Walter. *Engaging the Powers: Discernment and Resistance in a World of Domination.* Minneapolis: Fortress, 1992.

———. *Unmasking the Powers: The Invisible Forces that Determine Human Existence.* Philadelphia: Fortress, 1986.

Wright, N. T. *Revelation for Everyone.* Louisville: Westminster John Knox, 2011.

Yeatts, John R. *Revelation.* Scottdale, PA: Herald, 2003.

Young, Marilyn B. *The Vietnam Wars, 1945–1990.* New York: HarperCollins, 1991.

Zerzan, John. *Elements of Refusal.* 2nd ed. Columbia, MO: C.A.L., 1999.